The Practical Essence of Man

Historical Materialism Book Series

The Historical Materialism Book Series is a major publishing initiative of the radical left. The capitalist crisis of the twenty-first century has been met by a resurgence of interest in critical Marxist theory. At the same time, the publishing institutions committed to Marxism have contracted markedly since the high point of the 1970s. The Historical Materialism Book Series is dedicated to addressing this situation by making available important works of Marxist theory. The aim of the series is to publish important theoretical contributions as the basis for vigorous intellectual debate and exchange on the left.

The peer-reviewed series publishes original monographs, translated texts, and reprints of classics across the bounds of academic disciplinary agendas and across the divisions of the left. The series is particularly concerned to encourage the internationalization of Marxist debate and aims to translate significant studies from beyond the English-speaking world.

For a full list of titles in the Historical Materialism Book Series
available in paperback from Haymarket Books, visit:
https://www.haymarketbooks.org/series_collections/1-historical-materialism

The Practical Essence of Man

*The 'Activity Approach' in
Late Soviet Philosophy*

Edited by
Andrey Maidansky
Vesa Oittinen

Haymarket Books
Chicago, IL

First published in 2015 by Brill Academic Publishers, The Netherlands
© 2016 Koninklijke Brill NV, Leiden, The Netherlands

Published in paperback in 2017 by
Haymarket Books
P.O. Box 180165
Chicago, IL 60618
773-583-7884
www.haymarketbooks.org

ISBN: 978-1-60846-698-6

Trade distribution:
In the US, Consortium Book Sales, www.cbsd.com
In Canada, Publishers Group Canada, www.pgcbooks.ca
In the UK, Turnaround Publisher Services, www.turnaround-uk.com
In all other countries, Publishers Group Worldwide, www.pgw.com

Cover design by Jamie Kerry of Belle Étoile Studios and Ragina Johnson.

This book was published with the generous support of Lannan Foundation
and the Wallace Action Fund.

Printed in Canada by union labor.

10 9 8 7 6 5 4 3 2 1

Library of Congress Cataloging-in-Publication data is available.

Contents

      Piaget   154
          Pentti Määttänen

11   The Ideal and the Dream-World: Evald Ilyenkov and Walter Benjamin
      on the Significance of Material Objects   167
          Alex Levant

      Bibliography   189
      Index   202

Introduction

Andrey Maidansky and Vesa Oittinen

The 'activity theory' in Soviet psychology, represented by Lev S. Vygotsky and Aleksei Leontiev, is now known around the world. However, its sibling, the philosophical activity theory, which arose among Soviet philosophers in the 1960s, remains virtually unknown outside Russia. Among the many reasons for this could be the feeling that Soviet philosophical culture has nothing to offer to the present. This bias is shared by many contemporary Russian thinkers, who regard the 70 years of Soviet rule as nothing more than a black hole in the intellectual history of Russia. However, closer examination reveals that there is more to this picture. Such names as Bakhtin, Lotman, Mamardashvili and Ilyenkov have already established themselves, even in Western consciousness, and offer glimpses of a different kind of reality behind the allegedly monolithic façade of Marxist-Leninist ideology. The 'activity approach' presented in this volume was a further innovative undercurrent of the 'late Soviet' period that is worthy of reception and critical assessment even today. Its representatives posed important methodological questions concerning one of the main paradigms of Marxism and also of modern philosophy in general.

In this book, several Russian and Western scholars analyse the activity approach and its connections to similar approaches in other traditions, especially in Marxist philosophy and pragmatism. These contributions show that the scope of the activity approach is wider than that of Marxist philosophy, as it repeatedly contested the received ideas of Soviet Marxism-Leninism. This system of ideas represented a lacklustre interpretation of Marx's thought, which was – to cite Adolfo Sánchez Vázquez's now-classic exposition of the 'praxis-viewpoint' in Marxism – 'reduced to the old materialism fertilised by dialectics on the one hand, or a materialist metaphysics which is little more than an inverted idealism, on the other'. According to Sánchez Vázquez, this reduction was 'a result of the deliberate omission or rejection by some commentators of the centrality of the category of praxis'.[1] While this statement is correct, it requires further comment. Of course, the official Soviet ideology could not silence the idea of 'praxis', since it held such a prominent place in the corpus of classical Marxist texts, not only in the writings of Marx and Engels themselves, but also in those of Plekhanov and Lenin. However, the 'Diamat' view on praxis was as

---

1 Sánchez Vázquez 1977, p. 3.

lacklustre as its view on Marx's heritage in general: the concept of praxis was interpreted in a manner that did not differ greatly from the way the Pragmatists treated it, which meant that praxis as a criterion of truth was *de facto* identified with 'success' in action. Actually, it is surprising to find how few perceptive analyses there were in Soviet philosophy of the concept of praxis.

The emergence of the activity approach among Soviet philosophers from the early 1960s onwards, initially in the rather narrow circles of some Moscow intellectuals, represented a decisive break with the vulgarised Diamat ideas. In a sense, this current was a Soviet analogy to the Western 'Praxis' Marxism as it was expounded at around the same time by such Yugoslav philosophers as Mihajlo Marković, Milan Kangrga and Svetozar Stojanović. But there are also some important differences. First of all, the Soviet 'activity approach' was a much more heterogeneous (one could even say amorphous) current.

Another important characteristic of the Soviet activity approach-philosophy was that it developed quite independently from the Western theories of action. While both the philosophical theories of action in the Western world (such as Anscombe, Audi and von Wright) and the sociological theories (Max Weber, for example) were primarily interested in actions of individual agents from the viewpoint of teleological causality, the Soviet philosophers had a broader view of the subject-matter. They understood activity as the fundamental trait of man's relations with the surrounding world; in this sense, the concept of activity could be seen as forming the methodological basis of all human and social sciences (not only that of psychology, where it had proved especially fruitful thanks to the works of Vygotsky, Rubinshtein and the Leontievs).

Of course, this situation reflects the different philosophical backgrounds of Western and Soviet action-theories. The Western theories of action emerged mostly in the tradition of analytic philosophy, while the Soviet theories had their background in Marxism and its concept of praxis. However, the differences between the Western and Soviet approaches can be traced back even further into the history of philosophy, back to Aristotle. In fact, it is possible to extract at least two different action-theories from Aristotle. One is 'logical', based on the problematics of practical syllogism (action as a result of premises), and the other is 'anthropological' (action as realisation of human essence). The Western theories of action often start with Aristotle's idea of a practical syllogism, formulated in the seventh book of *Nicomachean Ethics*,[2] and thus focus on logical reasoning around different kinds and modes of activity. The Soviet Marxist tradition of praxis and activity-theories, in turn, relies on the

---

2   Compare *Ethica Nicomachea* VII.iii.9 et seq.

Aristotelian theory of *prâxis* and *poíêsis*, which not only concerns syllogistic judgement, but also refers to the actualisation of human essence itself.[3]

Although the Soviet philosophers tried to maintain a more or less convincing Marxist-Leninist façade in their publications, their divergent evolutionary paths soon brought them to face the abysses of fundamental philosophical questions in a manner that was quite different from that of the Yugoslav 'praxists', who had sketched a rather superficial and optimistic version of Marxism. Therefore, it is no surprise that some representatives of the Soviet 'activity approach', most notably Genrikh Batishchev, left the ground of Marxist thought as early as the 1970s.

These experiences of the late Soviet philosophy made it clear that a web of unresolved questions lay around the Marxist concept of 'praxis'. To this day, this concept has been hailed as a kind of panacea with which to solve man's age-old philosophical problems and his relationship to the world, especially in the theory of cognition. The Soviet Diamat had declared that the 'praxis-criterion' had solved the long-standing philosophical problems concerning the nature of truth and human knowledge and it should now remain only to continue to the 'shining future' following this secure path. Unfortunately, the discussions initiated by the activity approach-philosophers showed that the Marxist concepts of praxis and activity were only the latest in a long tradition that was rooted at least in the above-mentioned Aristotelian distinction between *prâxis* and *poíêsis* and continued in different kinds of philosophy of activity as a realisation of human 'essence'. In the modern era alone, this tradition has been represented by such thinkers as Bacon, Spinoza, Vico, Kant, the German idealists, Gentile and Croce.

Consequently, the Soviet activity approach-philosophers did not remain within the confines of the traditional Marxist textual corpus; instead, they leant towards other philosophical traditions. For example, Ilyenkov relied heavily on Spinoza, who had developed a coherent philosophy of action based on the dis-

---

3 In *Nicomachean Ethics*, Aristotle does not connect the problematics of practical syllogism in any coherent way with the action-theory (the famous *prâxis* versus *poíêsis* distinction) that he presents earlier in the same work (see *Ethica Nicomachea* VI.iv.1 et seq.). The way in which Aristotle connects human activity with the actualisation of essences is clearly visible in a beautiful but rarely-cited passage towards the end of the book: 'we exist in activity, since we exist by living and doing [*esmèn d'energeía (tô zên gàr kaì práttein)*]; and in a sense one who has made something exists actively [*energeía dè ho poiêsas tò érgon ésti*], and so he loves his handiwork because he loves existence. This is in fact a fundamental principle of nature: what a thing is potentially, that its work reveals in actuality' (*Ethica Nicomachea* IX.vii.4; English translation by H. Rackham).

tinction between *agere* and *pati,* and even formulated the famous and very Marxist-sounding thesis that man's ability to think (*cogitandi potentia*) derives directly from his ability to act (*agendi potentia*; compare *Eth.* III prop. 3). Others reverted to Kantian (or better, neo-Kantian) ideas, while most Soviet philosophers subscribed to the assertion of Marx in the first thesis on Feuerbach that 'idealism' (thus, above all, Hegel) developed the 'active side' of man, but only in an abstract manner. Therefore, Hegel was from the beginning seen as perhaps the most important extra-Marxist source of the activity approach as well.

The Emergence of the Soviet Philosophy of Activity

Discussions about the applicability of the category of 'activity' (in Russian, *deyatel'nost*; the term is roughly equivalent to the German *Tätigkeit* and has a more narrow scope than the English term 'activity', representing the primarily telos-oriented activity of the subject) peaked in the 1960s and 1970s. The first volume of the semi-official *Filosofskaya entsiklopediya* (1960) did not mention the term at all. However, it was introduced in a disguised form in the second volume, published in 1962, in the entry on the concept of the 'ideal', written by Evald Ilyenkov. This article became the first manifesto of the activity approach in philosophy. (As noted earlier, it had already been in use in psychology for a couple of decades, if not longer, by the Vygotsky–Leontiev school.)

According to Ilyenkov, the ideal (*ideal'noe*) is more than just a 'reflection' of the outer world in the brain and sense-organs, as Soviet Diamat considered it. The ideal is not a product of the subject's receptivity alone, but an *attribute of human activity*; it is the special, cultural-historical dimension of man as an active being. Everything that falls within the ambit of this activity receives the imprint of ideality and, as long as the activity continues, becomes a residence and instrument for the ideal. Ilyenkov defined the ideal as the 'reflection of the outer world in forms of human activity', or as the 'determinate being [*nalichnoe bytie*[4]] of an external thing in a phase of its entering into the activity of the [human] subject'.[5] The ideal is a form of activity that reproduces the form of a thing, or the form of a thing that has been separated from its own matter in the process of human activity. The ideal only exists at the very moment that the form of a thing is converted into the form of acti-

---

4 A Russian equivalent for Hegel's term *Dasein.*
5 Ilyenkov 1962, pp. 219, 222.

vity, and vice versa. As soon as human activity has stopped, the ideal fades away.

Ilyenkov was deeply influenced by the psychologists of the Vygotsky school. 'In the beginning was the *Deed*' – Vygotsky repeated this 'Goethe formula', as he called it, more than once.[6] His pupil A.N. Leontiev regarded *expressis verbis* the activity as the subject-matter of psychology.[7] Ilyenkov, who was on very good terms with Leontiev, engaged openly in the debate between the two parties of Soviet psychologists, which were headed by S.L. Rubinshtein and A.N. Leontiev, respectively, and proposed substantially alternative theories of activity. In his article 'O prirode sposobnosti' ('On the nature of the faculty'),[8] Ilyenkov defended Vygotsky's concept of 'interiorisation' against the critics. He argued that the individual becomes a human being, a person, solely through the process of 'ingrowing' (*vrashchivanie*; Vygotsky's term) of external cultural patterns of behaviour into the natural, animal psyche. Ilyenkov contested Rubinshtein's assertion about there being some 'inner, natural' subjectivity that can be traced as a 'core' of personality.

In the 1970s, Ilyenkov conducted a seminar at the psychological faculty of Moscow State University. In his report entitled 'Ponyatie "deyatel'nosti" i ego znachenie dlya pedagogiki' ('The Concept of "Activity" and its Significance for Pedagogy'), he compared this concept to a crystal, around which all theory and practice of education should be formed:

> Evidently, the concept of *activity* is indeed the key concept that alone makes it possible to unite the efforts of pedagogues, psychologists, and philosophers in accomplishing the central task of our entire education system – the task of organizing it on the basis of a clear system of theoretical ideas.[9]

However, the concept of activity should be interpreted more precisely. The form (scheme, mode) of human activity is determined by the nature of its object. Furthermore, not only real things but also *signs* of things (for example, words) may act as objects of activity. Such signs do not necessarily have anything in common with the things they denote. According to Ilyenkov, the logic of the

---

6 'Im Anfang war die *That*' (Goethe, *Faust*, I: 81).

7 Leontiev did say that psychology is interested only in the 'mediated activity, which is regulated by the subjective reflection of the world' (Leontiev 2001, p. 288).

8 The article was published 40 years later in a collection of Ilyenkov's works on psychology and pedagogics (Ilyenkov 2002a, pp. 62–71).

9 Ilyenkov 2007, p. 69.

objective activity is dialectics, while the *sign-symbolic* activity is guided by the laws of formal logic.

It is often difficult to distinguish an activity directed to the real object *by means of signs* from a merely formal activity *with the very signs*, which appear as a special object. In life, especially in the process of education, the latter kind of activity often substitutes for the truly objective activity.

> What takes place here is by no means the mastering of the *object* of knowledge (and knowledge can consist of nothing but this), but merely the mastering of *phrases* about this object, merely the mastering of the verbal shell of knowledge *in place of* knowledge.[10]

Such verbal quasi-knowledge requires verification, the special operation for comparing thought with object. However, the object could never be given to us *an sich*, in its naked form. We perceive only those objects with which we act and that act upon us. This is why Ilyenkov characterised the problem of comparing thought with object as 'insoluble in principle' and 'essentially absurd'.[11]

What is impossible to perform in the mind is sometimes feasible *in praxi*, where man is faced directly with reality. Unlike sensual perception and 'experience' (in a Kantian sense), objectively practical activity deals not with 'phenomena' but with things as they are 'in themselves'. Practical action subjectifies things and objectifies the phenomenon of consciousness appropriate to them. By representing this phenomenon as an external thing, praxis thereby sublates the difference between knowledge and thing.

> Identifying (that is, identity as an act, as acting, as a process, and not as a state of rest) of thought and reality is performed in practice and through practice.[12]

For such 'practically true'[13] knowledge, the problem of correspondence with an object does not arise at all: this knowledge is entirely *derived* from the object; it is extracted from the latter by human activity.

---

10   Ilyenkov 2007, p. 71.
11   Ibid.
12   Ilyenkov 1964, p. 51.
13   Marx's term: *praktisch wahr*.

So far as one has gained knowledge not from hearsay, but in the process of active mastering of a thing, the very thing becomes a source of certainty of knowledge and guarantees the verity of its idea.

> If the reference-point is a real action with object, accompanied by observation of the method of action ('reflection') ... knowledge then appears in the human mind exactly as *knowledge of the thing*, and not as a specific structure situated outside the thing, that still somehow has to be 'attached', 'applied' to this thing by performing some special actions.[14]

The logic of the objectively practical activity is dialectics (the teaching about identity of opposites) and primarily about the active identifying of subjective with objective, of thought with being. Dialectics against formal logic, the *logic of Deed* against the *logic of Word*: this collision determines the course of the entire history of philosophical thought. Ilyenkov's book *Dialectical Logic* (1974) is devoted to analysis of this collision.

The activistic concept of the ideal, as presented by Ilyenkov in his 1962 article, soon came into vogue. A great many young Soviet philosophers – the so-called *shestidesyatniki*, or the 'Sixties-Generation' – began to uphold its main tenets. Among the studies of the first wave are two small books written by Ilyenkov's pupils Yuri N. Davydov (1962) and Genrikh Batishchev (1963). At this early stage, the 'activity approach' was still viewed as a creative advance in Marxist thought, which in the short 'thaw' period of Khrushchev's so-called de-Stalinisation seemed finally able to free itself from the Procrustean bed of party-ideology. This renaissance of Marxism shared some common traits with the developments that also took place in Western intellectual life. In particular, the publication of the young Marx's Paris Notebooks gave a powerful incentive to activity-studies in the Soviet Union, just as they had stirred up the discussion of a 'humanistic' Marx in the West in the 1950s. What united these intellectual movements was the fact that Marx was being discovered, both in the USSR and in the West, as a theoretician of human subjectivity, of man as an actor and not merely a more or less passive executor of the objective laws of history. Marx's *Economic and Philosophic Manuscripts of 1844* saw the light of day in Russian in 1956 (they were originally published in 1932, but due to World War II their actual influence in the West began roughly at the same time as in the Soviet Union). The Russian translation of Marx's 'Notes on James Mill' were published even

---

14   Ilyenkov 2002a, p. 84.

later, in 1966, with Ilyenkov serving as a translator.[15] These notes are the first text in which Marx talks about the activistic essence of man, the alienation of labour and the need to overcome this alienation so that 'labour should be also *true, active property*'.[16]

Yuri Davydov's *Trud i svoboda* (*Labour and Freedom*, 1962) was one of the first Soviet books written on the young Marx's themes. It also applied the activity approach for the first time in the Soviet philosophy to social-historical and ethical problems (Ilyenkov's article on the ideal was situated on a more abstract-theoretical level). By 'freedom', Davydov primarily meant the 'active, vigorous manifestation, demonstration of the human essence',[17] that is, the demonstration of *social labour*, conceived as the production of not only useful things but, in the final analysis, of human beings as well, of social relations between men.

> Labour is *substance*, that is, the deepest essence, the foundation of human freedom. Labour appears here as Spinoza's *causa sui* (the cause of itself), as a universal relationship of Nature 'to itself'.[18]

Labour is as universal as Nature itself. Historically, however, this universality is realised in the reverse form – at the expense of reducing the activity of every single individual to the utmost narrow speciality. This historical process of the *division of labour*, in Marx's words, 'makes man a quite abstract being, a lathe, etc., and transforms him into a spiritual and physical freak'.[19]

The division of labour splits up the human essence into atoms, an effect of which is the *alienation* of man from man and, overall, the tearing off of an individual from the society to which he belongs as its particle. Davydov discussed the conditions that enable the sublation of the division of labour and the requirements for transforming labour into the free and autonomous activity (*samodeyatel'nost'*, *Selbsttätigkeit*) of a person.

Davydov always retained the communist ideal of Marx – the ideal of a versatile personality: laborious, healthy, clever, kind and having a subtle sense

---

15   Marx 1966, pp. 113–27.

16   Marx 1966, p. 127. 'Die Arbeit wäre also *wahres, tätiges Eigentum*' (Marx 1981, p. 466).

17   Davydov 1962, p. 28.

18   Davydov 1962, p. 45.

19   'Teilung der Arbeit, welche aus dem Menschen möglichst ein abstraktes Wesen, eine Drehmaschine etc. macht und bis zur geistigen und physischen Mißgeburt ihn umwandelt' (Marx 1981, p. 456).

of beauty. This ideal is a nod to the works of the humanists of the Renaissance and, even further, to the ancient classics.[20] Here is the aim of world-history, according to Marx; the subject of the labour-process, the human person, is to become the final end of this process.

Davydov cautiously restricted his research to an analysis of Marx's texts, avoiding the risk of comparing them with contemporary realities of 'developed socialism'. This was exactly the same for other adherents of the activity-approach. The only exception was Ilyenkov's 'Marks i zapadnyj mir' ('Marx and the Western World', 1965), which was originally a paper that was intended to be presented at a symposium at the University of Notre Dame (USA), to which Ilyenkov was invited. The author planned to speak about the alienation between people in socialist society. In his paper, he distinguished between public and state-property and defined the state as an 'impersonal organism, in opposition to every individual of which it consists'.[21] When the Communist Party censors became acquainted with the draft, they removed ideologically disloyal passages from the text and informed the organisers of the symposium that the author was ill and could not deliver the paper. Therefore, the version published in the symposium-volume is a censored one and does not reflect Ilyenkov's views to the full.[22]

The main orientation of the research-activities in the Ilyenkov school was towards dialectical logic, its categories as the *objective forms of practical activity* of man in nature.

In this spirit, Genrikh Batishchev interpreted the 'activistic' categories of Marxism in his 1963 book *Protivorechie kak kategoriya dialekticheskoy logiki* (*The Contradiction as a Category of Dialectical Logic*). These categories were alienation (*Entfremdung*) and reification (*Versachlichung, Verdinglichung*), objectification (*Vergegenständlichung*) and deobjectification (*Entgegenständlichung*):

> Categories generally must be considered ... as forms of human activity that, being the ideal ones, agree with forms of objects. This agreement is realised ... by the very activity and is immanent to it.[23]

---

20 'Der "Kommunismus" ist die geschichtliche Versprechung eines antiken Traumes des müßigen Menschen' (Priddat 2005, p. 129).
21 Ilyenkov 1988, p. 106.
22 See Ilyenkov 1967.
23 Batishchev 1963, pp. 9–10.

Another follower of Ilyenkov, N.N. Trubnikov, analysed the structure of human activity in his 1967 book *O kategoriyakh 'tsel', 'sredstvo', 'rezul'tat'* (*On the Categories 'Purpose', 'Means', 'Result'*). Here he declares the intention to build:

> an abstract model of the completed act of human activity, to describe its principal moments, to reveal the logic of such an act and, thus, to comprehend its epistemological and socially-historical sense.[24]

Trubnikov primarily focused on the correlation between the conscious aims of activity and its actual results, including the unforeseen social effects of man's interrelation. The very activity can be as a means of achieving some external purposes (such as receiving material benefits, power over people, and so on), as the *self-purpose*, the way of creatively self-realising a person. In the course of mankind's history, this latter kind of human activity has moved to the forefront, turning into the dominant factor of social development.

However, one of Ilyenkov's pupils, L.K. Naumenko, in his 1968 book *Monizm kak printsip dialekticheskoy logiki* (*Monism as the Principle of Dialectical Logic*), intended to show the objectively activistic nature of the basic categories of logic, such as substance, matter and form, essence and existence. Behind each of these logical forms there stands:

> a social form of sensually-practical activity, having its ideal shape in categories of thought. Rational cognition, logical thinking is the active reflection of the thing, according to its categorial, generalised practical objective meaning.[25]

Interestingly, Naumenko attempted to distinguish between an *objectively* activistic and a *formally* activistic methodology. His target is G.P. Shchedrovitsky, who several years earlier had started to elaborate a formal version of the activity approach. According to this version, the subject-matter (*predmet*) of knowledge 'is a product of human cognitive activity'. Knowledge itself forms, *creates*, its own subject-matter.[26] Naumenko argued against Shchedrovitsky's interpretation of the activity approach, which he felt was, in a Kantian sense, subjectivistic:

---

24   Trubnikov 1967, p. 12.
25   Naumenko 1968, pp. 36–7.
26   Shchedrovitsky 1964, pp. 14 ff.

It is not knowledge that creates a subject-matter from object, but the objective materially-practical productive activity, which at the same time creates the very knowledge as well ... The subject-matter of science itself arises in a system of things, and not in a system of 'things created by the science'.[27]

In the process of evolution, individual things and whole systems of things inter-lock one into another and transform into functions of more complicated forma-tions. Their own nature levels out and extinguishes individual peculiarities, insofar as they prevent the inclusion of such things in the structure of a new-born whole. According to Naumenko, this is the process of *real abstraction*, which is performed not in the head of the theoretician but in the very object of cognition. In that case, thought does not impose its subjective forms and purposes on things, but moves *according the logic of things*, tracing back the mode of entering this or that thing into the structure of reality of a superior grade.

In Shchedrovitsky's subjectivistic interpretation, the subject-matter of cog-nition is a result of the abstraction made by human activity, which proceeds following the purposes and tasks of the subject. Naumenko, on the other hand, distinguished between two different kinds of abstraction: artificial, *formal abstraction* that 'amounts to simple juxtaposition of different, heterogeneous things within our mind',[28] and *real, 'practically true' abstraction*, which 'is set not by our attitude to a thing, but by its objective position in a system of things, by its *objective function*'.[29]

Naumenko took the concept of real abstraction from Ilyenkov, who made reference to Marx:

The author of *Capital* persistently stresses that the reduction of differ-ent kinds of labour to uniform simple labour devoid of differences 'is an abstraction which is made every day in the social process of produc-tion'.[30]

27   Naumenko 1968, p. 157.

28   Naumenko 1968, p. 307.

29   Naumenko 1968, p. 55.

30   Ilyenkov 1960, pp. 8–9. Marx provided the following example of real abstraction from chemistry: 'Reduction of all commodities to labour-time is an abstraction not more, but at the same time not less real than the resolution of all the organic bodies into air' (Marx 1961, p. 18).

The distinctive trait of Ilyenkov's version of the activity approach consists of emphasising the *objective character* of both the content and the form of activity. That certainly applies only to the true, appropriate activity, not to the biased and tendentious activity which neglects the fact that its object has a function within a concrete whole.

The Activity Approach Comes of Age: The 1970s

The activity approach-movement of the 1960s received a mixed response. Several levels should be distinguished here. Despite the ideological control of the Communist Party and the hegemony of Marxism-Leninism, Soviet 'philosophical culture'[31] was not as monolithic as many in the West seem to think, even today. There were many niches in which relatively free discussion was allowed, and an uneasy kind of coexistence with the prevailing ideological dogmas was possible. Thus, Ilyenkov's activistic conception of the ideal had to confront various kinds of adversary. Many professional philosophers (that is, not party-ideologues) appealed to 'Lenin's theory of reflection', while others referred to the data of 'contemporary science' or simply censured Ilyenkov for his idealism and Hegelianism.

Of these controversies, the one between Ilyenkov and D.I. Dubrovsky became especially well known. Dubrovsky, an adherent of the analytic philosophy of mind, considered the ideal (as well as the consciousness and the mind) to be the function of the brain.[32] In the opinion of Dubrovsky, the activity

---

31   The expression 'Soviet philosophical culture' comes from the Dutch scholar Evert van der Zweerde, who has extensively analysed the forms of philosophical discourse in the Soviet Union. He saw in this discourse a form of culture that consists of its classics, its 'smaller' thinkers, its ideological boundary-conditions, traditions, educational and material bases (universities, academies, journals) and so on. In this context, Marxism-Leninism in itself was not a 'real' philosophy, but rather a legitimising instance of the concrete philosophical ideas of individual philosophers. As van der Zweerde pointed out wryly, 'This serves to explain the smooth transition of most Soviet philosophers to non-Marxist positions' after 1991 (see van der Zweerde 1994, pp. 5ff., 143). One could, *mutatis mutandis*, compare Soviet philosophy to the culture of medieval Scholasticism. Even here, the individual Schoolmen defended their logical or metaphysical ideas by referring in the last instance to the doctrines of the Church. However, their actual philosophical ideas and theories were not, as such, dependent on those doctrines, and although medieval Christian culture passed, the philosophical or logical ideas did not thereby automatically lose their relevance.

32   'The ideal is a piece of information, immediately given to the subject, about the external

approach detaches psychical phenomena from their material ground. Activity is 'programmed' by the brain so that the problem of the ideal can only be solved by neurophysiology and cybernetics analysing the processes of information-coding inside the brain. In contrast to the activity approach, Dubrovsky called his position the 'informational approach', which he claimed was the only way to understand how the mind and brain function.[33]

From the opposite standpoint, Ilyenkov's activistic conception of the ideal was criticised by his older friend M.A. Lifshits, a theoretician of Marxist aesthetics who in the 1930s collaborated with Georg Lukács, then in exile in Moscow. According to Lifshits, the ideal is a property of any natural phenomenon. This property only manifests itself in human activity, but it does not emerge in it and it is not limited by the sphere of activity. By the ideal, Lifshits understood:

> certain limits, that our sensual perception gives us in experience ... These limits are an ideal gas, an ideal [perfect] crystal – the real abstractions which one could approach, in the same way that a polygon with an infinitely growing number of sides approaches a circle. All the structure of the universe ... rests upon norms or patterns which can be reached only through infinite approximation.[34]

This abstract ideal, which is absolutely inaccessible in practice, owes much more to Kant than Marx. One could even say that, in Lifshits's hands, the ideal becomes a kind of immutable Platonic essence and human activity only 'recalls' these pre-existent ideas, just as the slave-boy in the famous Socratic dialogue found the eternal truths of geometry by drawing figures in the sand. Unfortunately, we cannot know what Ilyenkov thought about this interpretation, because Lifshits only came out against Ilyenkov's theory of the ideal after the latter's death. As for the party-ideology, the activity approach managed to keep up an uneasy coexistence with it by simply avoiding overemphasis on the possible ideological consequences of its main ideas. This seems to explain the strange fact that Soviet philosophical literature contained little discussion about the relationships between the categories of 'praxis' (*praktika*) and 'activity' (*deyatel'nost*). The category of 'praxis' belonged to the core arsenal of Marxism-Leninism and Diamat and was strongly ideologically charged.

---

world and himself ... The ideal (psychical) is exactly the property of the brain's definite neurodynamic structures' (Dubrovsky 1971, p. 108).

33   Dubrovsky 1971, p. 266. See also Dubrovsky 1976.
34   Lifshits 1984, p. 123.

In the 1970s, the Soviet state became slack and inactive, entering the so-called 'Era of Stagnation'. The promises of the 1960s were not fulfilled, which led to growing disappointment and even cynicism among the Soviet people and the intelligentsia. The attitude that socialism and, therefore, Marxist theory did not represent any convincing perspective for the future became increasingly widespread. A considerable number of philosophers, showing their loyalty to Marxism in words, began to carry out research in the spirit of analytical philosophy and post-positivist 'philosophy of science' (V.S. Gott, I.S. Narski, their numerous pupils and confederates). In the same vein, the activity approach lost its popularity. As before, many published works declared their fidelity to this approach, but the very concept of activity ceased to be concrete and became commonplace. Soviet philosophers were increasingly carried away by existential subjects, 'axiology' of a neo-Kantian shape, and even esoterism (G.S. Batishchev).

During the 1970s, the activity approach became an established part of Soviet philosophical discourse. Volume 8 of the official *Bol'shaya Sovetskaya Entsiklopediya* of 1972 included an extensive article on 'activity', which was reproduced in a slightly enlarged version in a third important reference book, *Filosofskiy entsiklopedicheskiy slovar'* (1983). Its authors, the young philosophers A.P. Ogurtsov and E.G. Yudin, declared that activity was 'the real moving force of social progress and the requisite of the existence of the society itself'. However, they added that the premises for activity – 'motifs, ideals and values' – are situated outside the sphere of activity as such, and that history knows even such 'types of culture' that do not regard activity as the highest value or 'the meaning of human existence'. These ambiguous clauses already essentially restricted the sphere of application of the activity approach and, on the whole, cast doubts over its fundamental character.

In the 1970s, almost the only new name associated with the activity-approach was V.M. Mezhuev, who as a student had been influenced by Ilyenkov. After the authorities had put an end to what they called 'gnoseological deviation' at the philosophical faculty of Moscow State University, Mezhuev was deprived of the opportunity to pursue philosophy for many years.[35] In the 1960s, Mezhuev fortuitously gained a place at the postgraduate school of the newly established Department of Culture at the Institute of Philosophy of the Academy of Sciences.

In his 1977 book *Kul'tura i istoriya* (*Culture and History*), Mezhuev aimed at a humanistic turn in Marxism, interpreting it as a 'philosophy of culture'. He defined 'culture', in line with the activity approach, as:

---

35   See Korovikov 1990, pp. 65–8.

the sphere of man's *historical activeness*, the sphere of his activity in the role of subject of the historical process ... In culture, man comes out thereby as *creative* being – not as the created, passive object of influence on the part of external and superior circumstances, but as a historical subject of changes and transformations, performed by his own efforts.[36]

The historical character of culture had been revealed and considered by the humanists of the Renaissance. History now appeared as the process of *self-activity*, as a form of man's creation of himself and human society in a whole.

Thus, *activity* is realised here as the only possible condition of the individual's entering into culture and his abiding in it.[37]

With this, man with his history is considered as a *universal* being who acts in accordance with the nature of all things and is capable of mastering all forces of nature. In this sense, a human being is a *speculum mundi*, a microcosm, and his activity appears to be the '*universal* principle of all the universe'.[38]

Mezhuev believed that the Renaissance ideal of a universal man-creator forms the cornerstone of Marx's theory. Marx discussed the *alienation* of objective wealth, which is created by people's activity, from its creators. In these circumstances, the very activity loses its free, creative, universal character. In the abstract labour of a factory-worker, freedom, creativity and culture itself die away. The purpose is to bring labour back to the bosom of culture. In Chapter 4 of *Kul'tura i istoriya*, 'The cultural mission of socialism', Mezhuev tried to demonstrate that, in socialist society, labour has already become cultured.[39] Overall, one could say that Mezhuev's train of thought approaches the Western variety of humanistic Marxism.

An unrestricted discussion on the category of activity became possible only towards the end of the Soviet epoch. The focus of the discussions moved instead to the relationship between the categories of activity and interaction (*obshchenie*). The 'absolutisation of activity' was increasingly criticised and the philosophical thought of the closing Soviet epoch turned to the search for

---

36 Mezhuev 1977, p. 60.

37 Mezhuev 1977, p. 26.

38 Ibid.

39 'If socialism has transformed culture into the public possessions, has made it accessible for everyone, then the new forms of labour, arising in the developed socialist society, make culture not only accessible, but also *necessary* for everyone, form the *want of culture*' (Mezhuev 1977, p. 193).

transcendent 'motives, ideals and values' beyond the scope of human activity. Both G.P. Shchedrovitsky and G.S. Batishchev abandoned their 'ultra-activist' views.

'Ne deyaniem odnim zhiv chelovek' ('Not action alone makes Man alive') was the title of Batishchev's article in the 1990 collection *Deyatel'nost: teorii, metodologiya, problemy* (Moskva: Politizdat), a book that attempted to summarise the threads of the discussions of the previous three decades. The volume, published in a series dedicated to the presentation of discussion themes among Soviet philosophy, offered a panorama of the divergent views on the subject-matter. The participants in the debate included philosophers and even well-known psychologists such as A.V. Brushlinsky and V.V. Davydov. However, although the book was published at a time when the Soviet Union still formally existed, it contains no fresh or original ideas. Soviet philosophy – and psychology too – had clearly had lost its vigour and enthusiasm, despite all it had shown in the 'golden decade' after 1960.

This volume is based on papers presented at the Aleksanteri Institute of the University of Helsinki in September 2010. The authors approached the subject of the activity approach from different points of view; however, the book has aimed to paint a coherent picture of this interesting phenomenon in Soviet philosophy. While Vesa Oittinen's paper discusses the utopian expectations invested in the idea of praxis during the first decades of Soviet philosophy and the uneasy coexistence of the concepts of 'praxis' and 'activity', other contributions focus mainly on the period between 1960 and 1980. Because the concept of activity developed in Soviet psychology is already widely known, even in the West, the papers concentrate only on the philosophical discussions (with the exception of the papers by Sergei Mareev and Pentti Määttänen, which take up certain connections between the philosophical ideas and questions of the method of psychology). The articles by Edward Swiderski, Vladislav Lektorsky, David Bakhurst and Andrey Maidansky deal with the 'grand' themes of the activity approach. For example, Swiderski questions the ability of this current to cope with the problems of metaphysics, while Elena Mareeva provides an informative survey of the tradition of the activity approach in Soviet Ukraine and Alex Levant traces the similarities between Ilyenkov and Walter Benjamin. The editors wish to thank all the writers for shedding light on a hitherto almost unknown aspect of late Soviet philosophy.

Helsinki/Belgorod, 15. August, 2015

CHAPTER 1

Activity and the Search for True Materialism

David Bakhurst

1   Introduction

When I began my studies of the philosophical culture of the USSR, one of the first things my Russian mentors made clear to me was that the key concept I had to understand was *activity*. This concept, they suggested, was critical to grasping the distinctive contribution of Soviet philosophy and psychology. This proved to be no easy task.[1] I had been brought up in the Anglo-American tradition of philosophy where there was plenty of talk about *action*, but precious little discussion of *activity*. Of course, I was familiar with discussions of *practices* among Aristotelians and Wittgensteinians, and of *practice* or *praxis* in Western Marxism, but the concept of activity in Soviet philosophy seemed to be more than merely a variation on those. Moreover, I gradually began to realise that there was no settled view within the Russian tradition of what the so-called 'activity approach' amounted to. Everyone conceded that the task was to heed Marx's call in the first of the 'Theses on Feuerbach' to develop a true materialism that would conceive of 'the thing, reality, sensuousness' not only 'in the form of *object or of contemplation*', but subjectively 'as *sensuous human activity*, practice',[2] but there was precious little agreement about what this would mean. This became evident to all towards the end of the Soviet era, when it was no longer necessary for philosophers to feign an appearance of unanimity, and radically different views of the concept of activity were openly expressed in the literature, together with a certain amount of scepticism about the notion's explanatory power.[3]

For all that, however, there can be no doubt that the concept of activity played a vital role in the history of Soviet thought. I have argued elsewhere that, in Soviet psychology, Vygotsky's followers insulated themselves against

---

1   The mentor who had the greatest influence on my work was Felix Mikhailov (see Bakhurst 2011b). I also profited enormously from discussions with Vladislav Lektorsky, Vladimir Bibler, Vasili Davydov and many others (see Bakhurst 1992, 1995).

2   Marx 1968 [1845], p. 28.

3   See, for example, the symposium presented in Lektorsky 1990, on which I draw extensively in this chapter.

the charges of idealism that were directed at Vygotsky himself by embracing the concept of object-oriented activity, and thereby succeeded in saving much of Vygotsky's legacy, albeit in transmuted form.[4] And in philosophy, because of its impeccable Marxist pedigree, the concept of activity was deployed to direct attention to some of the most philosophically interesting aspects of Marx's work – his philosophical anthropology and its Hegelian antecedents – thereby facilitating discussion of a range of philosophical topics, such as creativity, intelligence and alienation, epistemological issues of knowledge and justification, educational questions about 'hands-on' learning, and many more. In this way the concept served as a conduit for philosophical creativity in a difficult and repressive philosophical culture.

In this chapter, I wish to turn attention away from the role the concept of activity has played in the history of Russian thought and focus instead on its general philosophical significance. We need to ask whether the concept is of more than merely historical importance. Does what the Russians attempted to do with this concept represent a distinctive contribution to live philosophical questions?[5]

2   Ilyenkov: Activity as a Logical Category

Heeding my mentors' advice, I focused much of my research into Soviet philosophy on a thinker who gave the concept of activity pride of place, Evald Ilyenkov. So I propose to articulate a number of themes from Ilyenkov's work, where the concept of activity figures centrally, with a view to assessing whether they are of enduring philosophical relevance.

It is important to appreciate that the concept of activity, as Ilyenkov and many other Russian thinkers deploy it, is not an empirical concept, but something more fundamental: a logical category. That is, the activity approach, properly understood, does not set out to describe or characterise human activity as an anthropologist or empirical psychologist might, or even to provide a philosophical typology of different kinds of activity (object-oriented, material, intellectual, instrumental, communicative, interactive, or whatever). Rather, activity is supposed to be a basic explanatory category, charged with elucidating

---

4   Bakhurst 1990.
5   In what follows, I shall not be concerned with the influence of conceptions of activity on the development of 'activity theory' in the West. I discuss this undoubtedly important legacy of Soviet philosophy and psychology in Bakhurst 2009. My focus here is strictly on the philosophical significance of the concept of activity.

the relation between subject and object, thinking and being – with explaining the very possibility of a relation between mind and world. That is why it is central to the quest for true materialism. So when Ilyenkov says (echoing Marx) that 'both the *contemplating individual* and the *world contemplated* are products of history',[6] he means this not (or not only) as an empirical observation, but as a kind of transcendental claim: mind and world are possible only in and through activity.

3   Ten Ilyenkovian Theses

In a 2005 article, I tried to characterise some key moments of an Ilyenkovian approach in the form of ten theses.[7] Here they are, slightly revised:

i.   To understand our distinctively human mental powers, we must comprehend our ability to commune with what Ilyenkov calls 'the ideal', that is, with all those putatively non-material phenomena (such as ideas, meanings, values) that comprise the domain of the conceptual.

ii.   Our relation to the ideal is essentially normative in character; that is, ideal phenomena influence our thoughts and actions rationally rather than merely causally. To possess a concept is to understand a set of rational (often inferential) relations; to grasp the meaning of an expression is to know how it *ought* to be deployed; to recognise the value of some object, action or event is to appreciate something about what *ought* to be the case. The defining characteristic of human minded behaviour is that it is guided or determined by reasons, rather than merely dictated by causes.

iii.   To understand this, we must recognise that ideal requirements on thought and action have their authority independently of the consciousness and will of thinking subjects. In this sense, the ideal exists objectively. The realm of the ideal is not the projection of individual minds. On the contrary, the direction of explanation runs the other way: the objective existence of the ideal is a precondition of the possibility of individual minds, at least minds of the kind possessed by human beings.

iv.   This may look like a form of Platonism, but objectively existing ideal phenomena do not constitute a supersensible reality or group-mind. We

---

6   Ilyenkov 1974, p. 207.

7   Bakhurst 2005. I am grateful to Oxford University Press for permission to use this material here.

can think of them as elements of 'social consciousness', understood as a cultural formation, as something intelligible only in its relation to human activity.

v.   Cultural phenomena are embodied both in human practices and in the form the world takes on by virtue of human activity.

vi. If we adopt a 'genetic' perspective – one concerned with the origin of the ideal – we can say that ideal phenomena are 'objectifications' of human activity. By virtue of our engagement with the world, nature is lent significance and value; it is 'humanised' or 'enculturated'. (We should, however, not reify the ideal: it exists only in the dynamic interplay of activity and world, 'in the unceasing transformation of a form of activity into the form of a thing and back – the form of a thing into the form of activity').[8]

vii. The point is not just that our ontology must admit 'social objects' – artefacts and institutions, for example – understood as embodiments of human activity. Of course, any form of Marxism will acknowledge the reality of such objects and distinguish them from natural phenomena. Ilyenkov's claim, however, is that 'in man, all objects are idealised'; that is, all objects brought within the compass of our 'spiritual culture' are made meaningful, and our relation to them engages our conceptual powers.[9] The world is given to us insofar as it is brought within the realm of the conceptual.

viii. To be a thinking thing *just is* to have the capacity to commune with the ideal, to engage with the world normatively. We must orient epistemology away from what Elizabeth Anscombe called modern philosophy's 'incorrigibly contemplative conception of knowledge',[10] with its preoccupation with the representation or picturing of reality, and towards a conception of mind as a specific mode of active engagement with the world. As Ilyenkov liked to put it when sympathetically expounding Spinoza, thought is the mode of activity of a thinking body.

ix. Our distinctively human mental powers are not innate but are acquired through enculturation (*Bildung*). We become rational animals – persons in the full sense – as we appropriate the distinctively human forms of activity that manifest mindedness.

x.   This position aspires to explain both the nature of the world as a possible object of thought (that is, of rational engagement), and the nature and

---

8   Ilyenkov 1991a [1979], p. 269.
9   Ilyenkov 1974, p. 202.
10   Anscombe 1957, p. 57.

origin of the powers that constitute thinking, as emerging out of activity (or perhaps, in their essential relation to activity). It is thus a deduction (or dialectical derivation) of the distinction between subject and object, mind and world, in which the key concept – the 'cell', the 'arche', the 'unit' – is the concept of activity.

4   Batishchev Against Activity

I believe that these ten theses capture important elements of Ilyenkov's philosophy. Of course, since I have mined them, removed them from their context, and cast them in a rather different idiom from Ilyenkov's own, it might be questioned whether my reading of Ilyenkov is faithful to the original. Some might complain that this is more like 'Ilyenkhurst' than Ilyenkov. But suppose these ten theses express a viable Ilyenkov-inspired variant of the activity approach. Is it a live philosophical option?

It will help to consider some objections to the activity approach made by thinkers who were broadly sympathetic to it. The most interesting such objection is Genrikh Batishchev's claim that the activity approach is guilty of what he calls 'substantialism'. At first sight, this might appear to be the complaint that the activity approach treats object-oriented activity as a kind of material surrogate for Hegel's *Geist*. History, as the activity approach would have us see it, is not *Geist's* voyage to self-consciousness and absolute knowledge, but material activity's journey to free, self-determined fulfilment under communism.

The problematic character of such a vision was certainly part of the accusation of substantialism, but there was also a good deal more to Batishchev's concerns, which contain many overlapping themes. For example, another of Batishchev's targets was monism, understood not so much as substance-monism, but as what Paul Franks (2005) calls 'derivation monism' – the idea that all aspects of an adequate philosophical system are to be derived 'from a single, absolute first principle', which for the devotee of the activity approach is, naturally, activity.[11] But this, Batishchev argues, entails the 'shameless elevation' of

---

11   Franks (2005, p. 17) casts derivation-monism as a view about the derivation of the *a priori* conditions of experience. Such a view embraces Ilyenkov's philosophy, though Ilyenkov's explanatory ambitions are bolder. It is noteworthy that the entry on monism in volume 3 of the *Filosofskaya entsiklopediya* essentially defines monism in terms of derivation-monism (see the references in Davydov 1990a, p. 149).

activity into a 'supercategory' from which we are somehow to deduce all aspects of human life – mind, language, institutions, culture, art, religion, interpersonal relations, and so on.[12] Such a derivation might be relatively trivial, in that it is not hard to portray all these as aspects of human activity, but the activity approach's preoccupation with object-oriented, goal-directed activity paints far too instrumental a picture of our relation to the world, and to each other.[13] So Batishchev writes, distancing himself from views he once held, 'activity is not the only possible, universal, mode of being of man, culture, and sociality, and ... not the only and all-embracing mode of man's relation to the world'.[14] Any conception of activity needs to be complemented by other fundamental concepts such as, communication and community, that are simply irreducible to object-oriented activity.[15]

In addition, the activity approach does not simply distort our *relation* to reality; it offers a distorted conception of reality itself, portraying the world as merely the plaything of human activity. As Batishchev puts it, 'the whole of objective reality outside human consciousness [is] reduced to a world of objects – things that are axiomatically empty and a priori lower than man'.[16] Such radical anthropocentrism not only slights the independence of objective reality; it also perpetuates the myth that, as V.S. Shvyrev boldly puts it, 'humans are basically capable of taking control of any "space" in the world, any "sector" of existence'.[17] As such, the activity approach embraces a prometheanism that is as environmentally disastrous as it is philosophically baseless. Moreover, even as a form of anthropocentrism the activity approach is myopic in that its instrumentalism makes for a remarkably one-dimensional view of human beings.[18] Only consider the idea that the *Bildungsprocess* can be understood as a matter of the 'internalisation' of social forms of activity; indeed, it is sometimes claimed that internalisation accounts for the very genesis of the individual mind. But such a vision has no way to acknowledge an authentic form of subjectivity or genuine modes of creativity.

What Batishchev called 'substantialism' is thus code for a whole host of sins, incorporating monism, reductionism, anthropocentrism and instrumentalism,

---

12   Batishchev 1990a, p. 7.

13   See Batishchev 1990c, p. 171.

14   Batishchev 1990a, p. 9.

15   This was also a prominent theme in B.F. Lomov's reading of the activity approach in Soviet psychology.

16   Batishchev 1990a, p. 9.

17   Shvyrev 1990b, p. 3.

18   See Batishchev 1990c, p. 172.

which jointly preclude 'any sense of undiscovered possibility, anything beyond the limit, any mystery'.[19]

5   In Defence of Ilyenkov

There are certainly versions of the activity approach that warrant some or all of these criticisms. Indeed, there are those that invite the label 'substantialism' in its pure form. V.P. Zinchenko, for example, writes that 'activity as a whole is an organic system whereby, as in a living organism, everything is reflected in something else and that something else reflects everything in itself. But this is not enough. In addition, activity with its highly complex structure is constantly developing. An indispensable feature of an organically developing system is its capacity to create during the course of its development organs that it lacks.'[20] To conceive of activity as *subject*, as Zinchenko does in this passage, is undoubtedly problematic, but it is hard to see Ilyenkov as guilty of this kind of totalising vision. Ilyenkov is a substance-monist, but the substance is matter (understood as a dynamic system, not as human activity). Activity 'substantialises' itself in matter, but it is not itself substance, but form (or rather, that which creates form).

I also do not think that Ilyenkov gives the concept of activity all-encompassing explanatory pretensions. The concept plays a critical role in the solution to the problem of the ideal, which in turn explains the possibility of the relation between mind and world, but Ilyenkov is not committed to the view that the character of that relation, or of the relation between mind and mind, has to be understood exclusively in terms of activity. To become a thinking thing, the child must acquire the capacity to commune with the ideal, and this involves initiation into the practices of the community and, thereby, the appropriation of forms of activity which, as it were, bear ideality within them. A being that has acquired that capacity is able to engage in conceptual thought and communication, and to enter a meeting of minds with other such beings. Though this may be mediated by object-oriented activity, it does not *consist in* object-oriented activity, nor can it be reduced to object-oriented activity. Moreover, in the rare cases where Ilyenkov speaks of 'internalisation',[21] he is very clear that the appropriation of social forms of activity is to be understood

---

19   Batishchev 1990b, p. 90.
20   Zinchenko, quoted by Batishchev, 1990a, p. 11.
21   For example, Ilyenkov 2002b.

as a precondition of the emergence of self-determining subjects, who are by
no means 'products of society' in the pejorative sense. So there need be no
tension between the notion of internalisation and the idea of autonomy or creativity.

Of course, there are elements in Batishchev's criticisms that hit their mark.
The 'environmental' objection is spot on. The whole rhetoric of the activity
approach portrays nature as an object of aim-oriented activity, as a resource, as
the means of humanity's self-realisation. This is true of a great deal of Marxist
thinking. But though this comes naturally to the activity approach, I do not
think it *has* to see nature this way. If our active engagement with nature is the
source of our very rationality, it does not follow that we must portray the world
as subordinate to human ends. An ecologically saner perspective is perfectly
possible, one which acknowledges that we are parts of nature, not masters of
it.

Another serious issue is whether Ilyenkov's solution to the problem of the
ideal commits him to a form of anthropocentrism that slights the independence of objective reality. This is an objection I have tried to address in a number
of my writings, perhaps not entirely successfully.[22] Ilyenkov claims that the fundamental forms of thought that make possible our cognitive relation to the
world are not innate in individual minds, but are inherent in the practices of
the community – they are culturally, rather than psychologically, *a priori*. Each
child becomes a thinking thing by appropriating the practices constitutive of
those forms of thought. Does he not, therefore, confront analogous problems to
Kant? By what right does he think that our forms of thought disclose the world
to us 'as it is', rather than as it is relative to the forms of activity of beings like
us? Ilyenkov seems to hold that because our forms of thought are grounded in
the modes of activity of beings engaged with an objective world, those forms of
thought reflect the character of that world as much as they reflect our character
as agents. However, the theory is insufficiently developed and it is hard to say
whether this is an argument or an expression of faith. One might respond that
the contrast between the world as it is in itself, and the world as it is by virtue
of the influence of human activity, is a distinction that must be made *within*
the conception of the world that issues from the application of our concepts.
It is not as if the distinction can be drawn from some vantage-point *outside*
thought, from which we can compare the world as it is out of all relation to us
with the world as we find it. The problem of reality is one posed for us within

practice and is resolved practically, rather than philosophically, as the second of the 'Theses on Feuerbach' boldly affirms.[23]

Although this may seem an unsatisfying resolution, there is no doubt that we are in the terrain of live philosophical issues: how to understand the preconditions of our cognitive contact with a mind-independent world. It might be complained, however, that we have arrived at this live issue via a route that is full of obscurity. What does it really mean to say that ideality is activity objectified, or that the ideal exists in the interplay between the form of practice and the form of reality? It will not do just to show that the activity approach has live questions in view; it has to have something intelligible to say about them. Is this really true of Ilyenkov's contribution?

6   Activity and the Sources of Normativity

A natural response to this objection would be to present Ilyenkov's famous work on the ideal as addressing a question familiar from post-Kantian philosophy: what is the source of normative authority? As we saw above, the influence that the ideal has on thought and action is normative. The problem of the ideal is thus the problem of how norms are possible, or how rational determination is possible, and we can see Ilyenkov as arguing that normative authority is objective, relative to the individual, but ultimately instituted by social human activity. This brings Ilyenkov into dialogue with the social-pragmatist tradition (the leading exponent of which is Robert Brandom[24]).

On such a constructivist view, normativity is standardly thought of as brought into being by something like self-legislation, understood not as the exercise of pure practical reason, but as a matter of social recognition. Ultimately, there is nothing to being a norm other than being taken to be one. As Jeffrey Stout puts it:

> Our norms are our doing. Each time we apply a concept we contribute something to the evolution of our norms ... As subjects, we are products of the norms as they currently stand, just as our norms are products of

---

23   'The question whether objective truth can be attributed to human thinking is not a question of theory but is a practical question. Man must prove the truth – i.e. the reality and power, the this-sidedness of his thinking in practice. The dispute over the reality or non-reality of thinking that is isolated from practice is a purely *scholastic* question' (Marx 1968 [1845], p. 28).

24   See, for example, Brandom 1994.

the social practice in which our predecessors carried out their cognitive projects by applying concepts to things they considered worth talking about. The inheritance now rests in our hands.[25]

So Stout characterises a view that finds various forms of expression in the writings of many different philosophers. Ilyenkov's version, with its emphasis on the material instantiation of what Hegel calls 'objective spirit' through the objectification of activity, is rather different in character from the work of many contemporary pragmatists, but it is similar in inspiration and aim. It portrays the source of normative authority as ultimately residing in us.

It is certainly possible to see Ilyenkov as contributing to this style of thought. And this is hardly surprising, since the social-pragmatist tradition has its roots in Hegel, Ilyenkov's favourite philosopher.[26] I have reservations, however, about the idea that all normative authority issues from us. There is a good sense, for example, in which the rules of soccer are our norms, that we administer them, and so on. This is so because those norms are in the service of certain specifiable human interests and may be codified and modified to suit them. But things are not so straightforward when we consider norms of inquiry that are in the service of getting things right. Here the norms are as much a matter of discovery as the truths they enable us to disclose. In what sense, then, are they *ours*? They may be said to be so because we embrace them, thereby 'making them our own', but not because we put them into place. I believe we need to recognise a fundamental non-derivative kind of normative authority that is not constructed by us, but which we discover and to which we seek to conform our thoughts and actions. As John McDowell puts it, '[i]f self-legislation of rational norms is not to be a random leap in the dark, it must be seen as an acknowledgement of an authority that the norms have anyway'.[27]

---

25   Stout 2007, p. 30.

26   It is becoming popular to see the German idealist tradition as defined by its interest in solving what Terry Pinkard calls 'the Kantian paradox', namely, how the normative authority of, say, some maxim or principle is to issue wholly from self-legislation when it would appear to be rational to bind oneself only to principles for which there are good reasons – that is, reasons that are antecedent to, and provide grounds for, acts of self-legislation (see Pinkard 2002, pp. 59–60; Pinkard (p. 60n) attributes the first articulation of the paradox to Robert Pippin). Pinkard, Pippin and Brandom all see Hegel as resolving the paradox through a social theory of normativity. John McDowell provides a dissenting voice, with which I concur (see, for example, McDowell 2005).

27   McDowell 2005, p. 105.

Fortunately, we need not settle this issue here.[28] For present purposes it is enough to remark that if Ilyenkov's discussion of the problem of the ideal can be fruitfully read in relation to contemporary debates about the sources of normativity, then it is unmistakably a contribution to live philosophical issues, and moreover, one that addresses them with greater imagination than is found in the writings of many thinkers who struggle with these matters.

7 Conclusion: A Radical Proposal

I want to conclude by making a radical, even heretical, suggestion. Many of the problems of the activity approach, real or perceived, issue from the idea that activity is a category from which we can deduce the relation between subject and object, thinking and being. But suppose we forswear commitment to derivation-monism and appease Batishchev by adopting a more modest project. Let us think of ourselves as trying to characterise our form of life, or the human life-form, in a way analogous to the kind of natural-historical judgements by which we might characterise an animal species.[29] Any such account would have to describe our biological nature in terms anatomical, physiological, and so on. But it would also have to capture the distinctive character of human beings' modes of activity. Suppose we think of the philosophy of activity as trying to do just that. The task is not to give an empirical description of how human beings live or what they do, but to express the terms in which we must *think* human activity, the terms in which human activity must understand itself. Central to any such characterisation will be the idea that human beings are responsive to reasons, or that they commune with the ideal, as Ilyenkov might have said. It is not just that some of a human being's doings can, indeed must, be understood as guided or determined by reasons. It is that being subject to rational determination is an essential dimension of our mode of being. The ideas of object-oriented or goal-directed activity are in themselves less than adequate to capture this, for aim-oriented action as such is not distinctively human. What is critical is that a creature that is responsive to reasons is capable of deliberation, of making up its mind about what to think or do in light of an appreciation of what there is reason to think or do. Such a being is autonomous or self-determining. Its activity manifests freedom. Moreover, its freedom

---

28   For further discussion see Bakhurst 2011a.

29   This suggestion is inspired by Michael Thompson's recent work: see, for example, Thompson 2008.

presupposes that it is self-conscious, for it can think and act for reasons only insofar as it knows what it thinks and does. Now any attempt to characterise human activity along these lines must reckon with the fact that in the course of their lives human beings undergo a certain transformation. We are not born responsive to reasons, but attain this status in the course of coming to maturity. A human life is marked by *Bildung*, by the formation of reason.[30]

Suppose we give the philosophy of activity the task of continuing and deepening this characterisation, which picks up, of course, many of the themes in the ten Ilyenkovian theses I presented. Is this not really the project in which we have been engaged all along, once it is relieved of transcendental or Hegelian–Marxist baggage? It might be complained that Ilyenkov himself would not recognise the project. But I do not think that is true. For preserved in the approach is the idea, central to German idealism, that freedom, reason and self-consciousness are one, and hence the task of true materialism is to understand how a being that is self-conscious, free and responsive to reasons is, indeed can only be, a material substance. That is a question that Ilyenkov would definitely recognise as his own. Moreover, such an approach makes self-consciousness the primary object of philosophy: for the project of understanding how freedom, reason and self-consciousness are one is an exercise in self-knowledge, by thinking beings who understand their own nature as such. This issue, cast in this way, is very much alive in contemporary philosophy, thanks in part to Sebastian Rödl's impressive book *Self-Consciousness* (2007).

I think therefore that we can now conclude that the concept of activity is of more than merely historical significance. There is much in the activity approach, as exemplified by Ilyenkov, which engages with ideas prominent on the contemporary philosophical landscape. Indeed, I expect that as time goes on, and more and more lines of communication are opened between German idealism and Anglo-American styles of philosophy, the kind of theoretical insights that gripped Ilyenkov will come to seem increasingly relevant to our philosophical concerns, even as the political vision that inspired him becomes increasingly remote. Indeed, I suspect that the concept of activity, in one guise or another, may gradually edge its way towards the centre of philosophical attention and, with this, the reflections of Ilyenkov and like-minded Russian philosophers will come to seem strangely prescient. Whether I am right, only time will tell.

---

30   See McDowell, 1994, pp. 125–6; McDowell's philosophy is treated at length in Bakhurst 2011a.

CHAPTER 2

'Praxis' as the Criterion of Truth? The Aporias of Soviet Marxism and the Activity Approach

Vesa Oittinen

At first glance, the idea of the activity approach in Soviet philosophy from the 1960s onwards seems to continue the tradition of the theory of praxis that Marxist philosophy proposed. However, a closer look reveals greater complexity. Curiously, the concepts of 'praxis' (*praktika*) and 'activity' (*deyatel'nost'*) have mostly existed side by side, living their own lives in the discourses of Soviet philosophy. Even more astonishing, considering the central role the concept of praxis has played in discussions of Marxist philosophers, both in the Soviet Union and elsewhere, is the absence of a general survey of its place and fortunes in Soviet philosophy.

It is true that the history of Soviet philosophy remains insufficiently explored, but the reasons why this particular concept has not become the object of critical study probably lie deeper. Because the concept of praxis/practice[1] was such a cornerstone of Marxism-Leninism, all attempts to upset it would have rocked the boat of Soviet ideology. Consequently, attempts to rethink innovatively the role of praxis led to a bizarre dichotomy. While the new ideas about the active role of human subjectivity that emerged in the 'thaw' period of the late 1950s and early 1960s were discussed in different versions of the activity approach, these ideas had a much smaller influence, if any at all, on the status of the concept of praxis itself, which remained ideologically overcharged. Only after the demise of the Soviet Union and the specific 'form of life' it had created did an analysis of this situation become possible; thus, the old Hegelian wisdom of the owl of Minerva is applicable even here.

---

1   The Russian word *praktika*' seems to cover semantically both English concepts of 'practice' and 'praxis'. The two terms are used synonymously in this chapter.

Messianistic Expectations About 'Praxis'

In Marxist philosophy, the concept of praxis stems from two *loci classici*: from the 'Theses on Feuerbach', which Marx wrote in 1845, and from Engels's interpretation in his booklet *Ludwig Feuerbach and the End of Classical German Philosophy* (1886). Despite the fact that Marx's theses were first published in Engels's booklet, which means that both works were intimately connected, already a quick glance reveals that the young Marx and the old Engels stressed quite different sides in the idea of praxis. In 1845, Marx clearly used it as a *socio-philosophical* concept and polemised against both Feuerbach's ahistorical anthropologism and the subjectivism of the Young Hegelians; in 1886, Engels applied the concept of praxis to gnoseological problems, using it as a weapon against Kant's alleged 'agnosticism'. It was Engels, not Marx, who formulated the idea, which was later almost unanimously accepted among the theoreticians of the Second International, of praxis as a criterion of truth. In *Ludwig Feuerbach*, Engels claimed that in the process of practice things become 'things-for-us', thereby confuting the Kantian thesis of the unattainability of 'things-in-themselves'. In order to reinforce his assertion, Engels presented an argument that later gained renown as the 'alizarin example'. Engels wrote that the invention of synthetic alizarin, extracted from charcoal, replaced the madder-root that had previously been used to get red dye for the uniforms of English soldiers. Thus, Engels argued that modern chemistry showed that the chemical substances produced in the bodies of the plants were not any kind of 'things-in-themselves' but instead became 'things-for-us' as science and industry progressed. His general conclusion from the alizarin case reads, 'If we are able to prove the correctness of our conception of a natural process by making it ourselves, bringing it into being out of its conditions and using it for our own purposes into the bargain, then there is an end of the Kantian incomprehensible "thing-in-itself".'[2]

It may well be that Engels presented his alizarin-argument with tongue in cheek (indeed, reflecting on Engels's personal character, this is quite possible) but the Marxists of the Second International, followed by Plekhanov and Lenin, took it with an earnestness that was inherited by Soviet philosophy. Although it was quite *chic* to cite Marx's 'Theses on Feuerbach', the Soviet philosophers nevertheless interpreted the idea of praxis primarily in the sense of old Engels: not as a socio-philosophical approach, but as a universal doctrine with both ontological and gnoseological applicability. So the polemical works of Plekhanov,

---

2   Engels 1941 [1886], pp. 22–3.

the real founder of dialectical materialism, used the praxis-arguments of young Marx and old Engels indiscriminately, as if there were no differences between them.[3]

As a result of this approach, the idea of praxis became a seemingly omnipotent argument, which was able to topple all kinds of speculative metaphysics that theorised in an ivory tower, or of agnosticism that dared not say anything conclusive about the external reality surrounding us. In some cases, especially in the earlier phases of Soviet philosophy, the idea of praxis was filled with messianic expectations. A good example is the eulogy to 'praxis' by Nikolai Bukharin, who uniquely combined the roles of a Marxist intellectual and a party-man. In his *Prison Notebooks* of 1937, Bukharin wrote that Marx had revolutionised philosophy by introducing the concept of praxis, which had inaugurated a totally new epoch in the history of philosophy. The principle of praxis, which states that 'thought ... is the continuation of practice',[4] would actually lead to a replacement of the old discipline of gnoseology with a new discipline, which Bukharin called 'sociology of thought' and which 'acts as the prolegomena for any real philosophy'.[5]

The nod to Kant's *Prolegomena* is clear: Bukharin thinks that Marxism had brought about an upheaval in philosophy at least as great as the Kantian 'Copernican turn'. Indeed, philosophy in the old sense had ceased to exist because the idea of praxis solves the age-old issues of philosophy. Firstly, it shows that the Kantian idea of a 'thing-in-itself' is obsolete. Secondly, it points out that the ultimate criterion of truth is to be found in praxis. Bukharin cites Lenin from his *Philosophical Notebooks*: 'The result of activity is the test of subjective cognition and the criterion of *objectivity which truly is*.'[6] For Bukharin, the introduction of the concept of praxis was only one aspect of the total revolution of the life-

---

3   For example, in *Materialismus Militans*, Plekhanov, polemising against Bogdanov, unquestioningly accepts Engels's critique of the 'thing-in-itself', adding, 'The direct meaning of this is that experience presupposes interaction between the subject and the object *outside it*' (Plekhanov 1976a [1908–10], p. 218). In *Fundamental Problems of Marxism*, Plekhanov cites the first thesis on Feuerbach by Marx, according to which the 'chief defect of all hitherto existing materialism ... is that the thing, reality, sensuousness, is conceived only in the form of the *object or of contemplation*, but not as *sensuous human activity, practice*, not subjectively'. Plekhanov comments on this by saying that, for Marx, 'man is induced to think chiefly by the sensations he experiences' (Plekhanov 1976b [1907], p. 128). In both cases, Plekhanov sees the concept of praxis primarily as a moment of a philosophy of experience.

4   Bukharin 2005, p. 45. In the original: '*Myshlenie ... yest udlinenie praktiki*'.

5   Bukharin 2005, p. 213.

6   Bukharin 2005, p. 118.

conditions of humanity, which had begun in October 1917 and which would mean an end to what Marx had called the 'prehistory of human society'.

These messianic expectations about the revolutionising effects of the idea of praxis as the ultimate criterion of truth and a means to overcome the Kantian problem of things-in-themselves later became more moderate, but never vanished totally from Soviet philosophy. A typical example was the habit of dividing the textbooks of the history of philosophy into 'pre-Marxist' and 'Marxist' philosophy. This was a reminder that Bukharin's idea of the emergence of Marxism as a 'hinge' in the history of human thought was further taken seriously, although Bukharin himself became an 'unperson' in the Soviet Union. The ideological cliché of the superiority of Marxism-Leninism over all forms of 'bourgeois' thought was largely based on the idea of the revolutionising effect of the 'praxis-criterion'.

The official viewpoint is expressed in its 'mature' form in the standard work *Fundamentals of Marxism-Leninism* (second edition, 1963):

> In contrast to pre-Marxian materialism, Marxism *includes practice in the theory of knowledge*, viewing practice as the *basis and purpose* of the cognitive process and as the *criterion of the trustworthiness of knowledge*.
>
> By introducing the standpoint of life, of practice, into the theory of knowledge, Marxism directly connects cognition with industry and agriculture, with the research laboratory and the social activities of the masses. Marxism regards theory as the elucidation and generalisation of man's practical experience, and not as something differing in principle from practice.
>
> Practice and theory are opposites, just as man's material and mental activities are opposites. But these opposites penetrate each other and form a unity of two inseparably connected and interacting aspects of social life.[7]

And as to the theory of cognition:

> Indeed, man has no other means of establishing the truth of his knowledge except through practice. It is his practical activities – the basis and ultimate goal of cognition – that constitute the supreme yardstick with which to determine whether knowledge that has been gained is true or not. *Practice is the criterion of truth.*

---

7   *Fundamentals of Marxism-Leninism*, p. 91.

Dialectical materialism defines practice as a process in which man, a material being, acts upon his material environment. Practice is the entire activity of man in altering the world, and primarily his productive and social and revolutionary activity.

In industrial production, the most widespread form of practically verifying scientific and technological ideas is factory tests and the mass use of machines, instruments and technological processes.

In scientific research, practice often takes the form of *experiment*, i.e., man's active interference in natural phenomena, when on the strength of definite theoretical assumptions conditions are created artificially for reproducing or, reversely, terminating the phenomenon in question.[8]

It is noteworthy that these official Diamat definitions stress the role of 'industrial production' and 'experiment' in obtaining the truth, thus echoing Engels's old 'alizarin-thesis' and putting it at the fundaments of its theory of cognition.

'Praxis' in Soviet Philosophy – A Confused Concept

The 'official' view of Soviet ideologists was that fundamental problems of philosophy had already been solved by the introduction of the concept of praxis and there was no need for further discussions. From the 1960s on, however, an intellectual need appears to have arisen among Soviet philosophers to reinterpret the idea of practice and to develop it as a conceptual tool. In the books and articles published by professional philosophers, which usually had a restricted circulation, the Diamat concept of praxis was increasingly criticised, albeit very cautiously. For example, in 1973 the well-known Soviet logician D.P. Gorsky wrote:

One should not understand practice as criterion of truth in a primitive manner, but in the sense that every scientific assertion should be applied in practice and get confirmed by it. In the process of grounding the scientific assertions we are comparing the scientific assertions and scientific contexts with the reality using several mediated procedures ... which only in the last instance are connected with practice ... On the basis of the intrinsic laws of the development of fundamental sciences, there are cre-

---

8 *Fundamentals of Marxism-Leninism*, p. 109.

ated even such areas of knowledge, which in principle do not allow an immediate examination by means of practice.[9]

Gorsky and other 'logicians' followed the strategy of formally accepting the postulates of Diamat, but at the same time insisting on the necessity to pay attention to the relative autonomy of the 'sub-system of logico-gnoseological categories'.[10] Under this disguise, they then pursued research that, in principle, did not differ greatly from Western analytic philosophy of science or so-called scientific realism.[11]

The alternative strategy would have been to try to reform the Diamat concept of practice. However, such attempts were blocked by the concept's important ideological role. A revealing example of the difficulties to which this anomalous situation had led in the 1960s is the article on 'praxis' (*praktika*)[12] written by Aleksandr Ogurtsov in 1967 for the five-volume *Filosofskaya entsiklopediya*. The 18 and a half columns dedicated to this concept were a clear sign of its importance according to the editors of the encyclopaedia, whose main redactor was the then all-powerful Party philosopher F.V. Konstantinov. At the same time, however, Ogurtsov, a young philosopher of the post-Stalin *shestidesiatnik* generation, attempted to give some new life to the old concept.

Having defined 'praxis' as the 'sensuous-objective form of the life-activity of socially developed Man, a form which consists of the appropriation of natural or social forces and which expresses the specificity of the human relation to the world, the mode of existence of Man in the world',[13] Ogurtsov went on to give an historical account of the development of the concept, starting with Plato and Aristotle. The last third of the article is dedicated to the 'problem of praxis in Marxist philosophy'. There, the article's tone changes significantly, taking as its starting point the comment of Lenin in his *Philosophical Notebooks* that praxis forms the 'nodal point' of Marxist theory.[14] Ogurtsov then attempted to define the concept of praxis on the basis of Marx's 'Theses

---

9   Gorsky 1973, pp. 69–70. Cited here according to Oizerman 2003, p. 161.
10   The expression comes from Tiukhtin 1984, p. 12.
11   A telling example of this strategy is the above-mentioned book on scientific knowledge edited by Gorsky. He begins his short foreword to the volume by twice citing Marx's 'Theses on Feuerbach' and once Lenin's *Philosophical Notebooks*. The remainder of the 288-page volume, which deals with the logics of science, only includes occasional references to the ideologically relevant classics of Marxism (Gorsky 1984, pp. 3–4).
12   Ogurtsov 1967.
13   Ogurtsov 1967, p. 340.
14   Compare V.I. Lenin, *Sochinenija*, vol. 38, p. 275.

on Feuerbach' and declared that the structure of praxis is determined by the categories of objectivation and de-objectivation. Finally, he provided a survey of the different forms of praxis, among which he mentions 'praxis in the sphere of economic life', 'practical agency in a social group', 'practice of a class' and 'practice of building communism'. From the viewpoint of a philosophical analysis, the different forms of praxis can be classified on the basis of their relationship to theory, for example, as a traditional form of activity bound to certain institutions, or then as value-oriented or rationality-oriented forms of practice. Lastly, there are forms of practice related to scientific knowledge.[15]

The whole manner of the presentation in this encyclopaedia entry is somewhat haphazard. One gets the impression that the list of different forms of praxis given there is far from exhaustive and that almost all kinds of activity (or even mere change) might be labelled as some form of 'praxis'. Interestingly, the bibliography of Ogurtsov's 1967 entry contains several references to Yugoslav 'praxis-philosophers' who just at this time were provoking much international discussion among the Marxists, but he does not mention them in the text itself. This may be a subtle hint of the real sympathies of the author. A further interesting trait in Ogurtsov's article is that, by citing the 'classics' of Marxism-Leninism, he relies almost exclusively – with the exception of some obligatory quotations from Lenin – on the early works of Marx. He does not mention the works of the late Engels, particularly not *Ludwig Feuerbach*, in which Engels presented his famous 'alizarin argument'.

In sum, one could say that Ogurtsov's 1967 article exemplifies the difficulties of Soviet philosophy with regard to a strict definition of what should be understood by 'praxis'. Ultimately, these difficulties stem from the fact that the 'classics of Marxism' did not develop any coherent philosophical theory of praxis. As stated above, it should be obvious for any critical observer that Marx's ideas on '*sinnlich-menschliche Tätigkeit, Praxis*' in the 'Theses on Feuerbach' of 1845 must be read in a context other than Engels's 'practical' critique of Kant in his *Ludwig Feuerbach* of 1886. However, it was not possible in Soviet times to state this simple fact, for the reasons mentioned above. Hence the obscurities and grogginess around the concept of 'praxis'/'practice' in Soviet philosophy.

---

15   Ogurtsov 1967, pp. 347–8.

A Post-Soviet Refutation of 'Praxis'

Forty-three years later, in 2010, Aleksandr Ogurtsov published a new article on the concept of praxis, in the *Novaya filosofskaya entsiklopediya*.[16] This entry was several pages long, indicating that the editors regarded it as an important concept of philosophy, even though this new encyclopaedia was, unlike its predecessor from the 1960s, not conceived as specifically Marxist. The tone of Ogurtsov's 2010 article was quite unlike that of the previous one. All hesitations had disappeared, as if the owl of Minerva had realised that she could finally seize the opportunity to crush the old Diamat metaphysics of praxis. After a historical survey of the concept of practice, especially in Hegel, Ogurtsov turned to Marxism and wrote:

> The Marxist philosophy followed the lines started by Hegel, especially the universalisation of the practical relation to the world, the analysis of the structure of goal-setting, and so on. Marx and Engels saw the essence of the revolutionary turn in philosophy, which they allegedly had accomplished, in that they introduced praxis into the theory of knowledge and made it a basis and a criterion of true knowledge. One should, however, pay attention to the staleness of the concept of 'praxis' in Marxism, which was identified with the world-historical and transformative activity of mankind, especially of the proletariat. It found its means of concretisation only by examples, which were used in the course of its demonstration. Thanks to its staleness, the concept of practice may be used to justify anything whatsoever.[17]

Ogurtsov's 2010 article was above all critical of the Marxist-Leninist thesis of 'praxis as the criterion of truth':

> To this is related, too, a kind of opportunism, which is characteristic of all Marxist appeals to the criterion of praxis as a solution to theoretical and gnoseological questions. A non-discursive factor is intruding into the structure of the philosophical discourse, which obliterates even the act of demonstration itself. Because the 'practice' is an extra-cognitive and extra-discursive factor, it cannot serve as the criterion of truth. A grounding of knowledge by relying on structures which lie outside the

---

16   Ogurtsov 2010.
17   Ogurtsov 2010, p. 324.

sphere of gnoseology ... demands that the truth of the latter in turn gets grounded. In this manner, the procedure of grounding can never become completed; thus the grounding process turns out to be a bad infinity. From this one can conclude that a gnoseology which is based on such extra-cognitive and extra-discursive grounds is impossible.[18]

According to Ogurtsov, Marxist philosophy has had 'two principally different lines' regarding philosophical problems in general and to the idea of practice in particular:

> The one line, which emerges from the writings of the young Marx, who accentuated the universality of an intellectual-practical relationship to the world, was continued in the works of Antonio Gramsci, Karl Korsch and Georg Lukács, in the empiriomonism of Aleksandr Bogdanov, and in the latest *Philosophical Arabesques* of Bukharin, written in jail. The other line is represented by Russian Marxists, by Plekhanov, Lenin and their numerous adepts in the Soviet period.[19]

Ogurtsov's assertion about the existence of 'two lines' in Marxist philosophy is actually no more than the well-known distinction between 'Western Marxism' and 'Soviet Marxism'. His only original contribution in this respect is that he counts Bogdanov and the late Bukharin among the 'Western' Marxists. Although such a distinction is, of course, justifiable in general, it seems to me that, when applied to the problem of 'praxis', it is of less relevance than is often assumed. Let us take a closer look at Ogurtsov's theses.

In his critique of the Diamat idea of praxis, Ogurtsov refers in passing to the arguments of Leonard Nelson against the feasibility of 'extra-cognitive' arguments in gnoseology. This was a famous argument that Nelson, a mathematician and philosopher of the Jakob Fries school, presented at the International Congress for Philosophy in Bologna in 1911. In his paper, significantly titled 'Die Unmöglichkeit der Erkenntnistheorie' ('The Impossibility of the Theory of Knowledge'), Nelson stated that all attempts to solve the problem of the validity of knowledge break down because of a fundamental antinomy in the venture itself. We should use a certain criterion to judge whether our knowledge of something is valid. This criterion would itself be either cognition or

---

18 Ogurtsov 2010, p. 342. The mention of 'bad infinity' refers to Hegel's concept of *Schlechte Unendlichkeit*.

19 Ogurtsov 2010.

not cognition. If the criterion of validity is cognition, it would fall within the area of what is problematic; that is, the criterion of validity should be proved to be valid. If the criterion is not cognition, it should nevertheless have to be known, because otherwise we could not apply it; that is, we should know that it is a criterion of truth. In order to gain this knowledge, we should already have known beforehand that it is a criterion of truth.[20]

Although Nelson was not the first to detect the antinomies of the criterion of truth, he managed to present them in a form that seemed insurmountable for a conception of the criterion of truth such as Soviet Diamat possessed. The counter-argument, that practice is a continuous, unending process in which Man is only ever approaching the final truth, does not save the Diamat position, since the fault lies just in the fundament: in the assumption that practice should serve as the *general* criterion of truth.[21]

A second point in Ogurtsov's critique of mainstream Soviet philosophy's concept of praxis is that its ambiguities are shared even by the attempts to develop an alternative version of Marxist philosophy. Actually, *both* lines of Marxism mentioned by Ogurtsov – the 'Western' and the 'Soviet' ones – agree that praxis/practice makes the Kantian 'thing-in-itself' obsolete. Not only Plekhanov and Lenin repeat Engels's 'alizarin argument' against Kant and his alleged agnosticism; the same thesis is upheld by representatives of the other current such as Bogdanov and especially Bukharin, as the quotations from the start of this chapter show.

The truth is that both currents of Marxism have a distorted image of Kant, whom they misinterpret as an 'agnostician'. However, to speak of the doctrine of the 'things-in-themselves' as a kind of agnosticism is beside the point. The idea of a thing-in-itself is a necessary consequence as soon we take a gnoseological point of view. It says simply that we cannot have any knowledge of things that lie outside the subject–object relation constituting knowledge. In other words, it can be read as a tautology in the exact Wittgensteinian sense: we do not know that which lies outside the sphere of knowledge.

Moreover, the critique of the Marxists against Kant's 'thing-in-itself' overlooks the peculiar meaning Kant has given to the concept of 'knowledge'

---

20   I refer here to the abridged English translation of Nelson's Bologna paper by Thomas Brown, at http://www.friesian.com/theory.htm.

21   As Kant already pointed out, a general material criterion of truth cannot be given, since every case, in which the concept of truth should be applied, is different. We can have only a general formal criterion of truth, which according to Kant was that of the correspondence between the idea and the object; but this formal criterion is at the same time antinomic, as Nelson had shown.

(*Erkenntnis*): for him, all knowledge is constituted as a synthesis of sensual content and intellectual form. Therefore, when he says that there cannot be any knowledge of things in themselves, it means that we do not have sensual experience of them as they are *in themselves*, outside the subject–object relation. However, this does not exclude the possibility that we can *think* about things in themselves.[22]

I will not dwell upon the widespread Marxist misunderstandings of Kant's purported agnosticism as I have recently written elsewhere more extensively on the subject.[23] Suffice it to say that the idea of praxis does not make the gnoseological problems obsolete and that praxis cannot serve as the general criterion of truth. To that extent, Ogurtsov's critical comments in the encyclopaedia entry of 2010 – that 'because "practice" is an extra-cognitive and extra-discursive factor, it cannot serve as the criterion of truth' – are quite justified.

From 'Praxis' to Activity Approach

Despite its sketchiness, this brief survey of the history and the problems of the concept of praxis in Soviet philosophy does permit some conclusions. First of all, I believe that we should make a more accurate distinction than that made hitherto between praxis/practice as a *socio-philosophical* concept and the same as a *gnoseological* concept. It is striking that Marx seems to have mostly – or perhaps always – used the first meaning,[24] while it was Engels who, in his *Ludwig Feuerbach*, applied the concept of praxis/practice even to gnoseological

---

22   Compare, for example, the following passage from the *Prolegomena*: 'Es ist wahr: wir können über alle mögliche Erfahrung hinaus von dem, was Dinge an sich selbst sein mögen, keinen bestimmten Begriff geben. Wir sind aber dennoch nicht frei von der Nachfrage nach diesen, uns gänzlich derselben zu enthalten; denn Erfahrung thut der Vernunft niemals völlig Gnüge' (§ 57), in Kant 1968 [1783], p. 351.

23   See Oittinen 2009.

24   The 'Theses on Feuerbach' do not contradict my argument. In writing these theses, Marx was convinced that philosophy in the old sense was *passé*, thanks to Feuerbach's critique of Hegel. Thus, when Marx wrote in the first thesis that the 'chief defect of all hitherto existing materialism … is that the thing, reality, sensuousness, is conceived only in the form of the *object or of contemplation*, but not as *sensuous human activity, practice*, not subjectively', he cannot have thought of its special applicability to gnoseological questions, because these questions were philosophical questions and, in that sense, already obsolete.

problems, claiming that in the process of practice things become 'things-for-us' and that the Kantian thesis of the unattainability of 'things-in-themselves' is therefore destroyed.

Secondly, Ogurtsov may have been slightly too pessimistic when he concluded his 2010 article by saying:

> [T]o put hopes on 'praxis' in the manner the Marxists and Neo-Marxists did, when they saw in it the kernel of a revolutionary turn in philosophy, means to be exposed to the danger of falling into utopianism. Behind the cult of 'praxis' there lies always the temptation of a technocratic utopia.[25]

I would answer that it is not so much the 'cult of praxis' in itself that is chiefly responsible for such utopianism, but rather the idea that *philosophy* itself as a form of thinking and intellectual culture has grown old and can be liquidated and replaced by something else. From this point of view, the 'praxis-utopias' of the Marxists of twentieth century were not unique at all. Similar and often technocratically motivated utopias about the destruction of philosophy were cherished, for example, by the neo-positivists of the Vienna Circle or Wittgenstein (who claimed that all philosophical problems stem from the incorrect usage of words). In sum, it was the 'spirit of the epoch', the spirit of the 'short twentieth century' (Hobsbawm) that contributed to the utopian perception that philosophy in the traditional sense of the word could be replaced by 'praxis' or something else. Marx and Engels had a more ambivalent position to this question. Their critique of received forms of philosophy was not yet technocratically motivated. Rather, the main target for them was the speculative metaphysics which had culminated in Hegel's philosophy. They seemed to think that it might be possible to abandon the metaphysical 'system' of old philosophy, while retaining its achievement, the dialectics, as a 'method'. However, the experience of the twentieth-century Marxism, especially in its Soviet form, has shown that this is not so simple an operation as it may have seemed at first glance. As Antonio Gramsci stated, the assertion that philosophy has nothing to give to us is already in itself a strong philosophical thesis!

Ogurtsov does not seem to think that the idea of praxis can have any theoretical future of note. Perhaps he feels it has fatally compromised itself. However, one could ask whether the concept of praxis might yet be productive, provided one accepts its limitations and does not try to universalise it into a panacea as Soviet Marxism in particular did. This is, of course, too wide a subject to be dealt

---

25   Ogurtsov 2010, p. 325.

with here, but I think it is essential to realise the plurality of interpretations, none of which can claim to represent *the* Marxist point of view. An analysis of the Marxist literature soon reveals that it contains a vast amount of different ideas on praxis, not all of which are derived from early Marx or late Engels, but from some other sources. For example, Antonio Gramsci's *filosofia della prassi*, although used in his *Prison Notebooks* as a pseudonym for Marxism, does not only draw upon the laconic and somewhat enigmatic sketches of Marx's 'Theses on Feuerbach', but borrows, too, from the activist philosophy of his compatriots Giovanni Gentile and Benedetto Croce. Other examples abound. In Soviet philosophy, for instance, Evald Ilyenkov's ideas on practice and activity were reinforced by a Spinozistic connection (Spinoza's famous identification of *agendi potentia* and *cogitandi potentia*).

Of course, Gramsci and the other Western traditions of praxis-philosophy were known in the Soviet Union, but for ideological reasons they could not serve as the starting point of further development of the Diamat concepts. On the contrary, the ideological rigidity of the official theory of praxis caused the Soviet philosophers of the 1960s to the 1980s, who wanted to develop further the issue of human activity, to circumvent the Diamat concept of praxis altogether and develop a seemingly new theory – the 'activity approach' – independently of and parallel to it. This, I believe, is the main explanation for the apparently strange phenomenon that most Soviet philosophers of the activity approach seldom discussed how their theories related to the Marxist concept of praxis, although mandatory quotations from the 'classics' did of course occur.

CHAPTER 3

Reality as Activity: The Concept of Praxis in Soviet Philosophy

Andrey Maidansky

In an effort to emphasise how their materialistic theory was different from all those that came before, the authors of *The German Ideology* called themselves 'practical materialists' (praktische *Materialisten*, i.e., Kommunisten). They argued that the substance and subject of world-history is labour, man's practical transformation of external nature and of his own social relations. All of Marxism is built upon this axiom.

From the standpoint of common logic, however, this premise seems strange, given that labour is not a thing but an act, a process of human activity. Activity is the subject itself and things are its predicates – how is this possible? Idealist philosophers always stand on the idea that mind is a pure act that rules over the world. So, Marx asserted that 'the *active* side [*die* tätige *Seite*] ... was developed abstractly by idealism'.[1] All materialists regarded *the body, the physical thing* as the subject of any activity. Whereas Hegel rejected this logic within the physics itself, saying, 'We are used to considering motion as predicate, as a mode; but actually it is a self-being, the subject as subject.'[2]

Marx was the first materialist to give primacy to Action over Body. Everyone and everything in the history of mankind are modes of human labour. Marx felt that the main fault of all previous materialism was its lack of understanding of the objective reality 'as *sensuous human activity*', or 'subjectively',[3] that is, an inability to understand reality as activity and the activity itself as the subject. For Marx, every human thing is nothing other than objectified labour – the condensed and hardened lava of Action. Furthermore, all of the material conditions of labour, including the living bodies of men, are only the prerequisites and 'vanishing moments' of the labour-process.

---

1   *Thesen über Feuerbach*, I (MEW 3, S. 5).
2   'Wir sind gewohnt, sie als Prädikat, Zustand anzusehen; aber sie ist in der Tat das Selbst, das Subjekt als Subjekt' (Hegel 2000, § 261).
3   MEW 3, S. 5. The term 'subjective' here, of course, does not mean 'mental', but 'active' or 'being carried out by some subject'.

Vadim Mezhuev, who was one of the pioneers of the 'activity approach' in Soviet philosophy, correctly defined Marx's historical theory as a 'phenomenology of labour'. Marx's concept of labour replaced Hegel's *Geist* as the substance and subject of world-history. In fact, human labour is the sole personage of *Capital*. Labour, both abstract and concrete, living and objectified (capital), necessary and surplus, waged and free, private and social – in other words, every line of this entire book – represents the great metamorphosis of Labour in the bourgeois age.

Marxists mainly apprehended the '*active* side' of Marx's teaching in terms of revolutionary calls to liberate the working class from capitalist exploitation. However, it was not Marx who invented them; at that time, such slogans were already on the tongues of communists and socialists of every stripe. Marx's original philosophical principles, his *logic* of thought, remained unapprehended for a very long time.

Even Plekhanov and Lenin only had a superficial understanding of Marx's philosophy. Among the major ideas of *Materialism and Empiriocriticism*, no single considerable idea was unfamiliar to materialists before Marx. Therefore, this book contains no proper Marxism, no *practical* materialism. In particular, I doubt whether Marx was in favour of Lenin's notorious definition of matter as an objective reality given to man by sensations.[4] It was just the kind of materialism that Marx described as 'contemplative' (*der anschauende Materialismus*), for it took reality 'only in the form of object'. Like Lenin, English empiricists, French enlightenment thinkers and Feuerbach understood matter as a perceptible object – 'all the previous materialism' that was criticised in Marx's 'Theses'.

By means of 'sensations', one perceives not so much an objective reality as one's own practical *subjectivity*, transforming the objective reality and, with this, all our sensations. Lenin's definition of matter flatly lacked the 'active side'; that is, the practical ground. It replaced the *concept* of matter with *inadequate empirical abstraction*. Sensation gives reality to man in an abstract and inadequate way, like it does to each animal capable of sensing.

Marx discovered that the real world is given to man practically, in the form of his own labour-activity. Or, to be more precise, objective reality is *not given, but seized* from nature by human labour, by the sweat of a man's brow. Lenin's definition of matter, on the other hand, included 'sensations' in place of 'practice',

---

4   'Matter is a philosophical category denoting the objective reality which is given to man by his sensations, and which is copied, photographed, reflected by our sensations, while existing independently of them' (Lenin 1968, 18, p. 131).

as the definitions of all empiricists and sensualists had done in the centuries before Marx.

In Spinoza's terms, Lenin's definition of matter passes off one of the properties of matter (the property of objectivity) as its very essence. This definition has no more value than a definition of man as a 'two-legged unfeathered animal'. If you want to express the essence of matter, define what the matter *makes* and how it does so. A good definition must indicate the *modus operandi* of a thing, and not just its features, even the unique ones. As Aristotle wrote, '[e]ach object is defined by the action it performs and by the possibility to perform this action'.[5] This imperative is a cornerstone of the 'activity approach'. Surprisingly, as far as I know, none of the Soviet philosophers even attempted to offer an activistic definition of the category of matter. It is as if they were all hypnotised by Lenin's contemplative definition.

The heated polemics on the problem of the ideal lasted about half a century in our philosophy. Almost all of its participants considered themselves to be materialists and agreed that the ideal is a reflection of the material, an attribute of matter; therefore, the problem of the ideal cannot be solved without a clear and concrete understanding of the category of the material. In the course of a seminar on Ilyenkov in 2010, Vadim Mezhuev asked those present what exactly they meant by the 'material'. No answer followed. Lenin's definition of matter is of absolutely no help for solving the problem of the ideal. This is, of course, if we do not regard the ideal as 'copying-photographing' the external world by means of our senses.

Mezhuev rightly requires one to include the 'active side' in the definition of matter, to interpret matter not in a form of sensual contemplation but practically, 'subjectively'. I feel that the fact that this problem has not been raised onto such a plane until recently is a most serious omission.

Mezhuev expounded his own thoughts on this issue in a polemical article entitled 'Is There Matter on Mars?'. He believes that one has the right to speak of the 'material' only in respect to human activity. However, human beings have not yet lived on Mars. Mezhuev proposed a distinction between the categories of *material* and *natural*. The former characterises a substantial, objective aspect of human activity, while the latter characterises things by themselves; that is, what the old, contemplative materialism called 'matter'.

This is clearly an activistic approach to the understanding of the material and it deserves close attention. However, Mezhuev erroneously considered this approach to be strictly Marxist. The authors of *The German Ideology* derided

---

5   *Polit.* I, 11, 1253a.

the separation of the '*concept* of matter' (*der* Begriff *der Materie*) from the true nature (*der wirklichen Natur*) in the philosophy of 'Saint Bruno' (B. Bauer). In abstraction from the real world of nature, they argued, 'matter' is merely a 'philosophical phrase'.[6]

For Marx, nature (or matter, which is the same thing) is an *acting subject*. At the very beginning of *Critique of the Gotha Programme* Marx insisted that *nature* (he underlined this word) is a source of wealth just as much as labour, 'which itself is only the manifestation of a force of nature, human labour power'.[7] Here, the whole world, including human society with its history, can be seen as an action of nature itself, the outward appearance of the force of nature (*die Äußerung einer Naturkraft*). This is reminiscent of Spinoza.

For metaphysicians, nature is only a surrounding environment, the outer world in which man, the subject, acts. For dialecticians, nature is an acting subject, *natura naturans*, which manifests itself most comprehensively in the objective-practical activity of man.

In Soviet philosophy, Evald Ilyenkov stands closer than others to Marx's 'subjective' concept of nature-matter. Taken by Spinoza's philosophy, Ilyenkov went so far as to equate Spinoza's substance with the dialectical-materialistic category of matter. Indeed Ilyenkov went even further, declaring the subject of thought *not body, but action* – the process of labour: 'Labour ... is the "subject" to which thought as a "predicate" belongs.'[8]

The extent to which it is uncommon or difficult to understand this turn of thought may be judged by the fact that even Ilyenkov's closest disciples have appeared unready to accept it. In a recent discussion, almost all of them defended the concept of the 'thinking body', that is, the body as a subject of thought. The second, *inorganic* body of man has not been even mentioned.

Marx described *all nature* as the 'inorganic body of man', insofar as it is drawn into the process of human vital activity, into the orbit of *praxis*. Plants, animals, stones, air and light all 'in practical respect constitute a part of human life and human activity'.[9] Human practice unites and concentrates in itself all the powers of nature. Man is a 'practically universal' being, Marx concluded.

The universality of human activity also consists of its 'congruence' to each and every object. In any case, labour tends towards that. Since ancient times,

---

6   *MEW* 3, s. 89.

7   'Die Natur ist ebensosehr die Quelle der Gebrauchswerte ... als die Arbeit, die selbst nur die Äußerung einer Naturkraft ist, der menschlichen Arbeitskraft' (*MEW* 19, s. 15).

8   Ilyenkov 1974, p. 54.

9   *MEW* 40, s. 515.

this feature of human activity served as a definition of *reason*; wise men act according to the logic of things. Then the objective force of things turns into man's own subjective force, so the 'person himself ... is this inorganic nature as a subject'.[10]

These words are written by the mature Marx in *Grundrisse*. Again we see the 'subjective' concept of nature – *Natur als Subjekt*. As before, Marx cleaves to a principle of 'practical materialism': the reality must be 'seized not only in the form of object, or in the form of contemplation', but in the 'subjective' form of activity *par excellence*.

In Soviet philosophy, Genrikh Batishchev wrote a lot about the activistic grasp of objectivity. He constantly stressed that the object is not just a 'raw material' of human activity. In the process of work, man *meets* the world, deobjectifying (*raspredmechivaya*[11]) and adopting its 'objective dialectics'. The relationship requires the '*parity* and *reciprocity*' of both sides. The subjective violence to objectivity not only destroys and depreciates the latter, but also impoverishes the subject, man himself. 'The grade of actual perfection of a man can be measured exactly by the richness of his objective relations, by their complexity and multidimensionality.'[12]

According to Batishchev, objectivity is, to a certain degree, 'the foremost, initial and primordial' within the activity; objects not only fill and penetrate the activity, but also 'invigorate' it, turning activity into *creativity*. I believe it is more precise to speak not just of the activity approach, but of the *objective* activity approach or, likewise, of the *practical* one.

Batishchev regularly and insistently discerned two kinds of objective activity, that is, '*objektno-veshchnaya*' and '*predmetnaya*'. The English language may not allow a distinction between the terms '*predmet*' and '*objekt*' (in German, '*Gegenstand*' and '*Objekt*'), a distinction that was of essential importance for Batishchev. Moreover, Batishchev avoided referring to 'activity' as the unilateral impact on a certain object, introducing yet another distinction between '*deyatelnost*' and '*aktivnost*' (which again has no convenient equivalent in English; in German, '*Tätigkeit*' and '*Aktivität*').

In his 'subjective' (but by no means subjectivistic) interpretation of objectivity, which he declared in such an acute form, Batishchev followed Marx, arguing in tune with the first thesis on Feuerbach. Batishchev proposed that, in the process of practical activity, a human being changes not only an object

---

10   *MEW* 42, S. 396.

11   The verb was derived from Marx's term '*Entgegenständlichung*'.

12   Batishchev 1997, p. 67.

but himself as well, his own personality, and even human nature itself, if other people 'deobjectify' the fruits of his labour. Batishchev also borrowed this proposition directly from Marx. In the third thesis on Feuerbach, 'self-modification' (*Selbstveränderung*) is considered as one of the two poles of the definition of practice (*revolutionäre Praxis*). The same thought is repeated in the definitions of labour in *Capital* and *Grundrisse* in the course of analysis of the labour-process. Batishchev was quite right to contend that this moment of reflection of human activity into itself is constantly disregarded by adherents of the 'activity approach'.

Having burned his bridges, Batishchev broke from Marx when he rejected so-called 'substantialism'. Batishchev himself was convinced that he was fighting against Spinoza and contemporary Spinozists (in the person of Evald Ilyenkov). But there is no doubt that Marx himself was an ingrained, born-and-bred 'sub-stantialist'. Marxism simply could not exist without the concept of labour as the substance of social life and world-history in all of its hypostases. And, as is well known, *Capital* rests on the concept of abstract labour as a substance of value (*Wertsubstanz*).

Batishchev treated substance as an 'Absolute Object-Thing', in the spirit of the pre-Marxist, 'contemplative' materialism. There is no hint of dialectics in such a treatment of the category of substance, and it is entirely devoid of the 'active side'; Batishchev himself stressed this by defining substance as a 'dead subjectlessness' (*mertvaya bessubjektnost*).[13] Batishchev's 'substance' is simply a metaphysical scarecrow that has nothing in common with the form of thought, the dialectical category, that Spinoza, Marx and Ilyenkov referred to as 'substance'. Nothing, except the word 'substance', of course.

Batishchev reduced the concepts of labour, practice and production to 'sub-categorial elements of the objective activity'. The definitions of these elements in Batishchev's *Dialectics of Creativity* are rather unintelligible. For example, 'practice' is defined as a characteristic of the objective activity 'as being distinguished from its own, generated by this activity conventionally-ideal expressions – "echoes and gleams"'.[14] Marx himself could hardly have guessed that this florid phrase concealed a definition of practice.

Within the category of 'labour', Batishchev characterised 'the objective activity from the viewpoint of such *difficulties*,[15] which nourish it by an objective

---

13   Batishchev 1997, p. 408.

14   Batishchev 1997, p. 66.

15   A play on words. In Russian, the words 'labour' (*trud*) and 'difficulty' (*trudnost*) have the same root.

content and which are being solved in the process of this activity'.[16] It is difficult to take this philosophical quibble as a serious *concept of labour*, such as one may find in *Grundrisse* or in the fifth chapter of *Capital*.

Batishchev substituted the historically real content of the categories of labour, practice and so on through 'creative' wordplay. To my mind, Batishchev's philosophical investigations, starting from his first book about the dialectical contradiction, include a fair amount of negligence and arbitrariness in how they treat the venerable, classical categories of thought. This probably explains in part the astonishing 'freedom' with which Batishchev wandered from dialectical logic to existentialism, from atheism to Buddhism and, finally, to Orthodoxy with some 'cosmic status'.

Batishchev evaluated the 'activity approach', which was widespread in Soviet philosophy and psychology, quite critically. He mentioned that, in the course of its swift expansion, the category of activity (*deyatelnost*) had lost its *objective sense*. Any subjective activity (*aktivnost*) of an individual in the external world is regarded as *deyatelnost*. Batishchev disagreed with this 'crude activism, violating the dialectics', as well as with inactive 'substantialism'. Objective activity, as Batishchev treated it, cannot serve, in principle, as a basis of some 'approach' or 'paradigm' because such an activity is a pure *creativity*, undiluted by any algorithms. The real activity approach is simply the creative attitude to one's work.

In describing objective-creative activity, Batishchev elevated himself almost to the heights of poetry: 'It appears before us as a multidimensional harmonious process of meeting of many cultural proto-patterns [*praobraztsy*] or ideals – simultaneously, and for the sake of the deepest penetration into the former ones, and for the sake of creating the new ones, which bestow the spirit of rejuvenation to all their choir.'[17]

Surely, this formula can scarcely mean the process of labour of a carpenter or a shepherd. Apparently, Batishchev did not regard the labours of such workers as genuine *deyatelnost*. However, his formula conforms perfectly to the creative activity of some God-seeker or an armchair philosopher such as Batishchev himself.

Ilyenkov, Batishchev's former teacher, defined practice as the 'humanisation' of nature by labour. So clear and easy. While changing the external world in compliance with his needs, man exposes the 'pure forms' of things. In nature, as it is, the form of being of every thing is distorted or complicated by external

---

16   Batishchev 1997, p. 66.
17   Batishchev 1997, p. 196.

influences on the part of many other things. 'Man in his practice retrieves the own form and measure of a thing.'[18]

Ilyenkov understood practice as a process of refining the nature of any thing from external layers and admixtures, from everything that is accidental and inessential for this concrete thing. Practice turns natural phenomena inside out, bringing their essence to light. Therefore, in the practical activity of man, the nature of things uncovers itself, acquiring the pure (ideal) form of its expression, like metal in a melting pot. People perceive these pure forms as something *beautiful* that brings aesthetic delight to their senses. 'Under the form of beauty the universal nature of the given, concrete, singular thing is seized.'[19]

The practical changing of the world appears as a source and grounds not only artificial perception, but also logical thought and any other proper human ability. In practice, the melting and catharsis of the universal forms of things are performed within the 'retort of civilisation' and, later, forms should be perceived by human consciousness as the true and beautiful ones, that is, as somewhat 'ideal'.

> That is why all the definitions of freedom, as it is, are straight and direct definitions of the humanised nature, and in this sense they are 'anthropo-morphisms'. But these 'anthropomorphisms' absolutely do not contain, in themselves, anything 'specifically human', except of the only one thing – pure universality.[20]

Ilyenkov's conception of practice, as a primary source of the ideal, seems to me the most concrete and profound one in Soviet philosophy. It inherits Marx's idea of nature as the subject and the idea of a human being as a focal point of natural forces. Like Marx, Ilyenkov saw in humanity 'the true resurrection of nature – the accomplished naturalism of human beings and the accomplished humanism of nature'.[21]

The objectively activistic definition of nature (matter) is simultaneously the definition of a human being, and vice versa. In practical materialism, these two definitions are tightly linked to each other. If practice (human labour) makes *all of nature* an inorganic body of man, then the definition of a *labouring man*

---

18   Ilyenkov 1968, p. 261.
19   Ibid.
20   Ilyenkov 1984a, p. 259.
21   'Die wahre Resurrektion der Natur, der durchgeführte Naturalismus des Menschen und der durchgeführte Humanismus der Natur' (MEW 40, S. 538).

is, at the same time, the definition of all nature, or the definition of nature as a whole. Practice is a real dialectical conversion of the human and the natural, subjective and objective, historical and eternal.

'Im Anfang war die Tat' – Faust's formula also expresses the core of Marx's 'practical materialism'. Lev Vygotsky liked to repeat it, and he became a founder of the Marxist *objective* activity approach to mind, to the human psyche. Vygotsky's school, unlike the Ilyenkov school, has kept faith with the activity approach, having deepened and developed it in many respects (psychologists A. Leontiev, P. Galperin, D. Elkonin, V. Davydov and others).

Soviet philosophers, however, made interesting investigations of the practical origins of human language and theoretical thought. The two that seem to me the most considerable are *Monism as a Principle of Dialectical Logic* by Lev Naumenko and *The Riddle of the Self* by Felix Mikhailov.

Naumenko's book was published in Alma-Ata, where the author worked at the time in the Institute of Philosophy and Law of the Academy of Sciences, and promptly became rare. In my humble opinion, *Monism* belongs alongside Ilyenkov's works among the 'gold reserve' of Soviet philosophy. Several years later, in his prime, Naumenko unfortunately left 'big' philosophy for a prestigious job at the journal *The Communist*.[22]

The main thread of *Monism* is the search for a single *substance* of scientific knowledge, with its *attributes*, each of which outlines the domain of a particular science, and with *modes* of concrete scientific theories. Naumenko argued that differences between sciences are caused not by the subjective point of view but by the structure of human activity, transforming reality. This practical activity, in turn, exposes the internal structure of the reality itself, the 'logic of things'. Neither thought nor theory, but the very practice of 'splitting' reality into layers, makes cuts, which constitute the concrete subjects of the sciences.

In his famous introduction to *Grundrisse*, Marx spoke about the 'practically true' abstractions that reflect and express real human relations. Thus, the general abstraction of labour appears when its very subject, labour, has already become abstract, having lost its specificity: labour has broken its ties with the particular object and has boiled down to some relatively simple operations. This or that abstract category can leave an imprint within the human mind only on the condition that history has already *practically* performed the 'catharsis' of the object, which is expressed in the form of the given category.

---

22   The official journal of the Central Committee of Communist Party of the USSR. Its former title was *Bolshevik* (from 1924).

In the spirit of this practically-materialistic conception, Naumenko sought to comprehend the genesis of some of the simplest universal categories, which outline the scopes of subjects of philosophy, mathematics, linguistics and political economy. Practical activity, he wrote, 'unifies' real things, imparting to things that are diverse by their nature one common social function or another. As a rule, this practical genesis of the initial concepts of science remains hidden from the view of scientists.[23]

For example, mathematics studies the quantitative relations of things, taken in pure form, in abstraction from their sensually perceived qualities. But where does such a 'distillation' of the quantitative properties of things take place?

> There is only one sphere of reality in which the spatial form of bodies, their quantitative definiteness practically exists by itself – that is the practical activity of man for mastering the quantitative side of the world. The secret of paradoxes in mathematics consists of this very activity. The abstractness of the mathematical objects actually rests upon the practical *separability* of the quantitative side of things from this thing itself and upon its independent objective existence in this separateness.[24]

The primary, practical abstraction is an expression of some (quantitative, in the case of mathematics) properties of things by means of quite different things. This abstraction is a *real relation between things themselves*. Labour, the productive activity of things, places things in such a relation and only then can this relation become an object of thought.

The thing, through which the quantitative properties of other things are expressed, performs a function of *standard* (or, to use the language of *Capital*, *equivalent*). 'In the standard [*etalon*], form exists as separate actually, practically, and not only in imagination. Here it is actually isolated from the very thing; it appears objectively, materially.'[25]

The practice of measuring and calculation deals with things themselves, while science and scientific theory operate by substituting standards for things. Science uses standards to construct ideal models of reality, which causes the standards to lose their initial material character. In economics, a similar evolution occurs with money, which is dematerialised and emancipated from any

---

23   However, the name of geometry preserves a trace of its origin from agriculture, from the practice of 'measuring land'.

24   Naumenko 1968, p. 200.

25   Naumenko 1968, pp. 201–2.

ties with the practical usefulness, or 'use-value', of their material. Money is transformed into the paper-medium of exchange and even into a bodiless one. In mathematics, numbers and figures become such pure ideal standards; in language, sounds and letters, and so on.

As standards lose their materiality, their practical genealogy falls into oblivion. An illusion emerges that money, words and numbers are self-reliant and self-active entities, pure forms, *eide*, dominating matter. For theoretical thought, which is torn from practice by the force of division of labour, this illusion is as natural as the perception of the sun moving around the quiescent earth. Both are the objective 'reversed forms' of thought or, so to speak, the *practically false* abstractions. It is not the object, but the 'subject' with his egocentric angle of view that stands in the centre of such 'Ptolemaic' abstractions.

Naumenko insisted that 'practically true' abstractions do not simply express the relation of thought to its object but, first of all, the relationship of the given object to *itself*, that is, the interrelation of its various sides, 'layers', elements. Here is the difference between practically true and purely formal abstractions. The latter only grasp external correlations between things, the similarities and differences of their properties and the relation of things to an external 'subject'. By no means do they touch their inner nature, or 'substance'.

Naumenko interpreted this substance as a *subject of self-forming*.

> Under substance one should understand substratum, capable of self-movement, of imparting to itself a suitable form in the process of development. The form in this case appears as a *structure* of content, as a historically determinate and finite mode of existence of substance within the given conditions.[26]

The same objective substance is an actual subject of theoretical thought, which is not dependent on the scientist's 'angle of view'. On the contrary, it is our subjective angles of view that are entirely determined by the substance, by the real subject of inquiry. They express and fix certain aspects, phenomena and 'moments' of being of the substance as subject. An error only occurs if some of these abstract projections are passed off as the essence of matter, or if someone, such as a relativist, rejects the very existence of such an essence (substance), underlying any subjective assertions about the object.

In theoretical thought, substance is a 'universal logical space' and individual things are its finite modes or its internal boundaries. Naumenko felt that this

---

26   Naumenko 1968, p. 230.

method of thinking lies at the bottom of the *classical tradition* in philosophy and in science altogether. 'The cornerstone of this tradition is an understanding of the object not only as a matter of activity of a scientist, who manipulates it one way or the other, but also as the subject of all its own changes, as substance.'[27]

First, it is necessary to find the simplest and purest form of being of a substance, and then trace how the other, more complicated and concrete 'modes' have evolved and become differentiated from it. That is, in the most general form, the classical method of scientific cognition, as explicitly described by Descartes in his *Regulae ad directionem ingenii*. For Naumenko, the best pattern of its application is the deduction of the economic relations of capitalist society from the simple concept of the commodity in Marx's *Capital*.

In his analysis of language, Naumenko undoubtedly followed in the footsteps of Marx. *Monism* draws a strong analogy between commodity-relations and language as a form of communication, 'that is, the production and exchange of thoughts'.[28] Actually, it is more than an analogy, for word and commodity both have one and the same substance, namely, human labour. Within commodity-exchange, this substance reveals itself in a purely quantitative definition of *value*, whereas within word-exchange, labour appears in its strictly qualitative, ideal definition of *thought, idea*. The latter is, so to speak, an 'exchange-value of words' or their *meaning* in language.

At this point Naumenko openly formulated the activistic understanding of language:

> The genuine substance of it all is in no way substratum, but precisely the *social process*, the objectifying activity [*deyatel'nost opredmecheniya*]. The sound-matter is alien to thought, accidental with respect to thought. But this very accidentality is necessary: thought necessarily embodies itself in something that is opposed to it, in a material alien to its own nature; namely, in sound. At the necessary joining of these elements, which are completely heterogeneous and accidental with respect to each other, language is born, as a means of communication and as a means of expression of thoughts. Language is a materialised thought, a thought that has turned into sound-matter. The latter is a sound involved in the process of production and exchange of thoughts – a matter which *has become* a form.[29]

---

27   Naumenko 1968, p. 283.
28   Naumenko 1968, p. 234.
29   Ibid.

As shown above, Naumenko declared *activity* to be the substance of language, the 'social process' of objectifying thought in sound. Substance is a process, not a thing or a 'substratum'. Things are only forms of expression of Action, of the social labourprocess. It remains unclear how this 'practically materialistic' formula conforms with the definition provided earlier of substance as a 'substratum which moves itself'. Naumenko also left unaddressed the more general problem of whether substance is only the *social* process of activity, or whether the activity-principle has a universal sense. In other words, is an Action, a process of activity, only substantial within human society, or high and low in nature?

Today Naumenko is solidly in favour of the 'substratum', refusing point blank to admit that activity is the substance of anything whatsoever, including social phenomena. 'Only body, just a body' is the sole starting point that, in Naumenko's opinion, makes it possible 'to approach the understanding of thought and mind'.[30] He makes no mention now of labour, practical activity as a substance of thought, and the like. In his latest works, Naumenko considers not only natural phenomena, but also social ones, through the prism of 'body, just a body'. The activistic concept of substance is discarded now in the most harsh expressions, as 'ravings' and 'senseless tautology', which ruins the subject–predicate 'sense-structure'. Appealing to this formal structure as a criterion of truth, Naumenko betrays a secret of contemplative materialism, its proper *logic*. This is formal logic: hostile to dialectics always, now and forever.

Ever since Aristotle, formal logic has postulated that only things may be subjects of predication. But what could formal logic know about things? It is *formal* because it abstracts from things, from any concrete objects of thought. To pass judgements on *things* based on the subject–predicate structure of *propositions* would mean mixing words with things, the structure of speech with the structure of reality. For formal logic, the sole reality is verbal (and other symbolic) propositions; it has no idea about any other reality.

Having started once with the Marxist conception of the process of activity as substance and the subject of social phenomena, Naumenko has not maintained this dialectical peak. Instead, he has become a captive to formal-logical 'sense-structures' and rolled back on the position of pre-Marxian contemplative materialism. I would term this materialism a *somatic* one, since it refuses any other substance except for 'body, just a body', where body is Lenin's 'objective reality which is given to man by sensations'. The substance of somatic materialism is the *external, purely corporeal, sensually given* form of the practical activity of man in nature.

---

30   Naumenko 2008, pp. 67–8.

The revival of practical materialism and its confrontation with the prevailing somatic materialism is a leitmotif of the post-war history of Soviet philosophy. The small book by Felix Mikhailov entitled *The Riddle of the Self* became a conspicuous landmark in this confrontation. Its first edition came out in 1964 and the second 12 years later, in 1976.[31] There are significant differences between these editions and it is clear that the author considerably advanced his studies of the 'riddling Self' during this period.

Mikhailov's conception of 'Self' – that is, the human soul and personality – clearly shows the influence of L.S. Vygotsky's school, especially of the objectively-activistic theory of psyche of A.N. Leontiev, whose works are quoted frequently. According to Mikhailov, the inner world of a person is an *outer world* of objective culture and social relations, having been interiorised or, to use one of Vygotsky's favourite terms, 'enrooted' (*vrashchennyy*) inside the individual psyche. Objective artefacts, with their socially practical meanings, constitute a sort of language: 'the language of real life, exactly language, in the sense of a certain system of symbols, each of which – the subject or object of action – unites people, regulates their actions, guides their activity'.[32]

Mikhailov adopted the phrase 'language of real life' (*Sprache des wirklichen Lebens*) from *The German Ideology*. Marx and Engels described it as the 'material activity and material communication of people', *the social being*, which is reflected and expressed in human consciousness. From that *material* language came the *ideal* 'languages of politics, laws, morality, religion, metaphysics, etc.'.[33]

The language of material activity (practice) serves for the communication of people as among themselves, as with nature overall; in such a way Mikhailov continued the classics' train of thought. Man interrogates things in the language of Action, and things answer him by their own counter-action. If man is inactive, then things are mute as well. Being embodied in the sounds of human speech, schemata of objective actions form the *meanings of words*. Later, these meanings themselves become the objects of our purely mental, ideal actions. Words acquire a new life in the world of human communication. Having arisen as a medium in the communication of people with objects, words (similar to money) turn into a 'selfness'. Apart from their practical utility, their material 'use-value', words obtain an ideal 'exchange-value' with respect to other words.[34] Language is, so to speak, a 'market of words'. The parallel

---

31   There is an English translation of the second edition of the book (Mikhailov 1980).
32   Mikhailov 1964, p. 199.
33   *MEW* 3, S. 26.
34   Mikhailov 1964, p. 242.

between words and commodities indicates that Mikhailov, like Naumenko, followed *Capital* in his study of language.

Unlike Naumenko, Mikhailov did not confine himself to the logical analysis of linguistic ideas; he carried out his own investigations in the field which is now called 'psycholinguistics'. To me, that excursus seems dilettante; the author's erudition and wit is not enough. In the absence of substantial proof, Mikhailov's discussion on the genesis of human language looks more like philosophical speculation than a solid scientific theory.

In the second edition of *The Riddle*, Mikhailov revised his conception of the relation between language and thought. He had previously merged words and thoughts into one inseparable whole, up to the categorical denial of the possibility of the existence of thought outside language: 'We would not take, in principle, the assumption of thought without language [*bez"jazykovoe myshlenie*]. Thoughts are not formed in words; rather they are born together with words.'[35] This statement does not accord with the practically materialistic view on thought as a function of objective activity as the 'language of real life'.

Ilyenkov regards as an 'antique philosophical prejudice' the statement that language is the sole external form in which thought is expressed. It was Hegel who undermined this prejudice by pointing to the simple truth that thought manifests itself not only via language and other symbolic forms but also in practical actions, in 'acts of forming things'. The science of logic must explore 'the form of thought as such, in all its independence from the verbal, terminological or syntactical habiliments'.[36]

Mikhailov's acquaintance and personal contact with Ilyenkov shortly after the publication of *The Riddle* clearly played a part. From the second edition of the book, the passage about the joint birth of thought and word and the philosophical story of language of primitive man both disappeared, as did most of the chapter entitled 'The language of real life'. Instead there appeared the following typically Ilyenkovian turn of thought:

> Objective activity is the third that emerges as the integral "substance" in relation both to thought and to natural being of people ... Historically developing objective activity is the lap where the thinking human being, aware of himself and the rest of the world – our Self, or Ego – is being formed.[37]

---

35   Mikhailov 1964, p. 232.
36   See Ilyenkov 1979, pp. 123–5.
37   Mikhailov 1976, pp. 194–5.

It is interesting that the term 'objective activity' (*predmetnaya deyatel'nost*) was absent from the first edition of *The Riddle of the Self*, yet in the second edition it is highlighted, playing the role of 'substance' of the human being and thought. This substance expresses itself in two parallel forms – corporeal and mental: *una eademque est res, sed duobus modis expressa*, as Spinoza should say.[38]

In practical materialism, *activity* is substance, manifesting itself in corporeal form, whereas in somatic materialism, activity is a mere predicate of a body, and *body* is its subject. Herewith, somatic materialists occasionally write about activity, even about the 'revolutionary transformation of the world', treat practice as a criterion of truth, and so on. One can find whole chapters on these topics in any Soviet manual of Diamat (short for 'dialectical materialism').

Putting aside Marx's concept of activity (labour as substance), we acquire the old materialism of a Baconian type. Francis Bacon had glorified deeds as 'pledges of truth' (*opera ipsa ... sunt veritatis pignora*) and called for the joining of contemplation and actions by durable bonds. It is noticeable that in the Russian edition of Bacon's works, the term *opera* is regularly translated as 'practice', alongside with Bacon's own term *praxis*, which makes the empiricist and confirmed inductivist Bacon look like a precursor of Marx. With this, it becomes impossible to understand why Marx himself labelled all preceding materialism as 'contemplative'.

In general, it can be said that in Soviet philosophy, less the ritual Marxist phrases about practice, 'practical materialism', in a serious sense of this 'logotype', was not particularly common. In the late 1970s, the activity approach quickly lost its adherents. In his *Dialectics of Creativity*, Batishchev examined the philosophical and psychological conceptions that sought to either thought (S. Rubinshtein), the whole 'individual level of being' (K. Abulkhanova-Slavskaya), educational processes (A. Matyushkin and others), conscience (E. Yudin and A. Ogurtsov) or freedom (Yuri Davydov) and so on from the jurisdiction of the category of activity (*deyatelnost*).

In conclusion, I would note one fact that seems particularly meaningful. The 1960s marked the heyday of 'activity approach' studies, when the Soviet people enthusiastically tried to improve themselves and their state. As quickly as this historical endeavour failed, the category of activity went out of fashion, making way for various 'existentialities' or 'values', interpreted *à la* neo-Kantians. In March 1979, tormented and sick, Ilyenkov committed suicide and, with him, 'practical materialism' disappeared – or lapsed into a coma, at least. Soon thereafter, the Soviet state would repeat the fate of its Socrates, as had happened more than once already in history.

---

38   'One and the same thing, expressed in two ways' (*Ethica* II, propositio 7, scholium).

CHAPTER 4

The Category of Activity in Soviet Philosophy

Inna Titarenko

The post-Stalinist period of Soviet thought (the 1950s and 1960s) saw serious scientific interest in the category of activity (*deyatel'nost'*). At that time, Soviet society realised the need for transformation and to increase the effectiveness of socially significant kinds of activity, which included the economic, socio-political and scientific. Activity had to become the object of purposeful regulation and management. As is quite often the case, the interest in the problems of activity resulted in serious theoretical works (by E.V. Ilyenkov, G.S. Batishchev, G.P. Shchedrovitsky, E.G. Yudin and others) and a peculiar 'cult of activity' when the category was overemphasised and formed the basis of explanation of all phenomena of human life. This fact was recognised in the 1970s. In 1976, V.S. Shvyrev pointed out the widespread use of the word 'activity', as if it possessed some kind of magic, and which was not supported by corresponding conceptual analysis.[1]

Nevertheless, the theoretical conclusions of those who aimed at profound analysis, along with those who only yielded to the 'magic' of activity, both relied on the ideas of Karl Marx. Strangely, however, it not only led to dogmatism but, in a number of cases, assisted in the creative development of Marxism. It is worth recalling one well-known situation. At a conference on the problems of creative work held in autumn 1974, Arseni Gulyga, an eminent Soviet philosopher, was talking with E.S. Ventsel about the situation in modern philosophy. In Gulyga's opinion at that time, the serious philosophers included Hegelians (Ilyenkov and his followers), existentialists (Erikh Solov'ev, Piama Gaidenko), Kantians (among whom Gulyga ranked himself) and even Platonists (Aleksey Losev). When E.S. Ventsel responded incredulously, 'And what about Marxists?' Gulyga answered without hesitation, 'They are all Marxists.'[2] It seems as though the general meaning of the process that took place in the USSR's philosophy of the latter part of the twentieth century was grasped correctly in this dialogue.

The ideas of Marx have also influenced the formation of the activity-approach in Soviet philosophy. As is well known, Marx rethought the notion

---

1 Shvyrev 1976, p. 68.
2 Kuznecova and Shrejider 1999, pp. 182–3.

of 'activity', refuting the interpretation that was typical of German classical philosophy (Fichte, Schelling, Hegel) that activity was the immanent activity (*aktivnost'*) of consciousness. Instead, Marx began to consider activity as a proper human ability, determined by the objective world. Thus, Marx put into philosophical circulation the category of 'objective activity' (*gegenständliche Tätigkeit*; in Russian, *predmetnaya deyatel'nost'*), which formed the foundation of many of the Soviet philosophers' theoretical investigations. In its essence, activity in Marxism appears as objective, transforming and practical activity. Moreover, it is practical activity that underlies the explanation of theoretical, spiritual and contemplative human activity. Human nature itself is considered as object-active.

> It is just in his work upon the objective world, therefore, that man really proves himself to be a species-being. This production is his active species-life ... The object of labour is, therefore, the objectification of the species-life of man: for man produces himself not only intellectually, in his consciousness, but actively and actually, and he can therefore contemplate himself in a world he himself has created.[3]

In the process of practical activity, a man not only changes the external world but also transforms himself. It is a unity of two processes: changing of conditions and self-modification. This idea of Marx has become one of the most significant for Soviet philosophy. As Lektorsky said, 'The subject can transform himself only if he exposes himself outwardly, actively exteriorises himself, whatever the different forms of this exteriorisation are, beginning with a labour-activity and finishing with a moral act, an interaction with another person, creation of objects of spiritual culture.'[4]

E.G. Yudin

Marx's idea that the processes of changing the world and self-modification, exteriorisation and spiritual action are incorporated in practical activity, has allowed the possibility of extended interpretation of the category of activity for the Soviet philosophers. As E.G. Yudin noted, Marx's accentuation of the interconnection of theoretical and practical forms of activity appeared to be

---

3   Marx 1959 [1844], p. 76.
4   Lektorsky 1985, p. 32.

an overcoming of 'a gap between theory and practice, typical for all previous philosophy, and expressed a more extended interpretation of activity [*deyatel'nost'*] as a vital activity [*zhiznedeyatel'nost'*], including varied forms of human activity [*aktivnost'*]'.[5] The theory of Marx, who introduced only one possible way of explaining human life from the point of view of the activity approach, has become the starting point for multi-faceted research in Soviet philosophy.

At the same time, it should be noted that it was typical of the Soviet philosophers to comprehend the character of the category of 'activity' as polyfunctional. In the 1970s, Yudin stressed that this category belonged to the class of universal categories with a plurality of functions. However, this polyfunctionality of the category of activity is not obvious at all. It is determined by the high 'ontological' reliability of the given category, due to which it appears identical to itself, independent of context, and that is why it performs the same role every time. In fact, this role cannot always be the same. Thus, Yudin distinguished the five following functions of the category of activity in science:

- Activity as an explanatory principle, as a category with philosophical-methodological content expressing the universal basis (or, put more cautiously, the universal description) of the human world.
- Activity as a subject (*predmet*) of the objective scientific study, as something being divided and reproduced in a theoretical picture of the definite scientific discipline.
- Activity as an object of control, as something that must be organised into a system of functioning and development on the basis of the totality of settled principles.
- Activity as an object of projection (in the context of a revelation of the ways and conditions of the optimal realisation of definite, mainly new, types of activity).
- Activity as a value (in the context of analysis of the place it takes in different systems of culture).[6]

Yudin clearly showed that this category plays different parts in different theoretical constructions, and that the same word can have different meanings. He also argued that the list of functions is not closed.[7]

---

5   Yudin 1978, p. 289.
6   Yudin 1978, pp. 272–3.
7   Yudin 1978, p. 273.

Yudin put forward the explanatory principle as the most significant function: 'In modern cognition, especially the humanitarian one, the notion of activity plays the leading, methodologically central part, because with its help the universal description of the human world is given. Of course, this notion appears in any methodological analysis in different forms, and, in particular, no substantiation of the concrete object of humanitarian knowledge can do without it.'[8] According to Yudin, such a methodological role for the category of 'activity' is not accidental. This category allows social reality to be represented as an integral whole subordinated to definite regularities and interconnected inwardly. The activity provides the basis and the source of the social organisation. 'Activity' plays a great methodological part in explaining concrete social phenomena.

> The explanation of the phenomena of social reality by means of this notion makes it possible to avoid the psychologism that is typical for the traditional humanism. It reveals whole strata of a new, transindividual reality, and forces the introduction of new, formerly unknown lines of analysis.[9]

Yudin offered the example of an explanatory principle applied to activity and introduced the idea of scientific activity as a generating factor of knowledge, as well as the interpretation of mental phenomena through the objective activity in Soviet psychology.

Applying the explanatory principle to the category of 'activity' was connected with an understanding of the activity itself as a specifically human attitude to the world. The essence of the activity is an appropriate modification and fundamental change of this world on the basis of mastering and developing the present culture-forms. This thought was common for those who used this category as the explanatory principle. For example, G.S. Batishchev considered the subject of activity (*sub"ekt deyatel'nosti*) to be a cultural-historical subject. He noted that activity assumes the adoption of cultural norms, 'of all the content that was previously an organic part of "the cultivated lands" – of the culture'.[10] The same position was also clearly formulated by Yudin,[11] G.P. Shchedrovitsky[12] and E.S. Markaryan.[13] Activity (*deyatel'nost'*) is nothing

---

8   Yudin 1978, p. 266.
9   Yudin 1978, p. 294.
10 Batishchev 1985, p. 41.
11 Yudin 1978, pp. 266-7.
12 Shchedrovitsky 1995, pp. 688-9.
13 Markaryan 1972, p. 80; Markaryan 1983, pp. 96-8.

but a human activity (*aktivnost'*) in culture, which is determined by socio-cultural, not biological, programming. Thus, all followers of the methodology of activity, notwithstanding the differences between them, shared the conception of the interconnection of activity and culture in society. The activity happened to be connected with the cultural-historical conception of society and personality, was clearly oriented against naturalism, and proceeded from the primacy of the role and significance of social-cultural norms in the attitude of a man towards the world.[14]

G.P. Shchedrovitsky: Activity as a 'Supra-Human Substance'

It was thus natural for the followers of the methodology of activity to emphasise the significance of the analysis of education, upbringing, cultural norms and linguistic contacts. This feature was developed especially clearly in the works of G.P. Shchedrovitsky. While formulating the essence of the activity approach, Shchedrovitsky also proceeded from the idea of connecting activity and of the entire social-objective world created by a man: the world of culture.[15] Properties, tendencies, perspectives of the development of activity (and, more widely, of man) are determined by the properties and tendencies of the development of the means of human activity, such as language, thinking and art.[16] In this sense, Shchedrovitsky completely supported other representatives of the activity approach. He relied on Marx's well-known statement about the defect of all hitherto existing materialism, which consisted of examining objects only in the form of contemplation (*Anschauung*) instead of as human sensuous activity, practice.[17] At the same time, Shchedrovitsky noted that the activity approach is opposed to the naturalistic one. If the naturalistic approach directs a researcher towards the material of nature while examining the object, the activity approach directs him towards the means of activity itself, towards the material of culture.[18]

Shchedrovitsky noted that the reproduction-process of any activity in society necessarily also assumes reproduction and translation of the culture-mechanisms. The instruments and objects of labour, conditions and objects of utility,

---

14   Shvyrev 2001, p. 108.
15   Shchedrovitsky 1995, p. 279.
16   Shchedrovitsky 1995, p. 347.
17   Marx 1969a [1845], p. 13.
18   Shchedrovitsky 1995, p. 154.

human relations and organisational forms of activity must be reproduced.[19] It is only possible to reproduce one kind of activity or another by other people in new conditions of the social system if these people obtain the habits associated with this kind of activity, if they 'can do it'. For the reproduction of activity, people must be able to copy the activity of other people, or reconstruct it out of its products and the use of signs it assumes. Shchedrovitsky supposed that the teaching system appeared to provide exactly this ability in society.

> The function of teaching in the system of social reproduction consists of forming in individuals the activities according to the models represented in the sphere of culture as "vivid", really existing activity or as symbolic means and products of activity.[20]

Shchedrovitsky turned activity into the substance of social life, interpreting it as the collective, mass practice which embraces the entire social organism. He noted that if the totality of the social organism is studied as the unit of activity, this organism gets transformed into a 'universum of activity', which embraces things, people and the processes of their transformation.

This evident social and cultural fact, which in itself does not give rise to doubts, appears, however, to be the starting point for turning the activity into a kind of substance. According to this approach, man becomes a social being by associating himself with the activity carried out in the society. Shchedrovitsky describes the process as follows:

> After birth, everyone meets the already existing activity which is continually performed around him. One could say that the universum of social human activity opposes any child from the very beginning. In order to become a person, a child must be "attached" to the system of human activity; this means mastering definite kinds of activity and learning to put them into practice in cooperation with other people.[21]

This could be taken only as a constation of the obvious fact that, regardless of individual consciousness, there exists a material and spiritual culture of the society, which exerts influence upon the forming of individual consciousness, habits and skills. In itself this does not imply that activity should have the

---

19   Shchedrovitsky 1995, p. 199.
20   Shchedrovitsky 1995, p. 202.
21   Shchedrovitsky 1995, pp. 241–2.

character of an impersonal and supra-individual entity, nor that it should be transformed into a universal transpersonal substance. Nevertheless, Shchedrovitsky interpreted it in just this substantial sense:

> The universum of the social activity [*universum sotsial'noy deyatel'nosti*] cannot be considered as belonging to people as their attribute or property, even if we consider people as a crowd or organisation. On the contrary, the people find themselves as belonging to the activity, they are involved in it either as material or as elements together with mechanisms, things, signs, social organisations and so on.[22]

Consequently, according to Shchedrovitsky, people themselves become elements of activity.[23] He insisted that 'activity must not be considered as an attribute of a person, but as a basic universal integrity, a wholeness [*universal'naya tselostnost'*] that is more extensive than "people" themselves. Individuals do not create and produce activity; on the contrary, the very activity "absorbs" them and makes them act in one way or another.'[24] Thus, Shchedrovitsky converted activity into a kind of superhuman substance. Activity as a substance transforms the elements of society into an integral structure. Shchedrovitsky was clear when he said, 'There are no means of production, no signs, no works of art, and no people themselves beyond activity.'[25]

Shchedrovitsky's attempts to interpret various phenomena of social and individual life, based on the fundamental category of activity, had become the logical consequence of his proclivity to overemphasise activity. In his works, it is possible to find definitions of language, teaching, upbringing, performance, design, science and so on, all based on the activity approach. Thus, for example, Shchedrovitsky defined science as a special system of sign-elements of the research-activity that are its products and means.[26]

Shchedrovitsky paid special attention to the thinking process. In an attempt to explain the processes of thinking, he wrote:

> As a reality and as an object of research, thinking constitutes an element of the complicated organic whole – of the entire social human activity or, more precisely, his psychic activity. Thinking is inseparably linked

---

22   Shchedrovitsky 1995, p. 242.
23   Shchedrovitsky 1995, p. 198.
24   Shchedrovitsky 1995, p. 241.
25   Shchedrovitsky 1995, p. 201.
26   Shchedrovitsky 1995, p. 359.

with other aspects (elements) of the whole: with the labour-process, with sensible, volitional and emotional processes, with communication processes and so on. With one of them, it is connected directly and immediately; with the other, marginally and indirectly. It is only possible in abstraction to separate the process of thinking from other aspects of social human activity.[27]

Shchedrovitsky considered the process of thinking as the activity with signs that makes it possible to grasp the results of comparing objects of knowledge with the standards in sign-form (in other words, to grasp the content) and then to operate with this form as with the completely independent object. Shchedrovitsky formed the activistic-semiotic interpretation of thinking under the influence of Vygotsky's ideas. In an article written already in 1957, 'Yazikovye myshlenie i yego analiz' ('Language Thinking and its Analysis'), Shchedrovitsky criticised a number of Vygotsky's ideas, but only modified his conception of thinking.

Shchedrovitsky realised that the notions of 'activity' and 'action', as developed in psychological science, are extremely poor abstractions: '[T]he notions of "activity", and "action", if one puts aside their definition through the schemes of reproduction, come forward as expressions of powerful idealisations, extreme reductions and simplifications, which, in real life, correspond only to extremely rare, artificially created and exotic cases.'[28] He repeatedly underlined that, in real life, activity can exist only in inseparable connection with thinking, communication and language. That is why Shchedrovitsky introduced the notion of 'thought-activity [*mysledeyatel'nost'*]', focusing attention on the situation of involving thinking in the process of practical activity.[29]

Because of such integration of thinking and activity, Shchedrovitsky considered that the analysis of activity is, at the same time, aimed at research of thought-processes. Afterwards, however, as his disciples evidenced, Shchedrovitsky focused on other tasks, particularly on the description of thinking in the context of the ontology of activity.[30] Creation of the so-called 'general activity theory' became his universal task. Shchedrovitsky considered the construction of different schemes of activity to be based on the activity-methodology. His work contains a great number of graphical schemes, reflecting different kinds and processes of activity, establishing interconnections between

27   Shchedrovitsky 1995, p. 449.
28   Shchedrovitsky 1995, p. 297.
29   Shchedrovitsky 1995, p. 115.
30   See Rozin 2001, p. 104.

people participating in them, objects, signs.[31] The constructed schemes were declared as the activity-ontology (*ontologiya deyatel'nosti*), and the same methodological work was reduced to the construction of the normative instructions for the participants of one or another activity-process on the basis of these schemes. Thus, Shchedrovitsky ventured to consider the general activity theory as being basically constructed.[32] Unfortunately, such ascertaining was nothing but an attempt to present his desires as reality.

Batishchev's Critique of Shchedrovitsky

Evidently, Shchedrovitsky's theory is extremely categorical and based on the overemphasising of activity. Consequently, it was often subjected to criticism by followers of the activity-methodology. For instance, Batishchev wrote:

> Only concrete historical individuals can be cultural-historical subjects ... If the opposite statement was supposed – namely, the existence of the subject in his isolation and independence of persons – then the least appeared as only objects for this subject ... in such cases, the individual is reduced to a finite thing, submitted to the higher, powerful forces, and therefore deprived of his self-dependence and ability for creativity.[33]

It is important that the reduction of all vital human activity and social life to a unique abstract category can create an illusion of the ease of its projection, construction and programming. As the well-known Soviet psychologist V.P. Zinchenko noted, the illusion of ease is redoubled with the representation of the participants of such enterprise as impersonal subjects, deprived of their own self. From this point there is only a single step to subjectless activity (Shchedrovitsky's topic), to 'human material', 'cannon-fodder' and so on.[34]

It is worth pointing out that Shchedrovitsky himself recognised this difficulty in his overemphasis of the methodological role of activity. Transforming activity into substance, Shchedrovitsky did not, however, transform the person into a completely passive object of activity; he only emphasised the activity

31   Shchedrovitsky 1995; compare pp. 144, 145, 168, 169, 191, 202, 203, and so on.
32   Rozin 2001, p. 104.
33   Batishchev 1969, p. 90.
34   Zinchenko 2001, p. 85.

more than the person who is active. He admitted that people must be seen as active creators. The will to stimulate the active position of a man in social processes came forward as one of the tasks of activity-projection: 'We must not represent all social processes as natural, because this would give us no choice but to rest in a comfortable place and consider that history will do everything itself and that we need no management at all.'[35]

Another argument against Shchedrovitsky's methodological conception was that many aspects of human life – contemplation, emotional states – cannot be reduced to activity if they are to be understood exclusively as objectively real.[36] The way out from this difficulty could be, firstly, the refusal to overemphasise the methodological role of activity, and, secondly, giving to activity a more broad interpretation.

Shchedrovitsky himself, evidently, was inclined towards the second option. While he attached universal methodological importance to the category of activity, he did not reduce the same activity to objectively real activity only. This is evident from his analysis of 'thought-activity' and his interpretation of such phenomena as engineering, design and teaching.

It is important to note that the followers of the interpretation of activity as the explanatory principle quite often addressed the need for broad interpretation of activity or, on the contrary, the need to restrict the limits of methodological application of this category. This was particularly typical of Batishchev, who considered it possible to use the category of activity as the main explanatory principle. He noted that it was 'the methodologically important philosophical category', and its use in many branches of science, especially in humanitarian disciplines and in social science, was a positive phenomenon.[37] However, Batishchev stressed that it was impossible to reduce the entire activity to the objective-real, outside directed activity. Such activity falls into the 'subject–transformation–object' scheme. Under this interpretation, the objectification becomes the principal content of activity; it is reduced to an incarnation in external, material and separable results.[38] For such activity, the entire world is the equivalent of objects-things, means, useful instruments, material, equipment, background and so on. In this case, the process of objectification appears to be oversimplified, and the second very important process – deobjectification – is not even considered.

---

35   Shchedrovitsky 1995, p. 447.
36   See Lektorsky 1985, p. 31.
37   Batishchev 1985, p. 41.
38   Batishchev 1985, p. 42.

In contrast to this conception, it is important to note that activity is objective not in trivia, not in the meaning of its expansion and increase of a number of mastered objects-things, but in the sense that activity is capable of extending, without limitation, the process of meeting the inexhaustibly rich content of reality in any of its points and in any direction.[39]

As a man masters the 'book' of the reality, the union with cultural values takes place in activity. Objectification and deobjectification reveal the inner dynamism of material and spiritual culture as a living whole that exists only in the ceaseless process of its own production and reproduction through human activity. Objective activity, understood in such a way, becomes a creative process. 'Where there is no objective-activity process as the attitude and the actualised subjective being with its freedom, there is no creativity either.'[40] This many-sided process can certainly not be described only in terms of objectification.

However, by broadening the content of the category of activity, Batishchev also talked about the need to avoid overemphasising activity and transforming it into the substance of social being. This is especially typical of his later works: 'Activity is not the only possible universal way of a human being, culture, and sociality; is not the unique and universal way for a man to interconnect with the world.'[41] Absolutising the activity-principle represses the personality. In such cases, personality itself becomes an instrument of realising the substantial programmes of activity. It turns into one of many elements of the activity-universum. Again, such a reductionism was impossible for Batishchev:

> The subject-object relationship, taken as the only fundamental attitude of a man to the world, was the restricting principle, the necessary frame that did not leave a place for creativity and made reductionism necessary. It is the philosophical reductionism by means of which a man, as a subject, was reduced to something that originated from the object and ultimately from the absolute beginning. It is that substance that prescribes a man the readymade 'scenario of his life'. The substantialism is hostile to the creative subjectivity; its motto is: only substance is the subject and nothing besides it.[42]

---

39   Batishchev 1985, p. 41.
40   Batishchev 1997, p. 171.
41   Batishchev 1980a, pp. 23–4.
42   Batishchev 1997, p. 454.

Batishchev later reached the conclusion that activity in general could not generate a man's creative attitude towards the world and himself. On the contrary, creative attitude towards reality provided the grounds and conditions for creative activity. At the same time, Batishchev considered creative work as being oriented at a higher personal authority: at God. Of course, bringing the creative work beyond the bounds of activity and its location 'above' activity in this way did not allow Batishchev to stay within the limits of the activity approach.

While opposing substantialism, Batishchev was especially critical of the methodological conception of Shchedrovitsky, arguing that it lacked the axiological aspect of human activity, the freedom of choice of goals and means for their realisation, the human creative work. There were definite grounds for such criticism. Shchedrovitsky's methodological conception and his consistency in explaining social phenomena on the basis of activity have their advantages. However, it is also necessary to recognise that his interpretation of man was reductive. A human being, placed in the universum of social activity, represents the totality of the 'activities' he accomplishes. 'That is why cognising and describing "man" means analysing and describing the sets of activities [nabory deyatel'nostey] that he must accomplish in order to become "a social human being"'.[43]

Batishchev was not alone in his criticism of the overemphasis on the methodological possibilities of the category of activity, and also of the reductive interpretation of the role of the person. This was typical of many leading Soviet philosophers, including Yudin, to whom Batishchev referred as 'one of the eminent specialists in the activity approach'.[44]

Yudin considered the evaluation of the explanatory potential of the category of activity to be the obligatory condition of its use. According to him, 'the universality of this concept sometimes pushes a man to exaggerate its explanatory possibilities, to strive to answer with its help the questions that need different means of explanation'.[45] For instance, Yudin believed that not all manifestations of human existence (language, speech, higher psychic functions, creative work) can be explained exclusively as activity. The personality itself cannot be reduced to activity. The fact of a man becoming a personality via activity does not prove the ability of the category of activity to explain the variety of manifestations of personality.

---

43   Shchedrovitsky 1995, p. 388.
44   Batishchev 1985, p. 42.
45   Yudin 1978, p. 300.

Such a conclusion arises from the simple consideration that personality is not only the product, but also the condition for activity; it means that we must explain the very activity via personality. If we reject it, then we get "the activity" instead of activity, where personality acts only as a functional, and, consequently, in every concrete case, facultative appendage.[46]

However, the limitation of explanatory possibilities of the category of activity was not the only consequence of the difficulties that have appeared within this approach. In Soviet philosophy, the variant of the extended interpretation of activity was realised without reducing the methodological possibilities of this category. Thus, when considering the difficulties of the activity approach, V.S. Shvyrev kept the status of 'the universal description of the specifically human attitude towards reality' for activity.[47] The application of this category to explain the human world creates the possibility for philosophy to perceive this world as an integral whole. Besides, the category of activity is of great importance for other sciences which deal with the construction of theories of separate kinds of activity (including sociology, psychology and pedagogy).

In order to fulfil the role of the explanatory principle, this category cannot be reduced either to objective activity (*predmetnaya deyatel'nost'*) nor to activity (*aktivnost'*) nor to behaviour (*povedenie*). Shvyrev criticised approaches that considered activity as being a kind of behaviour different from that of animals, that is, caused not by biological but by cultural programmes or paradigms. Such an approach would lead to the exclusion of creativity from activity. Culture, on the other hand, consists not only of an adherence to definite 'programmes', but also of working out new programmes and their transformation. In other words, human cultural life has creativity as its presupposition.

> The reduction of activity to improved behaviour puts creativity aimed at perfection and development of these basic programmes outside activity and thereby destroys the inner unity of activity in the variety of its manifestations, its architectonics.'[48]

The creative potential of activity was in the same manner stressed by V.V. Davydov.[49]

---

46   Yudin 1978, p. 301.
47   Shvyrev 1985, p. 39.
48   Shvyrev 1985, p. 40.
49   Davydov 1990b, pp. 239–40.

Such a broad understanding of activity includes creativity, freedom, communication and purposefulness. For example, whatever definition of creative work is used, it must be assumed to be connected with the invention of new programmes of social-cultural activity, new attitudes towards reality, new paradigms of activity, new cultural meanings. In much the same way, freedom assumes the ability to create and fulfil its own programme of activity, to realise its creative possibilities in practice.[50] The entire history of human society, of the development of its material and spiritual culture, can be presented as the realisation of the creative attitude of a man towards the world, expressed in the construction of new modes and programmes of activity. Aimed at contemplation-empathy, the participation in something different, the deep-seated ontological communication about which Batishchev had written, it can be understood as the result of intensive inner work, as a deed, as activity in the extended sense of the word. Life in the world of culture is always a deed, an act; in other words, the demonstration of activity in the wider sense of the word.

Shvyrev included creative work in activity, while Batishchev, on the contrary, in his late period 'removed' it from activity. Shvyrev's theory, therefore, saved the methodological meaning of the category of 'activity'. Shvyrev expressed this position very clearly:

I am for the application of the category of activity for expressing the essence of the specifically human interaction with the world, provided the determinative characteristics of activity are understood broadly enough. For me, they are connected first of all with the 'openness' [otkrytost'] of activity to the surrounding world, both inside and outside man.[51]

It is evident that here activity is understood and described in a different way; it is activity in the extended sense of the word.

Speaking of the difficulties with the activity approach and the ways of overcoming them, the use of the category of activity as the methodological principle had an objectively positive meaning in philosophy and in a number of other sciences. Here I shall not consider the question of the significance of the activity approach for understanding psychological phenomena.[52] Instead, I will briefly note how the category of activity was used methodologically in analysing culture.

---

50   Shvyrev 2001, p. 111.
51   Shvyrev 1990b, p. 163.
52   See Zinchenko 2001, pp. 66–88; Lazarev 2001, pp. 33–47; Lomov 1979, pp. 34–47; Mikhailov 2001, pp. 10–26; Rozin 2001, pp. 96–106, and so on.

The Activity Approach and Culture: Vadim Mezhuev and Others

As seen above, the activity approach fixed the existence of the world of culture, material and spiritual values created by man, the existence of social-cultural programmes and norms. By virtue of this common purpose, the activity-approach has assumed the status of the basic methodological approach in the analysis of culture. As one of the outstanding Soviet philosophers, Vadim Mezhuev, wrote in his book *Kul'tura i istoriya* (*Culture and History*), recognising the connection of culture with human activity and, first of all, with material-practical activity, appears fundamental for its materialistic interpretation.[53]

Based on Marx's thesis of activity as sensuous-practical activity, Mezhuev considered any cultural form as the embodiment of human subjectivity to be the result of human activity. Therefore, 'culture is not a purely spiritual substance, limited by consciousness, but a special type of objective reality that, in contrast to natural reality, possesses a subjective (not in the sense of "conscious", but in the sense of "active") source of origin'.[54] This was the essential point in a materialistic interpretation of culture. The Soviet philosophers demonstrated the materiality of the cultural world, proving that only social subjects possess the ability for objective cultural activity. Social subjects, in contrast to 'transcendental' subjects and exclusively spiritual beings, can be the source of culture.

The use of the category of activity also made it possible to consider culture and all its phenomena as a whole, where material and spiritual values are connected. It is appropriate to mention Mezhuev's comments on the relativity of the dividing of culture into its material and spiritual constituents. Mezhuev considered such a division justifiable only within the question of the social division of labour. Under this aspect it is possible to distinguish between material and spiritual production. Even in such a case, however, the integral wholeness of the subject of cultural activity – a social human being who can realise himself in different kinds of material and spiritual production – is preserved, as well as the wholeness of the entire social production.

> As the product of specifically spiritual activity, culture, of course, has spiritual character. Yet, culture as a necessary expression of the total social-practical vital activity of a man, culture in all its subdivisions, represents phenomena with a common material source of origin.[55]

---

53   Mezhuev 1977, p. 67.
54   Mezhuev 1977, p. 70.
55   Mezhuev 1977, p. 71.

The important methodological role of the category of activity in the analysis of culture was also determined by the fact that it enabled the specification of social human life to be revealed, and also showed its substantial connection with biological life as a whole. A noteworthy conception of culture is the one presented by E.S. Markaryan. According to him, the principles of Marxist philosophy require that society is considered as an integral system which is not only principally distinct from biological life, but is also connected with this biological life.[56] Markaryan defined the concept of activity (*deyatel'nost'*) as the 'informational directed activity of living systems', which he placed at the same level with such concepts as 'self-organisation', 'informational directed activity [*aktivnost'*]', 'adaptation' and so on.[57] However, 'human activity [*deyatel'nost'*]' and 'culture' are the concepts that allow the social to be distinguished from the biological. Essentially, they can be explained only via each other. 'In the notion of "culture" we have the abstract expression of the mechanism of activity [*deyatel'nost'*] which is not given by biological organisation and which distinguishes the manifestations of specifically human activities.'[58] And the other way round, human activity is inherently a social activity, programmed and realised by means of cultural mechanisms. The presence of cultural mechanisms of regulation in human activity distinguishes it from the activity of animals. Human activity is stimulated, programmed, regulated and carried out exclusively via cultural mechanisms. Thus E.S. Markaryan defined culture as the specific mode of human activity which consists of 'supra-biologically' elaborated means of solution of the problems of life which men have to encounter. This functional definition of culture stresses an important feature of any cultural phenomenon: it must serve as a specific means of human activity. As Markaryan argued, the concept of human activity makes it possible to integrate all cultural phenomena into one class, independently from whether they are the manifestations of psyche, behaviour-acts, objectivated products, instruments of labour, or habits.[59]

Markaryan studied the question of whether the definition of culture, as a mode of activity, allows personality to be properly taken into account.[60] His answer is unquestionably positive. Any personality that, as an element of society, belongs to the class of the subjects of human activity, acquires during his life unique behavioural peculiarities. While these peculiarities shape the

---

56   Markaryan 1983, p. 91.
57   Markaryan 1983, p. 101.
58   Markaryan 1983, p. 97.
59   Markaryan 1983, pp. 114–23.
60   Markaryan 1983, pp. 99–110.

individual stereotypes, they also, as far as they were obtained in the process of socialisation, appear to be nothing but cultural phenomena. They belong to the definite way that activity exists in society.

Markaryan's ideas have played an important role in consolidating the activity-approach in studies of culture. It is important that they became one of the theoretical foundations of ethno-psychology. It is a good proof of the usefulness of the category of activity as an explanatory principle.

When analysing the role of the category of activity as the methodological principle in Soviet philosophy, it should be considered that discussions on the possibilities of applying it in investigations into the social reality have continued in Russia. The point of view, according to which the potentialities of the activity-methodology are not exhausted at all, is still convincing and reasoned enough (V.S. Shvyrev, V.A. Lektorsky, and so on). In the late 1970s, E.G. Yudin mentioned that the notion of activity as the explanatory principle is capable of fulfilling considerable structural work. At the same time, 'this notion fulfils real, not phantom, structural functions, at least when it receives objective interpretation either in this or that field of knowledge'.[61] Modern social research has only confirmed this conclusion.

Today, our conceptions of activity have broadened considerably and it is seen as a complicated, multivariate process. The extended interpretation of activity without any reductionism, analysis of the role of free reasoning and creative work, consideration of dialectics of the material and spiritual in different kinds of activity all create new methodological perspectives for the activity approach.

---

61   Yudin 1978, p. 298.

CHAPTER 5

The Activity Approach and Metaphysics

Edward M. Swiderski

Contemporary Russian philosophers and psychologists consider so-called activity theory to be among the few vital legacies of Soviet thought and therefore a viable resource for contemporary philosophy.[1] Activity-theory has thus been kept free of association with discredited Marxism-Leninism and can stand as a player in the global arena of scholarly exchange. As such, its arguments are open to analytic and comparative scrutiny by philosophers – among others – who pursue the kind of themes activity-theorists bring to the table.

The theme I wish to consider figures centrally in texts by activity-theorists, namely, man's transformation of reality, nature or the world (all these terms appear) where transformative activity is understood both in a generic sense and, more specifically, as labour. The generic sense pertains to the capacity humans are said to possess of effectively transforming both the world and themselves, whereas the specific form of activity, labour, is the central manifestation of this generic capacity. The reference to labour does suggest kinship with central theses of Marxism, including Marxism-Leninism. Indeed, it was usual to distinguish, in the context of the latter, between 'material transformative' and 'spiritual transformative' labour (or activity), that is, roughly speaking, between manual labour and cultural production. But of course the distinction was set into the context of ideological themes turning round the 'construction of socialism', the 'new man', and the like. The presumption is that these latter themes play no constitutive role within activity theory *per se*.[2] Nevertheless, it should not be inferred that in an examination of the foundations of activity the-

---

1   This is the conclusion at which Abdusalam Guseinov and Vladislav Lektorsky arrive in their conspectus of the state of philosophy in Russia today 'Filosofiya v Rossii: proshloe i nastojashchee' (2009a).

2   It is worth recalling that Soviet philosophers initiated a *perestroika* of their own in the late 1980s in the course of which most of the ideological components coming from '*nauchnyi kommunizm*' (scientific communism) were jettisoned and the basic principles of the world view were revised – philosophy would now be centred on man rather than 'matter in motion'. This development could only enhance the fortunes of decidedly anthropocentric activity theory. The programme and the initial formulations of the revisions were laid down in I.T. Frolov (ed.) 1989.

ory Marxian inspirations can be overlooked or ignored. In the end, therefore, there may be some ambiguity about activity theory's pedigree; whether, that is, it is a theory to be classified as thoroughly Marxist or not and, if so, to what degree.[3] My own view in this regard is that activity theory owes a great deal to Marxian inspirations, though not without certain ambiguities which are not easy to resolve. But to appreciate these ambiguities we need first to examine the central concept of activity theory, transformation.

1   Initial Statement of the Problem

A brief, straightforward characterisation of transformation (transformative activity) comes from a former leading activity-theorist, V.V. Davydov:

> The concept of activity focuses on the uniqueness of human social life, which consists of the fact that men purposively transform objective nature and social reality.[4]

If the statement is meant to be theoretical, in particular philosophical, rather than a statement drawn from common sense, then it is hardly unproblematic. My contention is that in the context of activity theory neither the concept of transformation nor the philosophy standing behind it is satisfactorily developed. Of course, much depends on how the focus on activity theory is adjusted, for the theory has two distinctive profiles. One, perhaps the most prominent among Western commentators, thanks to the standing of, among others, Lev Vygotsky, is the socio-psychological theory of personal development. The other is more properly philosophical, that is, metaphysical, with Evald Ilyenkov as its salient exponent. Ilyenkov the philosopher joined these two profiles of activity theory in a way that was more systematic, but, for that reason as well, more problematic, than that of the theorists typically associated with activity theory in its socio-psychological mode (Vygotsky, Leontiev, Rubinshtein, Davydov, and others).[5] In its metaphysical dimension activity theory

---

3 One strong case for this lineage was made by David Bakhurst in his *Consciousness and Revolution in Soviet Philosophy: From the Bolsheviks to Eval'd Ilyenkov*, Cambridge: Cambridge University Press, 1991. A recent consideration in Russia of the question is by Mareev (2008).

4 Davydov 1997, p. 57.

5 Ilyenkov has had his readership in the West for some time now. Other than the study by Bakhurst (compare the reference in note 3 above), there is a collection of articles arising out of conference held in the Aleksanteri Institute, Helsinki: Vesa Oittinen (ed.), *Eval'd Ilyenkov's*

emphasises the relation the subject entertains to that which lies outside her, to 'objective nature' and 'social reality', in Davydov's words. *Prima facie* it is a remarkable relation: the subject (individuals, social groups) is said to be able to change, transform the world at large, and these transformations are objectively real.

The trouble is that the formulations with which I am familiar provide statements of this idea which are hardly equivalent in import.[6] One way in which Ilyenkov puts it is this: 'The real object-related activity of man who transforms nature is in fact an act of identification or coordination of the form of man's activity with the form of the thing.'[7] Ilyenkov in this passage is parsing the Hegelian metaphysics of the identity of being and thinking more or less along Marxian lines, where 'labour' – and not Hegelian 'negativity' – stands as the mediating link between man and nature, producing the 'coordination', the alleged identity, of the 'forms'. Transformation then appears to amount to the coalescence of forms, those of activity and the things to which it is directed. But how should this be understood?[8]

David Bakhurst provides an account of Ilyenkov's intentions which, while suggesting an interpretation of transformation other than in terms of an 'identity of forms', raises further questions. In Bakhurst's words, 'Nature is organized, transformed, and "humanized" by action. From the sounds and shapes we employ in language to the structures that comprise our cities and towns, our world is full of *physical entities made meaningful through action*.'[9] Here the metaphysical import present in Ilyenkov's version appears to retreat behind a notion of meaningful action. The question immediately becomes: do we want to say that 'making physical entities meaningful through action' is what transformation is supposed to signify? But then would this mean that thanks to our transformative actions 'meaning' really is conferred, transmitted to the things which somehow come into possession of it? Or would it mean, perhaps some-

Philosophy Revisited, Helsinki: Kikimora Publications, 2000. A recent reconsideration in Russian of Ilyenkov's thinking is a thematic issue of the journal *Logos* (1 (69), 2009) prepared by the leading authority in Russia on Ilyenkov, Andrey Maidansky, including articles by, among others, Maidansky, Oittinen and Mareev, along with a text by Ilyenkov.

6 It would be more accurate to say that the idea is not systematically discussed in the literature with which I am familiar.

7 Ilyenkov 1997, p. 28.

8 The serious weakness in what follows is that I do not take into account and explore the concept of the ideal (*idealnoe*) which was central to Ilyenkov's account of activity. Bakhurst raises some questions about this concept in the study referenced in note 9 below.

9 Bakhurst 1997, p. 49.

what more intuitively, that relative to our interests – typically those in a socio-cultural setting – things take on now this meaning, now that, in relation to how we see and consider them?

This very short overview shows that there is certainly room here for questions and clarifications. With the passages cited in mind, I will start with some general considerations in the 'metaphysics of transformation' and then ask how activity theory stacks up in relation to them.

2   Some Conceptual Work

The sorts of intuitions that the idea of transformation (that is, transformative activity) excites concern at least the following aspects: the ontological 'scope' ('depth') of transformative activity, the ontological status of the transformed 'object', and the transforming activity itself. As to the first, we frequently say that by our actions we transform reality, that is, physical objects in space-time; as for the second, we talk as if by virtue of the transformational activity the nature of the objects has changed; and in the third case, we direct our attention to the capacity itself. The first and second aspects as well as their relations are of direct metaphysical import, the third perhaps less directly so. For the sake of the discussion I will distinguish a robust concept of transformation, a moderate, somewhat 'metaphorical' concept, and finally a weak view, which remains on the whole neutral or agnostic in regard to metaphysical issues.

1. With respect to the ontological 'scope' (or 'depth') of transformative activity, a strong position would be the following. Man has the capacity to transform nature as such; his activity is a genuine force in the world which brings about *substantial changes* in the very stuff of nature that nature alone, in man's absence, could not effect.
2. A weaker version leaves the question of substantial change open. In the weaker version man 'interposes' between himself and brute nature a realm of *artefacts* of various kinds; in this way man institutes, constitutes, 'his' human world which is distinct from brute 'nature'. The issue for this conception of transformative activity concerns the relationship of the 'human' to the extra-human, natural world. In particular, is the 'human world' an objectively real world in the manner of (brute) 'nature'?
3. The weakest version is restricted to activity itself. The 'transformation' under (2) presupposes the constitution and differentiation of *practices* thanks to which a diversified human world is possible in the first place. Talk of trans-

formation here may amount to a kind of socio-historical conception of culture, in case it is agreed that culture is or centrally involves diverse forms of practice.

(Ad. 1) The first version is, to repeat, strongly metaphysical in character. The formulation above, however, is ambiguous, in particular with regard to the question of how precisely man and world, that is, nature, stand in relation to each other. Is man entirely 'in' the world, such that the relevant metaphysics would be world-centred, materialist (naturalist), man being no exception within the overall metaphysical picture of the world? Or is man a being apart, a being to be characterised with reference to something other than the world (nature alone) to which by his agency he contributes some specific ingredients?

Once restated in terms such as these further questions are not long in coming. Chief among them is whether on the world-centred view the explanation of man's being does or should take a reductionist turn of some sort, for instance to accord with the scientific (physicalist) picture of the world. But this tack would be an embarrassment to a defender of 'transformative activity' on the strong reading; the latter concept would become toothless, a *façon de parler* and no more, in a reductionist, physicalist setting. Analogously, on the 'man-the-exception' view, explaining man's situation in the world would need to show that his exception is nevertheless compatible with the point at issue – that man can and does really transform the world. After all, the defender of transformative activity would want more than an epiphenomenal account of the capacity, a merely 'as if' kind of transformation.

However, it is safe to assume that neither of these tacks is a viable option. One reason for this is that the metaphysical backdrop of activity theory in Soviet Russia was after all dialectical materialism, that is, a view of the world which can be described as both naturalist and non-reductionist. Resorting to textbook terminology, on the standard formulations 'Diamat' is a 'metaphysical monism' (namely, 'materialism') but at the same time, ontologically, a non-reductionist 'categorical pluralism' (the world displays a rich variety of different kinds of things entertaining many and diverse relations of interdependency). The pluralism is anchored in a concept of emergence, which on this view is the engine of differentiation of kinds in the world to which the term 'dialectics' is applied. On this view, because human beings are no exception within the general causal order of the world they do, on the one hand, undergo the effects of causality even as, on the other, they are causal agents in their material environments. But according to Diamat – and activity-theorists follow suit – some of these direct influences by man on nature go beyond physical causality alone: some bring about real transformations, that is, novelties, in the world evincing characteristically 'human' properties (for lack of a better expression). And this is conceivable and possible only if man is seen as enjoying emergent powers of a kind which go beyond the 'merely' physical order of nature.[10]

To assess this view, we would of course need to know much more about these powers and what relation they bear to the physical basis upon which they arise and operate *sui generis*.[11]

Contemporary 'analytic' metaphysicians provide nice examples of the questions that need to be asked in these regards.

> Suppose that a carpenter shapes pieces of wood and arranges them together so as to compose a desk. In ontological strictness, what has happened? Is it just that certain pieces of wood or bundles of cellulose fibres have gotten arranged differently towards one another, or has some object different in kind from either the pieces or the bundles been created? Suppose that the desk gets crushed, perhaps by a collapsing roof, and no longer can function as a desk. Is this just a matter of certain objects being set in a new arrangement – perhaps very small objects, for example, cellulose molecules, if the crushing is severe – or is it a matter of some one object being destroyed?[12]

The challenge to the strong version of transformative activity consists precisely in finding a good argument to defend the claim that the carpenter has created an object different in *kind* from the materials to which he directs his energies.

We can see better what is involved in coming to some decision about this by pausing to consider the strictures Donald Davidson placed on the ontological scope of intentional action. Reflecting on the conditions of intentional action, Davidson concluded that '[w]e never do more than move our bodies, the rest is up to nature'.[13] Interpolating, if we believe that by acting, that is, intentionally acting in the manner of the carpenter, say, we bring about changes to things outside our bodies which really do come to display properties – call them either 'human' or 'intentional properties' – over and beyond those which nature bestows on 'brute' things, then Davidson at least would beg to demur.

---

10   I do not mean that this metaphysics was the theoretical ground of activity theory. My point
     is rather that Soviet philosophy was hostile to reductionism and thereby maintained a
     logical space congenial to the picture of transformative theory advanced by the psycholo-
     gical and metaphysical wings of activity theory.
11   More about this in section three below, 'Which "Marxism?"'.
12   Crawford Elder 2007, p. 33.
13   Davidson 2001 [1971].

The reason for his strong reservation is this. For Davidson, causality and intentionality do not mix, they cannot be conflated: the causal import of action is nothing other than what physics is able to tell us about it, that is to say, the physical impact of our bodies on environing objects, while – for Davidson – the intentional import of action *qua* intentional concerns no more than the agent's understanding of his behaviour, relative to his beliefs and desires, his reasons for action. From a Davidsonian perspective, out there, in the world, the desk the carpenter 'builds' is indeed nothing but a rearrangement of physical stuff resulting from what his hands do, even though in the intentional, that is, discursive sphere of reasons the carpenter describes (that is, understands) what his hands do and the rearrangements they effect with terms such as 'desk' and 'carpentry' which fall within the language-games of functionally significant practices.[14]

By contrast, someone who adopts the strong view of transformation would have to show how causality and intentionality bond in order to maintain that the carpenter has in fact brought into existence a new kind of object – and not merely rearranged pre-existing physical stuff. He would want to say, *pace* Davidson, that what happens outside our bodies when we act is not 'up to nature' alone. Transformative activity would bring about an object the substantial nature – the essence – of which cannot be categorised without remainder in physical terms alone.[15]

---

14   Presumably, Davidson would have taken exception to Marx's statement: 'Labour is, in the first place, a process in which both man and Nature participate, and in which man of his own accord starts, regulates, and controls the material re-actions between himself and Nature. He opposes himself to Nature as one of her own forces, setting in motion arms and legs, head and hands, the natural forces of his body, in order to appropriate Nature's productions in a form adapted to his own wants. By thus acting on the external world and changing it, he at the same time changes his own nature ... At the end of every labour-process, we get a result that already existed in the imagination of the labourer at its commencement. He not only effects a change of form in the material on which he works, but he also realises a purpose of his own that gives the law to his modus operandi, and to which he must subordinate his will.' *Kapital. Kritik der politischen Ökonomie*. 1. Der Produktionsprozess des Kapitals. 5. Arbeitsprozess und Verwertungsprozess (1969b, p. 148). The English version from Marx 1986, p. 76.

15   Does anyone maintain a position of this kind (requiring more detailed argument than I have presented here, certainly)? Perhaps those who believe that alongside physical particulars there are culturally *emergent* particulars as well, which are *embodied*, and therefore numerically equivalent, with their 'supporting' physical particulars. Particulars of this kind, on this conception, display 'cultural' or '*intentional*' properties. This has long been the position of Joseph Margolis (of his many and varied publications on the theme I cite only Margolis 1986 for a succinct formulation).

(Ad. 2) The weaker version of transformative activity, having to do with artefacts, brings its own questions and puzzles. This option softens the difficulty
faced by the first, strongly metaphysical variant. Artefacts are less a transformation of the world, in the sense of involving substantial change, than they are
rather additions to the world from the perspective of, and relative to, their
makers.

After all, artefacts involve their makers' concepts of what they are and what
interests and purposes they satisfy; their makers detain, on their side, all the
authority that is necessary and sufficient to stipulate what conditions have
to be satisfied for a given (kind of) artefact to 'exist'. The world seems to
have nothing to say in this regard. Artefacts, we can say, stand in a symbiotic
relation to their makers and users thanks to the particular mediating role of
intentionality: the way we think of and conceive artefacts is constitutive of what
they are for us, in the context of the practices in which they acquire and retain
significance.[16]

Despite this initial clarity, however, there is room for doubt. On the one hand,
we nurture a basic intuition about our artefacts: we believe that by producing
them we 'enrich' – transform – the world, and in the process occasion new
forms of experience and behaviour for ourselves. On the other hand, in a philosophising frame of mind, unless we go to the lengths our imagined defender
of the strong metaphysical conception of transformation appears willing to go,
we see that our basic intuition about artefacts turns out to be rather thin, ontologically. And the reason is this: on the metaphysically weak account what we
'bring about' by our transformative activity seems not in fact to incorporate,
intrinsically, a specific nature. And to the extent that there is no new embodied nature (essence) to pay testimony to the fruits of 'transformative activity', it
seems strained to want nevertheless to raise high the banner of our transformative potential.

---

16   Amie Thomasson has argued for this kind of ontology of artefacts in several publica-
      tions, including Thomasson 2007b. The difference between the first and second proposed
      meanings of transformation can be recast in ontological terms, with respect to different
      types of properties. The strong version (meaning 1) operates with a conception of mon-
      adic, intrinsic properties, which are empirically manifest in a single object to a properly
      disposed observer. The second meaning, pertaining to a 'human world' of artefacts, oper-
      ates with a notion of dyadic, relational properties, which something has only within a
      determinate context comprising along with the thing some agent or agents who maintain
      a relation to the thing; for instance they impute the property or properties to it. These
      would be typically functional properties: a table serves such and such purposes for so-
      and-so, a property it has only in relation to so-and-so.

The last remarks can be restated as a question in general metaphysics. Assuming that entities in a basic sense are what they are because they possess natures (essences), then the question is whether artefacts are entities in this basic sense. On the strong conception of transformation, the answer would have to be affirmative. But in the weaker version the answer appears to be 'No, artefacts don't have natures' (other than by convention, relative to how we identify and distinguish them, that is, relative to our practices).[17] Recalling Davidson's strictures on the ontological scope of intentional action, this conclusion would seem in fact to be compatible with Davidson's view, and it is also an answer to the question about the carpenter's undertakings – the outcome of his labour is not ontologically substantial; no new object comes into existence. But if so, then talk of transforming the world turns out to be more a matter of metaphor than a matter of fact, least of all 'ontological fact'.

A useful illustration of this kind of quasi-ontology of artefacts is found in Searle's ontology of institutional facts.[18] According to Searle, we 'interpret' such things as money into existence when, in the appropriate contexts, we 'understand' the metal discs, pieces of paper, blips on a computer screen, and the like as money in accord with commonly accepted rules, conventions – in short, we collectively institute money into existence. Generalising from this case, let us say that artefacts 'exist' when the 'transformations' we effect involve assigning collectively intelligible functions or statuses to 'mere ordinary things' or 'brute facts' (in Searle's terminology) which as such, in their material nature, remain entirely innocent of such imputations. As Searle puts it, artefacts (of the kind typified by money, marriages, works of art, and so on) are ontologically subjective, not objective, in their mode of existence: they depend on us, and the dependence involves a relation of meaning (with the 'world' in these cases coming to 'fit the mind', rather than the other way round). Out there in the world, outside the epidermis, beyond the pale of our socio-cultural spheres, the mere ordinary things, the brute facts, have not undergone any 'substantial' change. This is certainly why Searle and other social ontologists committed to his kind of thinking speak not of transformation (transformative activity) but

---

17   The two contemporary ontologists cited above, Elder and Thomasson, have grappled with this issue, arriving at opposite conclusions. Elder claims that artefacts do have essences (Elder 2005), while Thomasson believes they do not (Thomasson 2007a).

18   Searle eschews the term 'artefact' and spurns talk of 'social objects' (and similar). It seems to me, however, the kind of transformation in question here (meaning 2) falls within the purview of his institutional facts (Searle 1995).

rather of the 'construction' of social reality. It is only in a derivative sense at best that we speak of the things that make up, enter into a construction as having been 'transformed' (altered).

(Ad. 3) The third, and weakest, sense of 'transformation' seems to differ in kind from the first and second. It focuses not on entities, real or otherwise, but on human practices, with transformation understood as the development, the differentiation of practices. On this reading, talk of the 'transformation' of the world by human activity is redirected to the distinctive ways in which human beings come to make sense of their surroundings by creating patterns of significance for themselves. Clearly, it is but a step or two from here to talk about artefacts along the lines of the second option examined: practices and artefacts exhibit a symbiotic, mutually supportive relation. As such, what is at stake here is a notion of culture, for example in the way the neo-Kantians parsed the concept. A classic illustration comes from Max Weber:

> Culture arises when men attribute meaning and significance to some finite slice of the otherwise meaningless indeterminacy of the world's course ... Prostitution, religion as well as money are cultural phenomena only insofar as the historical existence and form they have assumed relate directly or indirectly to our historical interests, as they excite our cognitive orientation from the perspective of determinate values [*Wertideen*] which make the slice of reality to which they are directed meaningful ... The 'man of culture' is endowed with the capacity and the will deliberately to adopt an orientation to the world and in this way to attribute meaning to it.[19]

---

19   'Kultur ist ein vom Standpunkt des Menschen aus mit Sinn und Bedeutung bedachter
      endlicher Ausschnitt aus der sinnlosen Unendlichkeit des Weltgeschehens ... Eine Kul-
      turerscheinung ist die Prostitution so gut wie die Religion oder das Geld, alle drei deshalb
      und nur deshalb und nur soweit, als ihre Existenz und die Form, die sie historisch anneh-
      men, unsere Kulturinteressen direkt oder indirekt berühren, als sie unseren Erkenntnis-
      trieb unter Gesichtspunkten erregen, die hergeleitet sind aus den Wertideen, welche das
      Stuck Wirklichkeit, welches in jenen Begriffen gedacht wird, für uns bedeutsam machen
      ... Ein ,Kulturmensch' ... begabt [ist] mit der Fähigkeit und dem Willen, bewusst zur Welt
      Stellung zu nehmen und ihr einen Sinn zu verleihen.' Max Weber, 'Die Objektivität sozi-
      alwissenschaftlicher und sozialphilosophischer Erkenntnis' (1922). Quoted after Daniel
      2001. The English is my translation.

Weber's is a characterisation of the way cultural reality is brought into being and reproduced by way of what he calls meaningful action. It is worth noting that Weber sets culture off from the 'meaningless indeterminacy of the world's course'. His claim about the attribution of meaning is not to be understood in metaphysical terms, as a 'real' transformation of the meaningless indeterminacy of blind occurrences and lumps of matter, even though for the subject, the agent, the 'man of culture', relative to a given determinate socio-cultural matrix, it makes all the difference in the world (*sic*) that he experiences the world as meaningful, that is, a world organised into zones of significance demarcated by value-laden categories (his provocative yet telling examples of prostitution, religion and money).

The Weberian vision amounts to a historicist theory of the 'transformation' (that is, differentiation) of practices themselves, whereby practice is first of all parsed in terms of 'significance' or 'value' (Rickert's *Wertbeziehung*). It would appear, therefore, that, given the stark contrast with a meaningless 'world', it is first and foremost the *man of culture* who is in (ontological) fact both the subject as well as the primary object of 'transformation'. His world is his cultural reality and he is and understands himself to be what and how he is within the space of possibilities the cultural reality provides. Applied to our question about transformative activity, to say in this case that man in his activity 'transforms the world' would amount to an elliptical way of saying that ours is a cultural reality, which we 'make' and change, the fundamental constituent of which is patterns of meaning (values and their bearers in the many practices that make up our cultures).

3   Which 'Marxism'?

So what about activity theory, in its metaphysical guise? Which of these meanings of transformation would most plausibly apply to what I will call the 'standard' or 'average' concept of transformation among activity-theorists? To approach this question, let us consider the following passage which I take to be characteristic of the 'standard' account:

> Just what is the 'reality' with which man is concerned? It is the historical product of sensible practical activity by human individuals organized in collectivities. For that reason this reality, by being the objective incorpora- tion of the activity of the subject, appears to man not in the state of natural 'virginity' ... but in the form of a set of cultural-historical objects which have come to be regarded as the accumulation of the experiences, capacit-

ies ('essential powers'), and historical memory of generic man. The object is produced in activity as a human object or 'objectified man' (Marx), and therefore it is not merely the reflection of some physical stimulus. In the system of social relations it acquires a sensible-supra-sensible form which transmits to succeeding generations the human subjectivity objectified in it. A man who appropriates (*razpredmečivaet*) it in his activity becomes to a certain extent the 'other', he acquires the possibility of relating to his own activity from this perspective and by that fact becomes capable of self-development. Therefore, the reality that is conceived as a system of objects constituted by man and for man, and serves as the basis of his self-development as the measure of his act-practical universality ... is the very reality (the really existing essence) of culture.[20]

Of the three possible versions of transformation I have distinguished, the second and third are quite in evidence in this passage. Reality for man is by man, it is said to consist of 'cultural-historical' objects, that is, artefacts, and appropriation by man of this 'reality', termed here culture, promotes self-development, thereby reinforcing the status of culture as man's 'reality'. What about the first meaning, however, the strongly metaphysical meaning of transformation? The passage is ambiguous in this regard; conceptual slippage is detectable. In particular, what should we understand by 'objective incorporation of the activity of the subject', or by '[t]he object is produced in activity as a human object or "objectified man"'? Are we to understand that this 'objective incorporation' is tantamount to a 'substantial change' in the natural substrates 'out there', in the world, to which activity is directed? Or should we understand this phrase along the lines of the second version of transformative activity above, as interposing between man and brute nature a realm of artefacts, the existence of which is relative to the meanings we impute to objects? It is difficult to decide on the strength of this passage alone; it allows both interpretations. In short, the passage is ambiguous; no one sense of transformative activity clearly has the upper hand.

   Now I think that there is more to this ambiguity than conceptual sloppiness. It can be traced to a source, namely, the Marxian, and Marxist, background of activity theory. Earlier I alluded to Marxist-Leninist Diamat with its emergentist account of human capacities reaching beyond the 'mere' causal order of nature. This it was that kept suspicions at bay that activity theory could fall prey to reductionist-minded monist materialists. However, the Diamat account,

---

20   Mikhailov 1987, p. 32.

associated with mainstream Soviet philosophy, has often been portrayed as a distortion of Marx's own brand of 'materialism', the precise contours of which have, however, been a longstanding bone of contention among scholars. It is within this 'logical space' of questions about the concept of 'materialism' in Marx and his followers that the ambiguity besetting the notion of human transformative activity, as illustrated in the passage above, is rooted.[21]

There is no difficulty in acknowledging that the cues for the concept of transformative activity came in the main from Marx, indirectly therefore from Feuerbach and in the end Hegel. But the complicating factor has to do with the reception of this lineage in the course of the formation and consolidation of 'orthodox' Marxism-Leninism, in the guise of Soviet metaphysics. In order to explain what I have in mind, I will avail myself, for convenience sake, of the distinction Leszek Kołakowski drew between 'le marxisme de Marx' and 'le marxisme d'Engels' (he was of course neither the first nor alone in drawing attention to a difference).[22]

The first option concerning transformative activity, the strongly metaphysical one, could be read out of 'le marxisme d'Engels'. On this view, technology is given its ends by science which provides an objective, increasingly accurate picture of reality, thus affording man ever greater certainty of bringing about change, that is, impacting and transforming 'nature' for the sake of realising human purposes. We know that it was this 'marxisme' which in due course entered into the foundations of Soviet Marxism-Leninism, the other chief constituent thereof being the Leninist reflection-theory of knowledge with its insistence on the objective (realist) character of human knowing. As a result, the standard Soviet concepts of man, his powers and his capacities fit into the logical space of this 'marxisme'. The general idea is that man, in the course of his emergence (evolution), comes increasingly to do intentionally, with explicit designs in mind, what nature, in the course of its 'dialectical' development, had heretofore done 'blindly', that is to say, produce qualitative changes, new kinds of things and states of affairs. On this reading of the Marxist backdrop of activity theory, to say that man transforms the world is to say that nature, through the offices of man's transformative activity, as an emergent, 'higher form' of natural processes, transforms itself. Here there is room for speaking of 'substantial change' in relation to transformative activity, but characterised relative to possibilities in the world of which the human being is an emergent active constituent.

---

21   Compare Kline 1988, pp. 158–82.
22   Kołakowski 1978. In addition Schmidt 1971 and Jordan 1967.

The other 'marxisme', that of the 'young' Marx, centres on the notion of 'revolutionary practice' to which Kołakowski ascribed an altogether different 'ontology', which he dubs 'generic subjectivism' (the expression 'generic' answering to the German '*Gattung*' which appears in Marx's early writings as '*Gattungswesen*', usually translated as 'species-essence'). At first sight, this view on man and his relation to the world could be regarded as compatible with the second, moderate view of transformation: practices, their products – artefacts of diverse kinds – stand to each other in symbiotic relationships within a 'human world'. Of importance here is the adjective 'generic', signifying in effect 'social', the reference of which is not first of all to collectives or groups as higher-order entities, but rather to the properties individuals acquire and share in the course of the differentiation and organisation of their joint practices. And these practices, in turn, come about in the course of the 'social mediation of nature', whereby 'nature' is relative to the practices which embed these properties.

Now in Marx's early writings, there is no rift, no dualism, between a meaningless material world and social man, the meaning-bestowing agent, as in the example of the (neo-Kantian) philosophy of culture sketched above. One reason for this absence is Marx's initial reliance on the Hegel–Feuerbach line. Hegel's identity of thinking and being, concept and object, becomes in Feuerbach's reworking of Hegel's idealism man's rootedness in nature, though in a special understanding thereof. Individuals come in contact with nature – Feuerbach meant nature as experienced, sensuously – through the mediation of the *Gattungswesen*. Despite Marx's criticism, in his 'Theses on Feuerbach', of both Hegel and Feuerbach, his own notion of praxis preserves the gist, shall I say, of the 'philosophy of identity' which animated the thinking of his illustrious predecessors. Praxis, or labour, as the constitution *sui generis* of what is properly human, is a concept operating at two levels. On one level, praxis fixes the status of the individual in relation to specific configurations of social practices – witness the much quoted and incessantly examined thesis about the human essence being no abstract something inherent in each individual taken singly but the ensemble of the social relations. On another level these very 'social practices' – later in Marx, the mode of production – enclose, so to say, the 'world' (nature). Kołakowski interprets Marx to the effect that '*Il n'y a pas d'autre nature que celle qui est soumise à la praxis humaine*', such that, for any individual, at any time, the 'nature' always already 'socially mediated'.[23]

---

23   Kołakowski, ibid., p. 139. It is worth citing Kołakowski at length. 'Pour Marx ... "l'homme est la racine de l'homme". Il est pour soi-même l'ultime point de départ de toute explica-

Now my suggestion is that this divergence, the contrast of the two Marxisms and their respective 'ontologies', throws light on the passage with which I
started this section. It also throws light on Bakhurst's interpretation of Ilyenkov
quoted at the beginning of this chapter. I argued that in one and the other there
is a tension, an ambiguity in the characterisation of transformative activity. It is
the tension, in my terms, between the strong and the moderate conceptions of
transformative activity, or, in Kołakowski's reconstruction, between the Marxism of Engels and the Marxism of Marx. Bakhurst, we saw, takes Ilyenkov to be
saying that man has the capacity to create a meaningful world by attributing
meaning to physical objects, to his natural surroundings. He refers to this attribution as 'transformation', presumably because he understands labour to be
efficacious in transferring to physical objects characteristically human (socially
mediated) properties. Much the same can said of the passage I quoted at the
start of this section. Indeed, if anything, here the tension is even more marked:
the author is explicit about the 'objective incorporation of activity' (labour), on
the one hand, though, on the other, he identifies its results with culture, that is,
a world of meaning and value.[24]

In short, we find in these passages a tension, an unstable mix of meaning-
attribution and -transformation. Is there a way to resolve the tension between
the two? The short answer is no, at least not on Kołakowski's reading of Marx.

---

tion et ne saurait s'expliquer comme une des produits de la "Grande Nature". Cependant,
il ne part pas de l'acte de cogito, il ne se connaît pas lui-même sous forme d'une auto-
réflexion pure, sous la forme d'une conscience transparente pour elle-même. Il se connaît
comme sujet pratique et travaillant, mais il n'a pas d'autre objet que l'objet de sa pratique.
De même qu'il ne se connaît pas comme conscience autosuffisante, il ne connaît pas
non plus la nature comme objet autosuffisant: nous ne sommes donnés à nous-mêmes
qu'indissociablement sujets et objets de nos efforts, ni les sujets ni l'objet n'apparaissent
séparément à la pensée dans leur pureté autonome. C'est pourquoi la nature n'est con-
nue à l'homme qu'à l'intérieur de son horizon pratique, comme vis-à-vis de ses actions
conscientes. Elle apparaît à l'homme comme le prolongement de lui-même. Dans les rap-
ports sujet-objet, il n'y a donc aucune priorité absolue; dire que l'homme est le produit
de la nature est aussi justifiée que de reconnaître dans la nature le produit de l'homme:
la nature humanisée. Le contact actif de l'homme avec le monde est par conséquent un
point de repère que notre connaissance ne peut dépasser' (Kołakowski 1978, pp. 137–8).

24   With reference to note 16 above, we could say that the passage under examination here
runs together monadic (intrinsic) and dyadic (relational, 'cultural') properties.

4   Should We Retire 'Transformation' Talk?

Kołakowski's reconstruction and juxtaposition of the two 'Marxisms' are consistent with a radical conclusion concerning the theme under examination in this chapter. Rejecting the Engelsian take on the import and scope of labour as fundamentally out of tune with original Marxian themes, Kołakowski's characterisation of Marx's own position – as 'generic subjectivism' – is consistent with *giving up*, as empty, the very idea of transformation. Kołakowski is clear about Marx's anti-philosophical, that is, anti-speculative stance in this regard, in particular his rejection of the epistemological(-cum-metaphysical) problem of coming to know things as they are. What grounds do we have, he asks rhetorically, to assume that we can reflexively double-back on ourselves, step out of our skins, so to speak, assume the guise of a disembodied (transcendental) 'subject', and observe our 'objective' contact, including the impact of our supposedly transformative activities, from within our embodied mode, within 'brute' ('raw') nature?[25]

In effect, does not the praxical reorientation call for a revision of our standard, 'everyday metaphysics'? The semantics of our ordinary talk of transformation casts a picture of a 'raw stuff' (absolute or relative as the case may be) to which outside force, namely, causally efficacious agency (in the first place labour), is applied in order to bring about a result that was not there in the beginning, a result characterisable intrinsically in terms of (achieved) purposes, intentions, or similar. In other words, 'ordinary language' appears to sustain a metaphysically strong notion of transformation for which activity (labour) is understood as bringing about 'substantial change'.[26] By contrast, the praxist perspective, as Kołakowski understands it, amounts to a revision of this 'standard metaphysics', whatever the effects may otherwise be on our standard speech-patterns. The same applies *mutatis mutandis* to 'transformation' understood as meaning-attribution in a 'world' taken to be meaningless, however

---

25   Kołakowski had come to these conclusions well in advance of writing his history of
      Marxism, let alone the article I have relied on here. They were stated in his 'Karl Marx and
      the classical definition of truth', first published in Polish in 1959. The English translation
      appeared in Kołakowski 1968.

26   It is perhaps an embarrassment to the line put forward here that Marx provides an
      excellent example of this congenial marriage of transformation-metaphysics and ordinary
      parlance. See the quote from *Capital* in note 14 above. The anti-transformation thesis
      runs up against strong opposition from, among other sources, interpretations of Marx's
      concept of labour in Aristotelian terms, that is, in accordance with the logic of Aristotle's
      four 'causes'. For example, see Gould 1978.

ontologically weak this conception may in fact be. The dualistic picture this conception projects – the formative meaning (for example, value) and the formless (meaningless) 'stuff' – appears to be incompatible with the Marxian praxical 'man–nature' nexus. Here there are supposed to be no poles, no heterogeneous constants standing in opposition to one another, no 'subject–object' dichotomy, including the kind that activity theory appears to underwrite.

Have I driven this reasoning too far, beyond the limit of comprehension? Having signalled a tension afflicting 'standard' formulations of the transformation-thesis as advanced by activity-theorists and their commentators I have come to the seemingly counterintuitive 'conclusion' that, as regards the idea of transformative activity, neither a common-sense nor a high-flying metaphysical notion thereof withstands critical scrutiny and appraisal. It is a conclusion which appears to jettison a fundamental intuition about human capacities, our sense of ourselves as entities whose achievements, however they be evaluated, are real and effective, as demonstrated throughout the course of the civilisational process. Among other things, it appears to make nonsense of the scientific endeavour to accurately describe and come to understand the world we inhabit and our own situation within it.

Nevertheless, the argument has not been a random exercise in verbal dialectics. I began by distinguishing and considering successively three possible meanings of transformation of which the latter two were weighted in light of the first – the robust, substantial version according to which humans bring about real and substantial change in the world, thereby achieving, realising their purposes. The weighting meant that, should there be no grounds to adopt this robust notion, then the remaining, progressively weaker versions slide into relative insignificance, being hardly more than *façons de parler*, suggestive as metaphors perhaps, but little else.

Now, the Marxian concept of praxis, on Kołakowski's reading at least, questions this weighting, simply obviates the issue within the logical space of 'generic subjectivism'. On the Marxian account of activity, the human condition is such that, for any individual, his or her experience and forms of activity, including the objects, situations and other persons which they concern, are always already 'socially mediated', that is, they stand in mutually constitutive relationships ('the ensemble of the social relations'; the 'mode of production'; 'men inevitably enter into definite relations, which are independent of their will, namely relations of production appropriate to a given stage in the development of their material forces of production') which enclose (relativise) the nature–culture interface.

One way to test the significance of this thought is to shift to a phenomenological perspective in order to ask about the kind, the quality, of experience present to an individual. Is there some quality in experience, some phenomenologically essential datum (*Erlebnis*) of a 'normal' individual's experience, which an Engelsian account of consciousness and activity discriminates and articulates as constitutively salient for that experience and which would be absent from the Marxian account? Conversely, does the Marxian account of experience – 'consciousness' – pick out some phenomenologically significant datum to which the Engelsian perspective remains blind? Restating the question with recourse to textbook-terms, does the Engelsian 'cosmocentric' perspective sustain a phenomenology of experience different in kind from Marxian 'anthropocentric naturalism' (and inversely)? What kind of qualities might we be looking for, from either of these 'metaphysically' distinct perspectives?

An illustration of the issue is the following passage from Ilyenkov:

> From the standpoint of the individual, nature and humanized nature *fuse immediately* [my italics – EMS] into the surrounding world ... [N]ature 'in itself' is given to the individual only insofar as it has already been transformed into an object (*predmet*), material, a means of production of material life. Even the starry sky, in which labour alters nothing directly, becomes an object of man's attention (and contemplation) only where and when it is transformed into a natural clock, calendar, and compass, that is, a means and instrument of orientation in time and space.[27]

Ilyenkov employs a term, 'fusion', which seems to be phenomenologically significant. Does Ilyenkov mean that, in contact with the things in our milieu, those that are present to hand as extensions of our practices, we experience a 'fusional' quality of some kind, experience these things as 'humanised', a quality set off from yet dependent for its meaning on the contrasting quality of 'otherness' (brute nature)? However, it is open to doubt, I believe, whether we do experience 'fusion' *qua* fusion involving the pair of contrasting qualities. For one thing, this kind of talk fits far better with a genetic – that is, non-phenomenological – account of our experience. Rather than say that we experience fusion, it would be better to say that *what* we experience, the quality, in fact arises out of a 'fusion' of distinct, heterogeneous components, though below the threshold of the individual's 'living experience' (*Erlebnis*) with its many inflections in the course of interaction with her milieu. In addition, as formulated the passage builds on a redundancy. I suggest that Ilyenkov should

---

27   Ilyenkov 1997 (Bakhurst 1997 quotes this passage in the same issue, p. 50).

be taken as saying that all an individual experiences is 'humanised nature' *tout court* – though not *qua* humanised – rather than a curious amalgam consisting of 'humanised nature' along with, and distinct from, nature 'in itself'. I take it, in other words, that humanised nature 'comprises' all the 'nature' there is for the individual to experience, assuming of course that forms of experience – types and patterns of signification – are in their turn socially constituted relative to the practices, their histories, and so on.

Though it is gratuitous to do so, we can speculate that the Engelsian complement to the phenomenology of an individual's experience would speak of a fusion in experience of heterogeneous elements. After all, this corresponds, as we saw, to the strong, robust sense of transformational activity, which involves substantial change: first we experience a given thing now one way – in advance of our practical, transformative activity – then thereafter a new thing, the transformed thing, once our purposes are transferred beyond us, beyond our epidermis. The Engelsian account would want to build the transition, the transformation, into the experience – the 'dialectical passage from one quality to another',[28] where the latter is incommensurable, ontologically, and phenomenologically, with the former.[29]

Bakhurst, in turn, in his attempts to explicate Ilyenkov's position, falls into virtually the same 'phenomenological' predicament as Ilyenkov. As we have seen, Bakhurst thinks that, via activity (in the specific meaning of transformational activity), we convey meaning to physical objects. Though this kind of language is common – much like the language of labour creating new objects – it invites philosophical attention by reason of its implicit dualism. On one 'side', there is meaning, it seems; on the other, physical objects, the 'bridge' being activity. In other words, we discriminate the physical objects, and then we convey meaning to them. But is not the very discrimination itself already 'meaningful', is not the 'physical object' singled out in relation to a context of practices within which it is pre-constituted as significant, relative to a category such as a 'material for such-and-such an end', for instance? Ilyenkov's starry sky is beyond the reach of human hands, beyond labour, but is this not nevertheless a 'meaningful' beyond, a beyond relative to and dependent on the shifting boundaries of agency and their discursive articulation? Presumably, to use the stars to chart our direction is not to experience an amalgam of brilliant lights against a black

---

28   I set this phrase off in quotes because it refers to one of the three 'laws of the dialectics of nature', which is Engels's main contribution, perhaps, to metaphysics in a Marxist framework, broadly speaking.

29   On this account, the phenomenology sustains the position of the metaphysical realist, including as well the things humans have put into the world.

background as well as, in the same experience, a function imposed on, imputed to, this percept. It is just to engage in an activity the phenomenology of which shows it to be internally coherent in terms of its organising intentionality – to steer by the stars.

So it seems that, if these phenomenology-like reflections are sufficiently convincing, then we seem to confirm our suspicion that talk about transformational activity is miscast in case it is set into a metaphysical context supportive of the first meaning of transformation I distinguished. However, if the onus of activity theory's talk of transforming nature, the world, society, and so on, is shifted away from this version and towards the Marxian conception of praxis, with its distinctive anti-metaphysical (and anti-epistemological) tones, we arrive instead at a conception closer to the second meaning of transformation I proposed – that of a 'human world', where the mutually constitutive relation of practices and their products precludes any fixed outside ('transcendental') point of observation other than that provided by *historical* narrative within that very world – our history of our production.

In Lieu of a Long Conclusion

In closing it needs to be said that, despite the 'critical' remarks addressed to Bakhurst, his reading and reconstruction of Ilyenkov come close to this second reading of transformational activity. In Ilyenkov's name Bakhurst asks the question I have been worrying about throughout this chapter: 'How can minds "reach out" to the natural world when their natural currency is meaning ... yet objective reality seems to be bereft of meaning?' He answers, presumably in his own name as well as for Ilyenkov, 'Mind and world are made for one another because the world itself contains meaning',[30] though to explain how this is possible Ilyenkov had recourse to a virtually Platonist conception of ideal being. On this kind of account, there would indeed be a basis of speaking about experiencing things as 'infused' with meaning, that is, as an amalgam of meaningless stuff shot through with meaning conveyed to it by activity informed by the ideal.[31] Bakhurst is uneasy with that solution, preferring to set the reader on another path he thinks gets us closer to understanding how mind and world meet meaningfully, the path broken by Wittgenstein in regard to action and

---

30   Bakhurst 1997, p. 51.

31   The conception recalls the early Husserl's theory of meaning, out of a Fregean context, requiring the acceptance of 'ideal meanings'; this gave way in time of course to the noema, once Husserl came to clarity about constitutive intentionality.

practice. It is striking how he reads Wittgenstein: his take on Wittgenstein could be substituted for Kołakowski's reconstruction of the 'marxisme de Marx' and what follows from it, to drop talk of transformation altogether. Marx's praxis together with the consequences he drew with regard to idle, illusory 'philosophical' preoccupations – as if there is a privileged perspective from which to observe mind meeting matter – is equivalent to Wittgenstein–Bakhurst's 'forms of life': '[W]e must ... understand the character of our forms of life "from within," and this is to replace epistemology with cultural history and anthropology.'[32]

So it turns out that as regards its putative metaphysical profile activity theory has no claims to offer in this regard. What remains then is what attracts the attention of most commentators in any case – the psychological profile of activity theory. But then what are selves, minds, thinking and discourse – are they not 'real', and if as activity theory maintains selves, minds and all the rest of it undergo change, development, transformation, are we not back at the question with which we started?

---

32 Bakhurst 1997, p. 54.

CHAPTER 6

Abstract and Concrete Understanding of Activity: 'Activity' and 'Labour' in Soviet Philosophy

Sergei Mareev

There is a degree of confusion in Soviet philosophy and psychology regarding the notion of 'activity'. This confusion was caused mainly by insufficiently considered methodology, when philosophers tried to move from the abstract notion of 'activity in general' to specifically human activity. This is impossible to do, however – as impossible as moving from the notion of 'fruit in general' to the notion of 'pear', because the specific features of this concrete fruit disappear completely in the notion of 'fruit in general'.

The prominent Soviet psychologist S.L. Rubinshtein came very close to understanding the reasons for the confusion. 'The notion of activity is used now and then in a very wide and unclear meaning', he wrote. 'Like in physiology, where they speak about higher nervous activity, cardiac activity, secretory activity, and so on, in psychology we now discuss psychic activity, identifying activity as *deyatel'nost'* and as *aktivnost'*.'[1]

It is not entirely clear how the distinction can be made between *deyatel'nost'* and *aktivnost'*, which are almost synonymous in Russian but simply the same word in English. There is only one way to outdo the abstract notion of activity – by replacing it with the concrete notion of *labour*. Rubinshtein did not do this directly and, although he often spoke about labour, he continued to pack this idea into the abstract notion of 'activity': 'Activity, in the strict sense of the word, is an objective activity, it is practice. Activity and action imply impact, changing reality, creating an objectivised product of material or spiritual culture, which enters social circulation.'[2] However, such activity, which changes reality, is nothing else but labour. In reality, speaking cannot change anything, although it is also *deyatel'nost'* and *aktivnost'*.

'In the process of the historic development of social labour, which led to its division, different types of labour-activity were formed: production, man-

---

1   Rubinshtein 2005, p. 174.
2   Rubinshtein 2005, pp. 174–5.

ufacturing, pedagogical, scientific, artistic, and so on', continued Rubinshtein.[3] This is correct in general, although artistic activity is not usually called labour. Labour is mainly related to the field of *material* production while artistic creation is related to the field of *spiritual* production, where man himself is being made. In this context, Karl Marx spoke about emancipation from labour, saying that man would emancipate himself from producing things (it will be done for him by other things), but he will always make himself. In any case, we should start with the notion of labour, because only through labour can we explain the origin of all ideal senses and meanings that may be produced later in all fields of scientific and artistic activity. Evald Ilyenkov played an outstanding role here, showing how the *ideal*, as such, is produced directly within material activity, that is, in the labour-process. This link was missing in the works of A.N. Leontiev, the well-known psychologist, which is why he supported Ilyenkov so warmly.

Uncertainty regarding such notions as 'labour' and 'activity' provides the basis for such interpretation, when speaking (or communication) becomes the initial form of human activity. This uncertainty is aggravated by the *alienation* of labour, as a result of which labour-activity appears to be alien for the individual, uninteresting and unsatisfactory for his human demands, and provides only material living conditions.

'The primary form of activity', wrote E.G. Yudin, 'is labour that is characterised by both its specific forms of social organisation and its direct orientation to achieving a socially significant result.'[4]

'The primary form of activity' means that all other forms of human activity should be considered as being *derivative* of this basic form. It means that, in history, labour has preceded all other forms of human activity. For example, the activity of speaking should be considered as having its historical and logical source in labour. Only a scream is needed to give a signal of danger, but to explain to another person what they should do in a working process, articulate speech is required. We should make a distinction here between *symbolising* activities and *signalling* activities: symbols are always conditional, while signals are unconditional. Geese do not arrange for their leader's scream to indicate danger. But people can organise things so that a red flare means the beginning of an attack. Therefore, speaking cannot arise before labour-activity.

Labour is a form of activity that is *concrete* but at the same time *universal*. 'Universal' does not mean that it indicates similarity in the features of any acti-

---

3 Rubinshtein 2005, p. 475.
4 Yudin 1978, p. 268.

vity; it is universal as singular and concrete. Hegel called it *concrete universality*, in contrast to the abstract universality that is only a shortened expression for some set of singular objects of a certain kind. In his lectures on the history of philosophy, Hegel referred to Aristotle's example of a triangle as a *true universal* form of geometric figure. Porphyry, the neo-Platonist, used as an example a performance in a theatre, which is the same for all spectators and is therefore universal, although at the same time it is singular and quite concrete.

Most Soviet philosophers, including Yudin, could not apply this methodology of ascending from abstract to concrete to the notion of labour. Instead of passing from the abstract notion of activity to the concrete notion of labour, they stayed within this abstract notion of activity. 'The place and role of the notion of activity', Yudin wrote, 'are determined first of all by the fact that it belongs to the category of *universal ultimate* abstractions. Such abstractions embody a certain "through" sense: they provide substantial expression both to the most elementary acts of life and to its deepest foundations, and penetrating to these foundations they make the genuine integrity of the world reasonable.'[5]

Abstractions cannot be the deepest foundations of the world. The real basis is always concrete, otherwise nothing could be deduced from it in a logical way. Abstraction only makes it possible to *subsume* under it some set of phenomena, but this is not the same as deducing something. The formation of 'ultimate abstraction' is not a proper way to achieve something concrete. As Marx wrote, 'this way cannot provide considerable riches of definitions. A mineralogist, whose science would be limited by fixing the idea that all minerals in reality are "minerals in general", could become a mineralogist only in his own imagination. At the sight of every mineral, a speculative mineralogist would say: it is a "mineral", and his science would be limited by his repeated use of this word and he would use it as many times as there are real minerals.'[6]

The problem of the origination of speaking activity from labour was discussed by Lev Vygotsky, the founder of cultural and historic psychology. He proceeded from the idea of unity of thought and speech. In his work *Thought and Speech*, Vygotsky was armed with the formula of Abélard, which says that 'Word creates intellect and, at the same time, it is created by intellect'. One can only break this *Word–Thought–Word* cycle by turning the circle into a spiral. Unlike a circle, a spiral has a beginning, and its historical beginning is labour. However, it is only a *historical* beginning, for the *ontogenetic* beginning is the word. At first, a child masters speaking and only after that would he start working. The roles

5   Yudin 1978, p. 271.
6   *MEW* 2, s. 60.

are reversed here. But 'historically' means *essentially*. The essence of speech follows from the essence of labour, and it can be deduced from and explained by it only. This is the general idea and general method of the Vygotsky–Leontiev school.

'In the process of material production', wrote Leontyev, 'people also produce language that is not only a means of communication, but also a bearer of fixed socially developed meanings.'[7] As Vygotsky pointed out even earlier, '[p]ractical intellect is genetically older than the verbal one; action is prior to word, even clever action is prior to clever word.'[8] With reference to Karl Bühler's research, Vygotsky said that 'before speaking there exists instrumental thinking; that is, grasping mechanical couplings and inventing mechanical means for mechanical finite goals'.[9]

As for the genetic primacy of *practical* thinking in comparison to speaking, Vygotsky was quite clear. Thus, attributing some 'linguistic' or 'semiotic' approach to the analysis of human thinking to Vygotsky is inadmissible.[10] Apart from that, speaking activity that arises directly from a child's practical activity is not speech in its usual role as a means of *communication*. This speech, which is known as *autistic* or *egocentric*, serves as a peculiar accompaniment to objective practical activity. A child handles things, plays with them and, at the same time, accompanies his operations with things by denoting these things and operations with them.

However, this speech, which is generated by practical intellect, leads to intellect of a higher level. A child can more freely orientate in the visual field and can overcome its limits, which is not possible for a chimpanzee, as W. Köhler's experiments proved. In other words, even the simple denoting of a thing makes the attitude to it more free or, which is essentially the same, a *conscious* relation to this thing.

The ideal meaning is a form of human activity – labour – and only later a form of word, sign or symbol. A well-known experiment on teaching blind and dumb children conducted by A.I. Mescheryakov plainly demonstrated that a child could not memorise a word until he or she grasped the meaning of the thing that was denoted by the word. As demonstrated by Ilyenkov, the ideal is a form of *activity* that is objectified in the form of thing. Here we cannot manage

---

7   Leontiev 1975, p. 98.

8   Vygotsky 1984, vol. 6, p. 86.

9   Vygotsky 1984, vol. 6, p. 8.

10   As Aleksandr Surmava does (2009, p. 115 ff.), and some Western experts in psycholinguist-
        ics as well (Peeter Tulviste, Jim Wertsch, Dot Robbins, and others).

without activity, specifically *labour*-activity, because only labour can actually change the forms of things. The ideal meaning of a thing becomes the meaning of the word denoting this thing.

The desire to master words, in order to subordinate the objective world, is initiated by the experience of practical subordination in this world. 'This important fact', wrote Ilyenkov, 'was missed by American interpreters of the "Helen Keller phenomenon"'. Commenting on this phenomenon, they did not think it was necessary to mention the fact that before the girl could learn her first word (it turned out to be "water"), she had taken a serious course of "initial humanisation" under the direction of her friend, a black maidservant, who practically taught her to do the simple things connected with everyday life at her father's farm. This crucial fact allowed a gifted teacher named Ann Sullivan to teach Helen language. Being very religious, Sullivan ascribed the small black girl's merit to God, as she just could not understand how the girl managed to obtain "soul", which should be only "woken up by the power of words ... Herefrom, the religious-idealistic interpretation of this phenomenon started going up and down the world."[11]

Speech and speaking activity cannot change anything in the world; its aim is only to attend to the real activity which changes forms of things, that is, material production. Being formed historically in the process of the development of labour-activity, speaking activity now acquires an independent character and becomes the form of development of labour, so to say, in its 'otherness'. In such form, speaking develops thought.

B.F. Porshnev offered the exact opposite theory in his book *O nachale chelovecheskoy istorii* (*On the Origin of Human History*). Porshnev said that the first step is to explain 'word' and he felt that it had a materialistic solution. Notions such as 'activity' and 'labour' remain uncertain in his theory. Porshnev wrote, 'Let us assume the initial thesis of V.A. Zvegintsev: man speaks, thinks and acts; all these things together make up his activity.'[12]

This is also an abstract understanding of 'activity', which is just a common name for the whole range of activities. Furthermore, it is not clear what is primary here – speaking, action or thinking. As a starting point of history or the origin of man (which is the same), Porshnev chose speech and language, saying, 'The problem of *Homo sapiens*'s emergence is the problem of second-signalling-system emergence, of speech.'[13] Porshnev attempted to confirm his ideas using

---

11   Ilyenkov 1991b, p. 37.

12   Porshnev 2006, p. 99.

13   Porshnev 2006, p. 103.

the authority of Vygotsky. 'The psychological development of a child, as it is stated by our wise psychologist L. Vygotsky', wrote Porshnev, 'proceeds not from individual to social but from social to individual: man is social from his first words. It can be applied to the psychic transformation of people in history: they are social from the very beginning.'[14]

It is true that, according to Vygotsky, a child's speech is social from the very beginning, even when it is egocentric. But while the socialisation of a child starts when he learns his first words (though this is not exactly the case according to Vygotsky's point of view), this does not mean that historically social man commenced as man speaking and imitating animal language. The theories of Vygotsky and Porshnev diverge sharply at this point.

Porshnev developed the speech-theory of the origin of man and rejected the labour-theory. Labour is a *purposeful* activity, aimed at a certain goal, and that goal is the knowledge of things that are *non-existent as yet*; it is the image of a thing that is to be made. Plato referred to such images (or patterns) as 'ideas'. How can these ideas appear in the human head? Materialists tried to explain it by saying that ideas are 'reflections' of earthly things. But how can things that do not exist be 'reflected' in our mind?

Porshnev also became entangled by this problem. The solution to this problem can only be that human labour-activity *leads itself*, it begets the pattern which it follows. Human activity bifurcates into two moments – the pattern as such and the activity following the pattern. Before it splits into the idea, which exists only in the architect's head, and the material activity, conducted by a builder, carpenter, bricklayer, and so on, it *splits inside itself*. This concept was demonstrated lucidly by Ilyenkov, who said, 'Even completely corporal actions get split in the directly evident way: hand goes along an object, and eye, a bit earlier, goes along the curves (contours, geometry) of the outer body that faces the moving hand.'[15]

Here, a mutual correction of hand- and eye-movements takes place: the eye corrects the movement of the hand, while the hand corrects the movement of the eye. If the hand pushes against the obstacle that is invisible to the eye, then the eye corrects the movement of the hand in order to overcome the obstacle. Therefore, in the process of activity, hand and eye both learn to follow the texture of the material. For instance, the texture of wood can be seen accurately through the eye of the carpenter or joiner, which should be taken into account when choosing a proper tool and way of using it.

---

14   Porshnev 2006, p. 626.
15   Ilyenkov 1991b, p. 109.

No architect with a building project either in his head or on paper could exist if our distant ancestors had not constructed a hut without starting with any kind of 'project' and had, instead, 'projected' it in the very course of building. Man's eye and head are formed in the process of activity to such an extent that they become the eyes and head of the architect.

From a purely formal point of view, labour is only one type of activity, along with artistic, scientific and economic activity, and so on. 'Activity' is its genus and labour is defined through this nearest genus: labour is a purposeful activity in which a man places between himself and the object of labour some mechanical, chemical and other force of nature. *Historically*, however, we can see that one type of activity – labour – becomes its own genus. Now, different types of human activity can be considered as species of labour. This makes a dialectical difficulty, as from the formal point of view, the identity of genus and species is impossible; it is a 'paradox', a contradiction. It is the difficulty that prevents the development of the notion of activity. And labour is just formally subsumed under the notion of activity.

How labour engenders different types of human activity is a special problem that is to be solved in different ways in any concrete subject-field. With regard to speaking activity, this problem was posed and solved by L.S. Vygotsky. It should be underlined again that the difficulty consists in the fact that roles are reversed: condition becomes conditioned, cause appears to be determined by its own effect. Having given birth to a sign-symbol system, labour is now organised and directed by this system. Vygotsky analysed this reversion of the historical into the logical on the material of the intellectual development of a child.

The problem is not where articulate sounds and words come from. The problem is the origin of *meanings* of words. This problem of the ideal was resolved by E.V. Ilyenkov, who showed that material activity gives rise to the ideal in general, both in the form of activity-goal and in the form of idea, in the form of beauty and human moral sense. That is the concrete conception of activity that was attained by the Soviet philosophy represented by Ilyenkov.

CHAPTER 7

The Kiev Philosophical School in the Light of the Marxist Theory of Activity

Elena Mareeva

The Kiev philosophical school was formed in the 1960s and flourished in the 1970s and 1980s. Many Kiev philosophers – primarily the employees of the Institute of Philosophy of the Ukrainian National Academy of Science – still associate themselves with this school and insist that it is still alive, even though its form has changed.

Formation of the Kiev Philosophical School and Its Specific Features

P.V. Kopnin (1922–71) is considered one of the founders of the Kiev philosophical school. Kopnin arrived in Kiev from Moscow in 1958 and headed the Institute of Philosophy from 1962 to 1968. Although he later headed the Institute of Philosophy of the USSR Academy of Science for three years, his most productive period was when he lived in Kiev, as V.A. Lektorsky has noted.

Kopnin developed a new trend in Soviet philosophy called the 'logic of scientific cognition'. In his opinion, logic, the theory of cognition and dialectics did not belong to different spheres of research, but coincided in the light of the Marxist understanding of the method of scientific and theoretical thinking. Kopnin favoured an idea that was unusual for the official Marxist theory about the specificity of philosophical knowledge, namely that its subject-matter is man's relationship to the world.

This humanistic version of Marxism continued its development in Kiev even after Kopnin had left for Moscow. In 1968, V.I. Shinkaruk (1928–2001) became the head of the Institute of Philosophy of the Ukrainian Academy of Science. According to V.G. Tabachkovsky, Shinkaruk 'organised the anthropological turn' in the work of the Kiev philosophical school. Today, Ukrainian historians of philosophy consider Shinkaruk, rather than Kopnin, to be the real founder of the Kiev philosophical school, which focused on the problems of 'man and the world', mankind's specific individuality with all its emotional experience, and so on.

Many contemporary Ukrainian philosophers claim that the Kiev school continued 'humanistic traditions of Ukrainian philosophising'. Such claims ignore
the fact that it was mainly a Russian-speaking school and that Ukrainian and
Russian philosophy was a comprehensive whole. Today, Ukraine has attempted to introduce the Kiev philosophical school of the 1970s and 1980s within
the line started by the poet Taras Shevchenko. Ukraine-born philosophers such
as Pamphil Yurkevich, Nikolai Berdyaev and Lev Shestov are also attributed to
this school. Existential motifs in their works are interpreted as a threshold of
the Kiev philosophical school of the second half of the twentieth century.[1]

In light of modern preferences, the Kiev philosophical school is referred to
as 'world-outlook – anthropologic', and its initial core is considered to contain
some 'existential anthropology' (V.G. Tabachkovsky).[2] All these assessments
and interpretations were initiated in order to contrast the Kiev philosophical
school of that period not only to the official Soviet philosophy, but to Marxist theory in general. In my view, however, it is necessary to pay attention to
those Ukrainian philosophers who consider the school to be a *synthesis* of
Marxism and existentialism. More precisely, the Kiev school came into life
through attempts to *rebuild* Marxism under the influence of modern philosophy, particularly existentialism. Bringing Marxism and modern philosophy
closer together, representatives of this school were inspired mainly by Marx's
manuscripts of 1844, which were published quite late and provided an opportunity to place new accents in his legacy.

The combined efforts of the Ukrainian philosophers of the Institute of Philosophy were presented in monographs and collections of articles, issued by the
Naukova Dumka publishing house in the 1970s and 1980s. The topics of these
books were typical of Marxist philosophy in the USSR, dealing with the structure of world-outlook, cognition and practice, with the system of categories,
forming of personality, and so on. However, changes in its treatments are very
important, for they allow us to speak about the specific features of the Kiev
school.

The Soviet philosophers of Kiev unanimously repudiated Hegel. In 1993,
V.G. Tabachkovsky announced that Marxism inherited 'hyperactivism' from
the German classics and underestimated 'various essential layers, which could
hardly be reduced only to social activity'.[3] Of course, such negative assessments
of the social essence of man could not be stated in Tabachkovsky's works during

1 See Melkov 2008.
2 Since V.I. Shinkaruk and up to the present day, the Ukrainian Institute of Philosophy has been
   headed by M.V. Popovich.
3 Tabachkovsky 1993, pp. 18–19.

Soviet times. During that period, however, he criticised the 'gnoseological dis-tortion of culture and activity', which he believed was rooted in Hegel's ration-alism. In the monograph *Kritika idealisticheskikh interpretatsiy praktiki* (*Cri-tique of the Idealistic Interpretations of Practice*), Tabachkovsky accused Hegel of referring to science – rather than everyday life – as the genuine sphere of human existence.[4] He wrote that, in idealism, the relationship between man and the world was reduced to that between subject and object.[5] It is natural that Marx, as a materialist, would support those who saw the departure-point of philosophy in studying the 'life-position of concrete individuals'.

Tabachkovsky sympathised with Schelling, who seems to have turned away from the 'gnoseological distortion' of human activity when it is examined through a prism of cognitive attitude; he aspired to understand man as a living whole. The Schelling of the later period seemed more convincing to Tabachkovsky than Hegel did; however, even at earlier stages, Schelling was on the threshold of an 'existential turn', when the practical is opposed to the intellectual, and a return to the forgotten individual ego occurs.[6]

The reason why I expound Tabachkovsky's views so thoroughly is because his argumentation can illustrate those emphases that were placed in the history of philosophy by the vanguard of the Kiev philosophical school of the 1970s and 1980s. Such a version of Marxism, of course, differed from the officially estab-lished one, as well as from Kopnin's version. For many Kiev philosophers, the very idea of the 'practical' is filled with some over-rational or, to be more pre-cise, pre-rational content. Practice is now treated as activity that corresponds to pre-reflexive and emotional forms of world-perception. This interpretation of practice is used to fit the Marxist discourse, as if it were retrieved from the works of Marx and Lenin.

Other categories of Marxism have undergone similar transformation. The main idea of the Kiev philosophical school is that knowledge is not enough to form personality. While official Marxism spoke about a scientific world-outlook, the acquisition of which leads an individual to become not only a personality but also a citizen, the Kiev interpretation of world-outlook focuses on 'practically-spiritual mastering of the world', which precedes the scientific mind and in which the level of world-outlook appears to be embedded into the real life-process.[7] According to Kiev philosophers, such a 'world-experience'

---

4   Tabachkovsky 1976, p. 32.
5   Tabachkovsky 1976, p. 86.
6   See Tabachkovsky 1976, pp. 131–4.
7   *Kategorial'naja struktura poznanija i praktiki* 1986, pp. 17–18.

has advantages over a scientific 'world-outlook'. Marx is portrayed as a philosopher who rejected abstract theory in favour of practice that involved an immediate and pre-reflexive world-outlook.

Even the most highly qualified Kiev Marxists of that period were forced (or maybe inclined) to work within the frameworks of the adopted dichotomies: particular–general, immediate–mediated, irrational–rational, and so on. According to V.P. Ivanov, the assistant-director of the Institute of Philosophy of the Ukrainian Academy of Science in the early 1980s, philosophy and science are not the only ways to develop a world-outlook. Knowledge is universal, he wrote, and beliefs are personal; knowledge is descriptive and beliefs are imperative; knowledge is objective and beliefs are subjectively individual. Thus, a world-outlook must, first of all, express a 'life-sense-position' (*smyslozhiznennaya pozitsiya*).[8] M.A. Bulatov, an expert in philosophical classics, paid particular attention to the fact that analysing categories, in the context of life-problem, 'made Hegel go beyond the limits of pure logic and introduce another, non-logical types of categories'.[9]

It is clear that the general direction of the discussion of practice, world-outlook and culture was predetermined by V.I. Shinkaruk, the head of the Institute of Philosophy. Shinkaruk wrote that 'faith, hope, dream, spiritual emotions (the positive manifestation of all these feelings is love in the widest meaning of the word) are extremely important categories of the spiritual life of man and society, and therefore, of spiritual culture'.[10] One should pay special attention to the title of the collection of articles from which this quotation was taken. The title deals with categories of materialistic dialectics, by which Marxists meant *something* and *nothing*, *quality*, *quantity* and *measure*, *possibility* and *reality*, and so on. Shinkaruk, however, interpreted them as certain 'categories of spiritual culture'.

This shift of interest from the objective to the subjective point of view in world-outlook-orientation can be discerned in the foreword Shinkaruk wrote to the collective work *Chelovek i mir cheloveka* (*Man and Man's World*, Kiev 1977). Here the world-outlook is an expression of a choice of life-goals and - evaluations, and thus it serves as a tool of 'changing the world',[11] where no distinction is made between the individual and the human species. While the

---

8   Ivanov 1986, pp. 11–12.

9   Bulatov 1984, p. 133.

10   *Mirovozzrencheskoe soderzhanie kategorij i zakonov materialisticheskoj dialektiki* 1981, p. 23.

11   Compare *Chelovek i mir cheloveka. Kategorii "chelovek" i "mir" v sisteme nauchnogo mirovozzreniya* 1977, p. 18.

official Diamat regarded the categories as forms of organising the world out-side Man, in the works of Shinkaruk of this period the categories were not conceived of as forms of organising the world of nature, but the world of cul-ture, the core of which consists of human actions, goals, values and exper-iences. According to this position, man creates culture from nature, follow-ing his own laws and forms. However, the question of how the objective and the subjective, the individual and the generic are interrelated in this kind of practical activity and in the world of culture was not elaborated very percep-tively.

The same shift can be observed with the majority of the representatives of the Kiev philosophical school, who considered it as a 'humanisation' of dia-lectical materialism. In this context, they speak about 'practical categories', 'culture-categories' and 'world-outlook-categories' as universal forms of 'con-sciousness in general', that is, categories of everyday consciousness. Tabach-kovsky made a distinction between categories of culture, categories of world-outlook and categories of scientific consciousness. He saw the peculiarity of culture-categories in the fact that they demonstrate 'the primary conceptual-isation of the transition from nature to culture'. He also mentioned that culture-categories are definitions of 'everyday life' rather than definitions of thinking process, but that all three types of category are kinds of 'thinking categorisation' (*myslitel'naya kategorizatsiya*).[12] This is typical of the Kiev school's uncertainty in interpreting 'logical', 'rational' 'thinking'.[13]

If Kopnin tried to orientate Kiev philosophers towards the logic of scientific cognition and a scientific worldview, then Shinkaruk made extra-scientific forms of world-outlook the dominant theme for the members of the Kiev Institute of Philosophy. Some departments continued studying natural science and scientific methodology but they were very far from Kopnin's dialectical logic.

Thus, the 1970s and 1980s, a group of Shinkaruk's followers was formed in the institute. These people became known as the Kiev philosophical school, which was a unique phenomenon in Soviet philosophy. Despite the claims of Kiev philosophers that the school still exists, it has in fact passed into history. The

---

12   See *Chelovek i mir cheloveka. Kategorii "chelovek" i "mir" v sisteme nauchnogo mirovozzren-iya* 1977, pp. 81–2.

13   One should, however, mention here the interesting works of A.I. Yatsenko, which deal with the dialectics of objectivation and de-objectivation, innovation and tradition, and the categories of 'goal', 'freedom', 'choice', 'existence' and 'duty' as forms of human activity (compare Yatsenko 1977). However, Yatsenko relies heavily on Marx's *Economic and Philo-sophic Manuscripts of 1844* and does not transcend their problematics.

school attempted to transcend the limits of Marxism in terms of understanding practical activity, world-outlook and culture. The only available way to do that in those days was through a camouflaged synthesis of Marxism with modern philosophy.

The most frequently used terms in the works of the Kiev philosophers were 'activity' and 'practice', as well as 'world-outlook' and 'culture'; however, these philosophers did not develop a comprehensive theory of activity. At best, one can speak of the *research programme* concerning the problem of activity, which can be found in the monographs published by Naukova Dumka in the 1970s and 1980s.

The Concept of Activity: Vadim Ivanov's Criticism of the System-Approach

The activity approach in most of the works by the Kiev philosophers appeared as a set of generalised statements concerning activity, practice and labour, which filled Soviet textbooks on dialectical and historical materialism. The Kiev school supplemented those statements with its own typical considerations of extra-logical or pre-logical forms of human activity. Only one Kiev philosopher, V.P. Ivanov (1933–91), developed a more or less original theory of activity. Although he called his approach a 'philosophical worldview' (*filosofsko-mirovozzrencheskiy*), his book *Chelovecheskaya deyatel'nost – poznanie – iskusstvo* (*Human Activity – Cognition – Art*, 1977) offers a distinctive version of the activity approach.

In this book, Ivanov substantiated his own understanding of the nature of art and, at the same time, refuted 'gnoseologism'. The book contains other signs of his belonging to the Kiev philosophical school, but we are interested mainly in his concept of activity. Ivanov's position shows itself most sharply in the course of his criticism of M.S. Kagan and E.S. Markaryan.[14]

Moisei Kagan belonged to the Leningrad philosophical school, and Eduard Markaryan was a well-known Armenian philosopher. Ivanov attributed himself to the dialectical tradition, while Kagan and Markaryan adhered to the system-approach. Terms such as 'system-approach', 'system-structural approach', 'functional approach', 'system-analysis' and 'system-structural analysis' veiled the

---

14   Witty criticism of Kagan's system-theory was offered by Mikhail Lifshits (see Lifshits 1985).
     The work of Vadim Mezhuev (Mezhuev 1977) also provides detailed criticism of Kagan and
     Markaryan.

methodology that had been perceived in the USSR since the 1960s as the last word in scientific methodology.[15] The insufficiency of this methodology in terms of researching human activity was shown by Ivanov in the above-mentioned book in a section entitled 'The category of activity and specific features of its philosophic consideration'.

Kagan was one of the first Soviet philosophers to raise the question of the structure of human activity. He also developed an original classification of human-activity types: transformative, cognitive, value-orientating and communicative activity, as well as artistic activity, which combines the four previous types.[16]

Acknowledging some logic in this model, Ivanov pointed out that this only made it possible to show some 'structural profile of certain society's vital activities'.[17] However, this historically concrete profile was passed for social structure in general and, thus, society was depicted as a finite and static system. The same happens to human activity. The nature of the human attitude to the world implies *historical changes* in the very structure of activity. Within the frame of the system-analysis, meanwhile, this structure, for instance Kagan's 'pentamerous formula' (*pyatichlenka*), is represented as constant.

Ivanov showed the contradictions between the understanding of activity developed by the system-approach and its understanding in dialectical philosophy. He underlined that the system-approach is anti-historical, which is difficult to deny. It is enough to mention sociological theories that widely apply this approach. Even if a sociologist passes from statics to dynamics, these schemes of social development provide no opportunity to understand the real facts and route of history.

Ivanov elaborated on the notion of activity. This raises the question of how it is possible to proceed from cognition of certain types of activity to knowledge of human activity in general, to activity as a philosophical category. Ivanov wrote that a system-approach-perspective implies the knowledge of integral features and functions of the whole system. Having gained knowledge of some features of the elements, their functions and interrelations, it is necessary to pass over to an idea of functions and features of the whole. This integral function (system-quality) is always more complicated than the sum-total of the initial elements, as was proved by systems-theory.

---

15   In some cases, representatives of the system-approach interpreted it as an element of materialistic dialectics (M.S. Kagan, V.G. Afanasiev, V.N. Sagatovsky, A.I. Uëmov).

16   See Kagan 1974.

17   See Ivanov 1977, p. 66.

Following the procedure offered by Kagan, however, would produce the opposite results. In this case, 'elements turn out to be richer than the system to which they belong, for, apart from its general characteristics, they have their own specific features, such as transformation, cognition, and so on'.[18]

Ivanov reached the unequivocal conclusion that activity is a reality that cannot be studied through system-structural analysis. 'Here is the relationship between genus and species (even the universal and single), but not between structure and its elements.'[19] Specifying the content of activity as the human essence, he added, 'The system-organisation, stipulating for the adequate method of analysis, deals only with the level of reality, that is, *being*, its substance and structure, but not the level of essence. It becomes more evident when we speak about the essence of man, which is not an ordinary objective essence, but activity in the endless field of its subject-realisations.'[20]

According to Ivanov, by focusing on the general notion of activity, representatives of the system-approach look to answer the wrong question. This was the case with Markaryan, whose notion of activity coincides with the way of functioning of any 'living systems', including biological, social and some 'technical systems self-capable of reproduction'.[21] The latters Markaryan referred to the distant future. But most important here is that activity implies not only a *human* attitude to the world. Markaryan treated activity as the adaptation of any living system to the environment. With this, any living system, in contrast to a lifeless one, adapts itself to the environment through the negentropy effect, that is, making its organisation and behaviour more complicated but not simplifying it.

In Ivanov's opinion, the methodological foundation of all these constructions is 'a bizarre combination of ideas and notions from systems-analysis, cybernetics, information theory and thermodynamics'.[22] Such theories have become 'commonplace in works that are equally far both from physics and biology, and that offer, instead of adequate analysis of the specific features of an object, some pompous theses of universal scale'.[23] It should be emphasised that these words, written more than 30 years ago, also characterise today's prevalence of pseudoscientific 'universal' theories. One could here refer, for instance, to synergetics, when it pretends to explain all and everything.

---

18   Ivanov 1977, p. 66.
19   Ivanov 1977, p. 65.
20   Ivanov 1977, pp. 69–70.
21   See Markaryan 1973, p. 13.
22   Ivanov 1977, p. 71.
23   Ivanov 1977, p. 66.

In Soviet times, Markaryan was well known as an expert on culture, although he considered culture not to be substance but only a means of adaptation to the environment. He distinguished biological (similar to animal) ways from socio-cultural ways of human activity, which meant that culture is nothing more than a mechanism and potency of activity. Diversity of activity-types is stipulated by a 'component-structure of society', which depends on a subject, object and method of activity.

Markaryan's explanations contain a vicious circle. The variety of types of human activity depends on the definite social structure and, conversely, the social structure depends on a type of this activity. The boundaries of this vicious circle can only be overcome, Ivanov wrote, by turning to the real history of mankind, taking into account man's active or, to be more precise, *practical* attitude to the world. Here we can retrace the genesis of real types of activity. Anti-historical explanations result in the designing of speculative schemes, for which some real equivalents are sought out afterwards.

Relying upon abstract schemes, instead of historical facts, Markaryan 'washes away' activity, in Ivanov's words, depriving it of a specifically human sense. As a result, activity can be understood as striving for anything what-soever. On the other hand, the variant of the system-approach offered by Markaryan refers to human relations as real 'systems', in which man himself is an ordinary component.[24]

However, as Ivanov stressed, human activity is not a species that belongs to a certain genus. Ivanov was strongly opposed to the opinion that an animal or technical system is a subject of activity. Only a human attitude to the world can be defined as 'activity' in the strict sense of the word; there is no activity except for human activity.

Kagan and Markaryan both postulated activity with a finite set of functions, which is a typical feature of the system-approach. In the variant of the system-approach advanced by Kagan, the general idea of activity emerges as a result of summing up notions of various types of human activity. Through such a method, a very poor notion of the 'general' is formed. By subtracting its trans-formative, cognitive, artistic and other elements from activity, we obtain some abstract 'action in general' with an undefined object and an uncertain goal.

In accordance with the empiricist tradition in philosophy, this type of 'general' can exist only in our mind as an idea about 'general features' of single bodies. Does this mean that 'activity in general' can also be only abstract and does not exist in reality?

---

24   See Markaryan 1973, p. 13.

In discussing this question, Ivanov reproduced the arguments of Feuerbach, who insisted that there is no general activity, that there are only concrete activities: individuals establish sensual contacts with concrete objects. General features of activity can be abstracted but they are not as real as concrete activities. Feuerbach maintained that only idealistic and religious consciousness ascribes real being to abstractions.

The idea of activity, wrote Ivanov, is not 'just a mental *abstraction* from real activities'.[25] There are a lot of 'acts' but 'activity is the only one, it is comprehensive, universal, and it shows itself in these acts but it is not formed by them, since its definitions are depicted in general characteristics of the human attitude to the world'.[26]

We should agree with Ivanov that, in the case of the notion of activity, we pass over to the sphere of relations between general and singular, essence and phenomenon, but not the relationship between a system and its elements. However, Ivanov does not clearly explain in what sense the essence of human activity is 'real' and 'the only one'.

Activity and Labour: V.P. Ivanov and E.V. Ilyenkov

V.P. Ivanov elaborated his version of the activity approach in the frame of the Marxist dialectical tradition in philosophy, which was most brightly represented by E.V. Ilyenkov. The philosophers sometimes communicated directly when Ivanov came to the Institute of Philosophy of the USSR Academy of Science. Their common friends say that Ilyenkov did not go into any great depth regarding the differences in their views. At that time, when Ilyenkov's opponents outnumbered those who agreed with him, Ilyenkov preferred to concentrate on the times when their positions were similar.

Ivanov's attitude to Ilyenkov, I should say, was cautious enough. Ivanov acted as an official opponent at the defence of my dissertation in 1983. It took place at the Philosophy Faculty of the Rostov University, where Ivanov arrived from Kiev. The Rostov philosophical community was seriously influenced by Ilyenkov's views, initially by the agency of his friend A.V. Potemkin. Ilyenkov and Potemkin defended two doctoral dissertations, but neither of them was approved by the Higher Attestation Board of the USSR. Potemkin's book *O spetsifike filosofskogo znaniya* (*On the Specificity of Philosophical Knowledge,*

---

25   Ivanov 1977, p. 67.
26   Ivanov 1977, p. 69.

1973) was condemned for 'gnoseologism' – reducing the subject of philosophy to the laws and categories of thought. It was the same charge that had been brought against Ilyenkov in 1955, which had led to the young lecturer being driven out of Moscow University.

In 1983, Ivanov criticised my dissertation, which was also influenced by Ilyenkov, because of its focus on the tool-nature of human activity. Ivanov argued that one should accentuate the fact that activity is always immersed in the system of social relations, by which it is essentially determined. Although Ilyenkov's name was not mentioned, it was certainly implied.

The Kiev philosophical school put forward the idea of the so-called 'socially relational' (social'no-otnoshencheskoye) content of human activity. In accordance with Marx's thesis that the essence of man is an 'ensemble of social relations', Ivanov argued that the essence of man is not finite; it is not included in his body but acquired by an individual from the outer world through the creation of his social qualities. In this way, each of us appropriates an 'embodied link of individuals'; that is, 'sociality', which is the 'genuine cradle of activity'.[27] It is difficult to say whether this means that typically human activity arises due to our social linkage, although Ivanov insisted that it is sociality that turns an individual into the subject of activity. Moreover, it is not the kind of social work that 'makes individual a man, but sociality itself, allowing him later to master any kind of work'.[28]

According to Ivanov, consciousness and self-consciousness are formed in the course of mastering social relations, together with embedded cultural senses. At this point, Ivanov's stand differs from Ilyenkov's conception of the socialisation of an individual as mastering the concrete kinds of human activity. Ilyenkov rested on data from the experiment conducted by a teacher named A.I. Mescheryakov, who worked in the Institute of Blind-deaf Pedagogy. Mescheryakov proceeded from the fact that blind-deaf children only start to shape their psyche and consciousness through 'joint-shared activity' (sovmestno-razdelennaya deyatel'nost') with a teacher. The starting point here is everyday activity for ordinary self-attendance. Ilyenkov considered this special case to be the demonstration of a general rule: the establishment of the human attitude to the world takes place within activity with things made by man for man.

It might seem as though Ilyenkov and Ivanov are speaking about the same thing. However, the difference becomes acute when they speak about labour and its role in the formation of man. For Ivanov, the key point in becoming a

---

27   Ivanov 1977, p. 100.
28   Ivanov 1977, p. 8.

human being is mastering *sociality*, which determines human activity. Ilyenkov, in the spirit of the materialistic understanding of history, believed *labour* to be the 'cell' that gives rise to the diversity of types of human activity. Concrete labour-activity, rather than abstract 'sociality', creates human beings (although, of course, labour always has a social character). Labour, having come into being as a *special* attitude of our ancestors to the environment, later became a *general* foundation of human life.

According to Ilyenkov, any essence, including the essence of man, is nothing other than a *concrete universal relation* between phenomena, or the law of their interlacement within the concrete whole, in which they are essentially 'kindred' due to their common genesis. They have a common essence insofar as they are modifications of the same real 'substance'.[29]

It is obvious that the disclosure of such a necessary relationship (the 'concrete universal', in Ilyenkov's terms) does not mean the abstraction of similarities, but a *concrete analysis* of how one is connected with the other. As for the human essence, Ilyenkov noted that Marx supported Franklin's definition of man as a tool-making animal.

> Formally, Ilyenkov wrote, this definition refers only to a narrow circle of individuals, namely workers of machine-building plants or workshops. Even workers who do not make, but only use these machines will not fit, formally, the frames of this definition. So, old logic, with its understanding of the "general", should justly assess this definition not as "general" but as particular, not as a definition of "man in general" but as a definition of a particular profession.[30]

In dialectical logic 'generality', as the essential unity, can be determined not by presence but by the absence of a certain feature. 'And *this absence of a certain feature can bind one individual to another even stronger than presence of this feature in both of them.*'[31] It follows that general definitions, which express the essence of genus, should not be perceived as individual features, or 'predicates', of each and every representative of this genus.

Here we can see a significant difference between the views of Ivanov and those of Ilyenkov. Though the latter sees in labour the common human essence, he does not mean that every human being labours. According to Ivanov, how-

29   See Ilyenkov 1991c, p. 327.
30   Ilyenkov 1991c, p. 334.
31   Ilyenkov 1991c, p. 324.

ever, activity as such, which constitutes the human essence, reveals itself necessarily in the concrete activities of every individual. 'Activity as such has its own historical-cultural forms – its properties are "absolute" and stand "outside" any historical variations, though these properties may be expressed tangibly only in a historical form.'[32] Pure activity historically realises itself in practical transformation of the world, which breaks up into material and spiritual activity and, further, into labour, cognitive, artistic and other types of human activity.

It seems that, by characterising practice as the objective-transformative relationship of man to the world, Ivanov fills the notion of practice with a more lofty meaning than simply making tools of labour and means of living. In contrast to Ilyenkov, Ivanov considered abstract definitions of activity, such as freedom, universality, creativity and setting goals, to be the driving force of development of real activity. Ilyenkov, for his part, treated the internal 'strain of contradiction' within labour itself as a motive power of self-development of labour and a cause of its differentiation and division into particular kinds of human activity.[33]

According to Ivanov, activity, as such, virtually contains its future modifications, which are largely predetermined by its nature, in spite of their own openness and incompleteness. Activity has a limited circle of possibilities. In characterising activity in this way, with its intrinsic parameters, Ivanov's rhetoric sometimes begins to sound somewhat Fichtean:

> In contrast to their products, which drag out a transient objective existence, activity as human essence ... exists insofar as it modifies, forms, transforms, and it does not reach its final realisation and completion in any of its particular forms. Permanently creating, it *lives* only in frailty of its incarnations. It is the very *creating motion*, but not the result of this motion at a certain time, certain place and in a certain quality. It makes up its most general dialectics and also its (as well as the human) *generic* attitude to the whole world that faces it and that is modified by it.[34]

Ivanov specified that he was referring here to activity in its ultimate meaning, where it coincides with sociality as some 'potential force of social tie'.

---

32   Ivanov 1977, p. 98.
33   See Ilyenkov, 1991c, p. 334.
34   Ivanov 1977, p. 89.

The notion of labour occupies only three pages in Ivanov's book. Well-known ideas of Marx's *Capital* are interpreted here in an unusual manner. Ivanov repeats several times that labour gave birth to man, but this standard Marxist phrase sounds rather allegorical coming from Ivanov. Ivanov actually located labour in the same category as cognitive, artistic and other types of human activity. Nevertheless, in this brief section of his book, Ivanov states that 'labour in general' is not only a theoretical abstraction but 'a practical reality which was attained by human being at a certain point of development'.[35] He was referring to capitalism, which formed indifference to concrete types of labour when individuals passed from one type of labour to another easily, as Marx showed. Labour became a means of making wealth in general, once it was no longer interwoven with individuals, which had been typical of pre-capitalist formations.

Ivanov offered an original and rather unexpected appraisal of this historical fact. He asserted that, by turning labour into abstract activity, capitalism 'actually raises labour to its deepest substantial foundation – activity, and transforms it, within a system of certain productive relations, from the aggregate of specific man's skills to the *universal force of creation*, equal to the total creative power of individuals or, which is the same, to their sociality'.[36]

The statement that labour, having become abstract, returns to activity in general, corresponds with Ivanov's logic. In Marx's own theory, the characteristic that Ivanov attributes to abstract labour would fit better with 'universal labour' (*allgemeine Arbeit*), which is opposed to private labour in capitalist society. Private labour deprives the individual of personal qualities, brings complicated activity to simple tasks and turns individuals into a screw of technological process. On the contrary, universal labour, as a creative work of human intellect (of a scientist, for example), does not lose its integral, social nature even if it is carried out by a man alone.

The final chapter of Ivanov's book is devoted to art, which expresses the general nature of activity better than any other concrete form. According to Ivanov, the world of culture has its own 'over-natural' (*nadprirodnaya*) logic, which is objectified in the system of cultural meanings. The individual masters these meanings (which Ivanov referred to as the 'value canons of culture') in the form of subjective emotional experience. Art, with all its 'impracticality', allows us not only to deobjectify any available 'cultural fund', but also to seize the universal principles of creativity.

---

35   Ivanov 1977, p. 110.
36   Ivanov 1977, p. 111.

So, the sense of beauty (in contrast to the long-standing tradition) cannot be reduced to the sum of qualities and measures of objective reality and the ability to reproduce the latter. Beauty is connected with resolving general problems of cultural creativity, with the process of socially historical transformation of the objective world into the human world. Beauty, in this sense, can provide the name for the most optimal and reasonable extension of the reality in human practice, stipulated by the existing system of culture.[37]

Beauty in art derives from improving reality in practice, while practical activity is, by definition, creative.

It would be strange if Ilyenkov had denied the creative essence of art. However, he openly supported Ivanov's idea that 'tradition existed for a long time'. Ivanov pointed out that improving the world of culture is stipulated by the existing system of culture. But how is that possible? By and large, Ivanov included the essence of human creativity in the very notion of activity, as its universal definition. The creative nature of activity is simply certified by Ivanov, as if it needs no explanation; for Ilyenkov, however, it creates a serious problem.

Ilyenkov proceeds from the postulate that the 'existing system of culture' is based on the ability to act in accordance with a measure of any kind and it takes place primarily in labour. Practical re-creation of both external form and essential ties of natural things is the foundation of the 'inorganic body' of civilisation; we call it 'material culture'. However, human activity is universal and creative, because, in labour, people synthesise measures of things and such synthesis cannot be found in external nature.

According to Ilyenkov, artistic creative work can be explained by such components of labour as setting goals (*tselepolaganie*). Free activity of man that aims at socially important goals has its own form and logic, which is as objective as the laws of nature.

Thus, the real "anthropomorphisation of nature", that is, imparting "human forms" to nature, is not a matter of "imagination". It is simply the essence of labour, the essence of producing material conditions for human life. By changing nature in accordance with his own goals, man humanises it.[38]

---

37   Ivanov 1977, p. 224.
38   Ilyenkov 1984b, p. 258.

It is clear that the objectivity of social laws and forms of human activity differ from the objectivity of the laws of nature. A sense of beauty allows us to apply to nature the measure of creativity and freedom that was previously formed in labour. Ilyenkov constantly reminded us about the unity of beauty and freedom. He underlined that the ideal of beauty expresses not man's arbitrary will, but the measure of freedom in our activity. In the projection of this human ideal on nature, man sees features similar to his own freedom and goals.

The archive of S.N. Mareev, Ilyenkov's pupil and friend, included the collective monograph entitled *Kul'tura i razvitie cheloveka* (*Culture and Human Development* Kiev, 1989), with an inscription by Ivanov that read, 'To Sergey Mareev from representatives of a different philosophical school to get acquainted and regarded with favour.' As we can see, representatives of the Kiev philosophical school deliberately dissociated themselves from other philosophical schools, including that of Ilyenkov.

The first chapter in this book, written by V.P. Ivanov, criticises E.S. Markaryan, N.S. Zlobin and V.M. Mezhuev. Ivanov appraised the works of the two latter authors as the best in Soviet philosophy in terms of dealing with cultural issues (they both use and elaborate on the activity approach). However, commenting on the notion of 'universal labour' in Mezhuev, Ivanov wrote of the impossibility of explaining culture on the basis of labour. The notion of culture requires 'more general interpretation of the activity-principle itself', substantiated by analysis of 'the fabric of the life-process'.[39] Although the terminological emphasis here shifted from 'sociality' to 'life', the line of thinking remained the same. Morality and arts are the 'forces of man's sociality' and 'the forces of social form of life' but not the 'forces of labour' at all.

Having been born on Marxist soil, Ivanov's theory of activity recedes from the basic Marxist principle that man makes himself by his labour. In addition, Ivanov assigns the leading role in human life to art, which is in the common spirit of the Kiev school.

I see the key paradox of Ivanov's methodology as follows. Having criticised the system-approach for designing speculative schemes, Ivanov then claims that human essence is an abstraction of activity in general. In line with Markaryan, Ivanov characterises 'activity in general' as a source of the concrete diversity of human activities; in other words, this diversity is a realisation of the initial abstraction. Therefore, Ivanov's dialectical method shares a speculative character with the system-approach of M.S. Kagan and E.S. Markaryan.

---

39   *Kul'tura i razvitie cheloveka* 1989, p. 88.

The Kiev philosophical school continues its researches, and the Institute of Philosophy remains its centre as before, though neither the activity approach nor Marxism remains there. Its affinity with the Soviet Kiev school goes no further than an accent on worldview and existential aspects, but it is now connected with the national self-consciousness. Consequently, the Kiev philosophical school of the 1970s and 1980s, as well as V.P. Ivanov's theory of activity, is now only a subject of historical-philosophical analysis.

CHAPTER 8

The Evolution of Batishchev's Views on the Nature of Objective Activity, and the Limits of the Activity Approach

Aleksandr Khamidov

Marx formulated the principle of objective activity (*gegenständliche Tätigkeit*; in Russian, *predmetnaya deyatel'nost'*) in his notebook while he worked with Engels on *The German Ideology*. However, he had already applied this principle earlier in his *Economic and Philosophic Manuscripts of 1844*. Marx used this principle to formulate his own philosophical concept of man, to create the concept of alienation and to develop his system of political economy.

In early Soviet philosophy, before the country was subjected to the 'wisdom' of Stalin's work *Dialectical and Historical Materialism*, P.L. Kucherov substantiated the value of the category of activity for Marxism, relying also on Hegel's works (especially *The Phenomenology of Mind*).[1] The talented Georgian philosopher K.R. Megrelidze applied this category, along with the cultural-historical approach, to the analysis of thinking. His book, *Osnovnye problemy sotsiologii myshleniya* (The Main Problems of the Sociology of Thinking), had been written in 1936 but was only published for the first time in 1965 (and even then with abridgements) and reprinted in full in 1973.

In his well-known article 'The Ideal', written for the *Filosofskaya entsiklopediya* (1962), Evald Ilyenkov demonstrated the heuristic potential of the objective activity-principle. His pupil Genrikh Batishchev (21 May 1932–31 October 1990) worked in the same sector of the Institute of Philosophy of the Academy of Sciences of USSR as Ilyenkov. The central theme and focus of Batishchev's philosophical writings is the problem of *human creativity*, in its ontological, epistemological, anthropological and axiological aspects and dimensions. Batishchev's work falls into two main areas: (1) the theory of dialectics, its essence and its categories (primarily the category of *contradiction*); and (2) the essence of man, his being in the world and delusive forms of existence (especially *alienation*).

A characteristic of Batishchev's philosophical work was its constant *transcendence*, but it did not transcend the limits of just one world-outlook, as is

---

1 See Kucherov 1930.

common among philosophers, even the great ones. While these philosophers changed and developed, they did not move *beyond* a certain accepted scale. Batishchev, on the other hand, transcended not only small but also large *worldview* paradigms. He overcame them and left them behind once he understood their boundaries and limitations. Batishchev was not just guided by the accepted paradigm – he *thrived* on it. For Batishchev, the crisis of the adopted paradigm was not only epistemological or methodological, but also a *world-related* (*mirootnoshencheskiy*), existential crisis. On each occasion it was his own personal life-drama, and his attitude to the category of objective activity was equally dramatic.

Batishchev realised his movement from one paradigm to another both fully and clearly. He considered the path of his own thought as a transition from *substantialism* (the philosophical principle that absolutises substance to the detriment of subject) towards *anti-substantialism* (the opposite principle, which absolutises subject to the detriment of substance) and, finally, to a new philosophical position, which he defined as *intersubjective* and *polyphonising*.[2] In fact, it was not a Hegelian triad of the negation of negation, as Batishchev himself was inclined to depict it.[3]

Regardless of Marx's true philosophy, the official Soviet philosophy – Diamat and Histomat – was a kind of 'substantialism'. Batishchev, too, started from this point, but he also managed to understand and appreciate the principle of objective activity, as well as Marx's concept of alienation and its overcoming. As early as his postgraduate years, Batishchev had started to study the problem of human activity, as well as the problem of contradiction (the topic of his PhD thesis). Batishchev's interpretation of the category of activity in this period is clearly presented in his monograph, entitled *Protivorechie kak kategoriya dialekticheskoy logiki* (Contradiction as Category of Dialectical Logic).[4] Like Marx, Batishchev understood human activity primarily as an objective activity: 'The very first attribute of activity is its objectivity [*predmetnost'*; Marx's term *Gegenständlichkeit*].'[5] Three years later, he offered the following detailed definition:

> Objectivity is universal and, if one does not stop at intermediate links, it is the only source of creative power of human act; the one true power

---

2 See Batishchev 1990f, pp. 328–9, and more explicitly in Batishchev 2002.
3 See Khamidov 2009.
4 See Batishchev 1963.
5 Batishchev 1966, p. 249.

that creates something historically priceless and everlasting. Objectivity pervades the activity and forms its own *first* definition.[6]

During his 'substantialist' period, Batishchev highlighted *objectification* and *deobjectification* (*Vergegenständlichung* and *Entgegenständlichung* in Marx) as the main attributes of objective activity. It is the process of transitioning the objective content of activity from its only potential existence, as an ability to act, to the form of fixed thingness, and vice versa. As Batishchev said, '[o]bjectification and deobjectification form a genuine dialectical *unity* of the interpenetrating *opposites*. And this unity of opposites *is* the activity in its concrete definiteness.'[7]

Batishchev followed Marx in his interpretation of *objectification*, but the case is different with regard to *deobjectification*. In the *Economic and Philosophic Manuscripts of 1844*, Marx used the term '*Entgegenständlichung*' as a form of activity that is *opposed* to objectification, as a form of *alienation*, or dehumanisation (*Entmenschlichung*). Batishchev, for his part, gave this term a *deeply positive* sense and, in so doing, moved far beyond Marx.

According to P.L. Kucherov, the same interpretation was developed by the above long before Batishchev. In 1930, Kucherov wrote:

> Exposing the essence of subject, practical activity also reveals the being of its object. Transition of activity into the object reveals the objective being for the activity. The object loses its extraneity to the subject, it is being bared in the action of the subject, it displays its real objective nature, 'deobjectifies' (Marx's expression) its nature. The disclosure of the object to the subject ('deobjectification') is found in the practice of 'objectification'; that is, entering subjective activity into an object. The penetration into the object, the transition from a form of activity into a form of being is, at the same time, the opening of the object. The transition of a subjective activity into being (objectification) and revealing the object to the subject represent a single process – the process of practice, of the objective activity. 'Objectification' is to be understood as 'deobjectification'; both processes are in accord with each other. The essence of the subject reveals itself in this unity of two processes within labour; the subject is a form of practice, of the objective activity.[8]

---

6 Batishchev 1969, p. 81.
7 Batishchev 1963, p. 14.
8 Kucherov 1930, p. 76.

The above quotation shows that, although P.L. Kucherov repeated Marx's expression that 'objectification appears as deobjectification', Kucherov, unlike Marx, added a positive sense to these concepts. E.V. Ilyenkov did the same in his article 'The Ideal'. 'Ideal', he wrote, 'as a form of subjective activity, is assimilated only through the active work with the object and product of this activity; that is, through the form of its product, through the objective form of thing, through its active "deobjectification".'[9] As in Kucherov, the word 'deobjectification' is in quotes, although Ilyenkov used it as a *metaphor*, that is, not in a strictly conceptual sense. In this regard, Batishchev developed a similar view on deobjectification as Kucherov.

Until the end of 1965, Batishchev was indeed a 'substantialist', in some sense of the word. 'Activity', he wrote, 'is a true universal "ether" of the new form of development, its substance-subject, as Hegel would say; that is, a self-developing being.'[10] Batishchev continued:

> In fact, this category is nothing more than a basic *social* connection, a very simple *social* relationship within which activity as labour and activity as communication still coincide and are not divided into relatively independent realms. This is a *"cell"* (both historical and logical), that is, extremely abstract concreteness of all social processes, of the entire social form of movement. This "cell" appears as a content of all the material and spiritual culture of mankind, for activity is the *façon d'être* of culture, its way of life and development.[11]

The above quotation means that objective activity is the substance of *culture*. According to late Batishchev, it is nothing else than *activistic reductionism* and some latent *anthropocentrism*. Early Batishchev follows a tradition that dates back to Kant and considers activity to be a *subject–object* dialectical relation.

In Batishchev's work from this period, another aspect of substantialism may be pointed out. The accent on the subject–object relation promotes the substantialistic conception of activity. In particular, Batishchev wrote:

> For a social man, the subject–object relation appears not as a 'fragment' or 'part' of reality, but as a practical, real implementation of the universality of the very nature. Man is a universal, substantial being and universality

9   Ilyenkov 1962, p. 226.
10   Batishchev 1963, p. 13.
11   Batishchev 1963, p. 15.

is an ultimate background of freedom. With respect to any finite object of nature, it serves as the representative of the infinite nature, its universality, its integrity, of the total law, as the universal power of nature itself. And that is why man, as a subject, makes everything the object of his activity, rather than simply interacting with it as a thing with a thing.[12]

All things in Nature are finite, limited by their own peculiarity, and only human beings are universal like Nature itself, as a representative of Nature. In its activity, Nature achieves its concrete universality. In finalising the logic of this conception (though Batishchev himself never did so), man as a subject is the highest stage of development of a universal substance. If even a hint of such substantial reductionism took place in Batishchev's philosophical outlook, it did not last long.

Deeper attention to human activity in general, and creativity in particular, gradually led Batishchev to understand the limitations of his position, and he soon departed from the substantialist paradigm. For some reason, he later believed that he had been *wholly* in the power of this paradigm and consistently followed it in his studies of the first period. In fact, this is not the case. Let us now take a look at whether Batishchev was right to feel that he had proceeded to quite the opposite paradigm – anti-substantialism.

The second period of Batishchev's philosophical evolution started in 1966 and lasted until about 1974. He presented his new position in an extensive article entitled 'The Active Essence of Man as a Philosophical Principle'. Here Batishchev noted that human activity, as a process self-caused by its own past results, 'is the real *causa sui*'.[13] The anti-substantialist motif can be easily discerned here. However, other assertions can be found, such as: 'Social man becomes a subject so long as he accepts in his activity, making them *his own*, the definitions of *substance*.'[14] This formula clearly contradicts the pure anti-substantialism according to which the man-subject produces all the definitions of his own activity *by himself*, and they are only revealed in acts of their objectification.

In the same article, Batishchev reconstructed, in the most complete form, the architectonics of objective activity, formulating and resolving five consecutive antinomies of such activity. He also expounded, and somewhat advanced, Marx's theory of alienation; no one could have excelled Batishchev at this

---

12   Batishchev 1967, p. 96.
13   Batishchev 1966, p. 249.
14   Batishchev 1966, p. 251.

point. Finally, the same article demonstrated the *work* of dialectical contradiction within cognition. By exploring the architectonics of objective activity, Batishchev formulated a meaningful antinomy, resolved it and moved on to another formulation of the antinomy and its resolution, and so on.

The following quote from Batishchev reveals one of these antinomies:

> Activity is performed and can be carried out only *according* to the logic of *each* particular object, but at the same time, it is not performed and cannot be carried out according to the logic of *none* of the particular objects. In other words, man *finds himself in the world of objects* [*predmetnyy mir*], and only in it alone, but *not* as one of its objects or their whole set. He conditions himself by *objectivity* and by nothing else, but at the same time, it is *he* who conditions *himself*; otherwise it should not be *ob*-jectivity [*predmetnost'*] for him.
>
> It is only possible to resolve this antinomy by establishing such determinations of human activity, in which the logic of any particular object appears exactly as a particular in relation to it, and owing to which it may determine itself by that peculiar logic. However, every particular is particular only for universal totality [*universal'naya vseobshchnost'*], for substantiality. Equally, self-conditioning is possible only as inherent to the universal totality and substantiality. To treat each particular object as a particular, taken in its own logic, in its immanent measure and essence, and to determine himself by the object as a particular, man should *turn the universally-total* determinations of all the reality into forms of *his own activity* and should *assume into himself*, as a master of activity, their *substantial character.*[15]

But man does not simply adopt determinations of substance; his activity overbuilds them. By deobjectifying and mastering the world of particular objects, man creates his own world that is not reducible to the world of Nature.

> Human objective activity is the process in which substantiality of nature 'overbuilds' itself [*dostraivaetsya*] *creatively* up to something that is impossible in its very nature and, at the same time, masters nature as it exists. This mastering and inheritance of nature by man presupposes the creative enrichment of nature and its 'overbuilding' on the inherited foundation. Likewise, creativity presupposes mastery of this foundation.

---

15   Batishchev 1969, p. 86.

That is why human reality is a realm of the *creative mastering of substanti-ality* of nature and, at the same time, the mastering *of creative work, which inherits nature*. This is a realm of *culture*.

Objective activity is the building of culture as unity and identity of mas-tering and creativity.[16]

Objective activity has two vectors: (1) the proper activity, aimed at a certain object and implemented with that object, that is, the *subject–object* relation (Batishchev designates this kind of activity with the term '*aktivnost*'); and (2) the relation to another person, that is, the *subject–subject* relation, communica-tion (*obshchenie*). These two vectors are inseparable, although one or the other of them prevails in a concrete activity-process. Carrying out activity and creat-ing its product, the subject addresses it to other people; in so doing, he realises his human relation to them by means of this object. During this period, Bat-ishchev still did not distinguish between *communication* and *social relations*.

In subsequent years, Batishchev concretised his concept of activity. He began to distinguish between activity as *deyatel'nost* and *aktivnost* and later introduced the concept of *object-thingish* (*objektno-veshchnaya*) activity as a *degenerate* form of activity. This is a hypertrophied subject–object relation-ship, having gone beyond the mark of its relevance. The objective activity is relevant only in respect to a lower, coarse-thingish level of reality, that is, to inorganic nature. When applied to the higher levels, it appears to be destruct-ive. Batishchev explained the difference between the proper objective activity and the object-thingish one as follows:

> Within the activity as such, according to its nature and concept, the subjective process of self-changing takes precedence over the objective process: a person transforms circumstances in order to modify himself. Within the object-thingish activity, on the contrary, all is turned upside down: object-thingish tasks appear as self-sufficient and self-aimed, and people just have to take into account the demands that performing such tasks every time makes on the subject, and they have to adapt to such demands more or less outwardly, to adjust themselves under them.[17]

The material object-thingish activity is characterised by the fact that self-creation and self-transformation of subjects appears to be an *indirect, incid-*

---

16   Batishchev 1969, p. 89.
17   Batishchev 1984, p. 8.

ental result, and it is not a goal in any case. Transformation of the thingish activity into the universal explanatory principle makes it impossible to explain many phenomena of reality. Indeed, this principle obliges one to see everywhere but the world of objects-things, including other subjects. In light of the thingish activity, the *objective* content, which is a materialised activity of the subject and its objective attitude to another subject, is annihilated, being reduced to its object-thingish form of expression. The very subject–subject relation is interpreted as a *kind* of thingish activity.

Batishchev also revised his earlier interpretation of the union of subject–object and subject–subject relations within objective activity. Having previously regarded them as relatively equal, or attributes that were equally worthy of objective activity, he then gave priority to subject–subject relations. He argued that 'the subject–object relationship appears here not as something self-reliant and rooted in itself, but only as a moment that belongs, as a subordinate, to the context of subject–subject relations; only the latter attaches to this moment the final rationality and deeper sense.'[18]

Batishchev should have elaborated more concretely at this point about the priority of the subject–subject relationship as compared to the subject–object relationship. Batishchev felt that the genuine

> activity [*deyatel'nost'*] – as opposed to the object-thingish activity [*aktivnost'*] as its converted, wrong form – *commences* not with a thing but with *another subject*, and *concludes* itself, with equal necessity, not by the thing itself but in fates of *another subjects*, to whom it is addressed also by its objectified being. In other words ... *deyatel'nost'* is an *intersubjective* essential power.[19]

In addition, Batishchev noted, 'Between the subject, taken in its peculiar being, and the object ... there exists one more, third, intermediate kind of being – the *artifiable* [*proizvedencheskoe*] being.'[20] Consequently, 'the synthetic, unifying formula appears: *subject-work of art-object-work of art-subject*'.[21] Furthermore, at this point Batishchev insisted on the prevalence of deobjectification over objectification.

Within the very being of the subject, Batishchev indicated three levels, or fields. He applied the term 'field' in the sense of a magnetic field. Batishchev argued for the existence of the following three fields:

---

18   Batishchev 1977, p. 169.
19   Batishchev 1997, p. 68.
20   Batishchev 1989, p. 23.
21   Batishchev 1989, p. 24.

a. *The field of utilities*, which corresponds to the autonomous field of the subject–object relations and the *logic of finalising* (*okonechivanie*);
b. *The field of aspirations*, in which thingish relations are sublated by the more concrete intersubjective relations, opened into infinity;
c. *The field of creating* the infinite aspirations themselves, or creativity in the proper sense of the word, as a cosmic universal existential co-authorship ...

In the field of utilities, subject is to be the subject of needs, the holder of its own scale, summarising the code of claims that man set up to the thingish world. Here, the life of man has a vector to itself as the final being which at the same time finalises itself. All the remaining serves to him only as a means with which to achieve his goal ... In the field of infinite aspirations, the subject has such a value and target quality of his activity direction, which is beyond the influence of even the most intensive utilities. Here man is an 'end in itself', as Marx called it. It is a direction from itself towards infinite points or ideals of creativeness ... Finally, only in the field of creating the infinite aspirations does the subject ascend to the absolute problematisation of the world, for he ascends to the complete problematisation of himself and renounces not only any *self-centrism* but also any pre-selection of values [*tsennostnaya predizbrannost'*] of his relationship to the world.[22]

Within the first field, the subject is *appropriating*; within the second field, the subject is *mastering*; and finally, within the third field, the subject is *accepting into himself* (*v-sebya-priemlyushchiy*). Consequently, value is an objective phenomenon that cannot be reduced to any utility. Usefulness as it is conforms to a certain need, and value is not that which is consumed but that to which man *aspires*. People strive for values, measure themselves and reality by values, commune with values, but they do not subordinate values to themselves, like useful things. Absolutisation of the first field leads to rampant *utilitarianism*. Absolutisation of the field of values can lead to *dogmatism* and even *fanaticism*. Only the highest level does not allow any absolutisation.

For a long time, Batishchev did not *radically* bring into question the theoretical status of the principle of objective activity. He still believed that activity was the only way of being of the man-subject and his culture, his sole relation to the world. The radical change in Batishchev's views occurred after he became

---

22   Batishchev 1979, pp. 120–1.

acquainted with two doctrines: Agni Yoga (Living Ethics) and A.A. Ukhtomsky's theory of a cortical dominanta.

In the early 1970s, Batishchev was strongly influenced by the ideas of *The Secret Doctrine* by Helena Blavatsky, *Letters* by Helena Roerich and related theosophical texts. From that point on, Batishchev revised his entire philosophical outlook and definitively moved away from Marx. Having said that, he had broken up with his former Marxist colleagues, including Ilyenkov, several years earlier, when he severely criticised their 'substantialism'.

Batishchev's conceptual break with his former Marxist beliefs was fixed in an unpublished essay entitled 'Theses not to Feuerbach', which was written in 1974 and then improved and rewritten until 1980. The essay provides a clue to all of Batishchev's philosophical works, although, even in its final form, it remains heterogeneous and ambiguous. In 1977, Batishchev accepted Orthodoxy and, over the next three years, tried to *synthesise* it with Agni Yoga's ideas and way of life. Having realised the impossibility of such a synthesis, he abandoned Agni Yoga and went over to Orthodox Christian positions once and for all.

The text of 'Theses not to Feuerbach' is divided into two columns. The left-hand column is entitled 'Theses to Feuerbach, complemented by the most significant excerpts from other texts of their author. 1837–1845, 1845–1883'. The right-hand column is entitled 'Theses *not* to Feuerbach, trying to extract a lucid sense from embrace of darkness. 1974–1980'. Each thesis, with additions in the left-hand column, corresponds to the right *counter*-thesis (but not *anti*-thesis, which might be, in its union with thesis, sublated by synthesis, according to Hegelian logic).

Under the direct influence of Agni Yoga, Batishchev fought against *anthropocentrism*, which was interpreted as a belief that humanity is the sole rational community in the Universe, and that it represents the highest stage of cosmic evolution.

> Man ... pretends to be, by himself, a "root" and a "sun". With his goals and values, he tries to behave irrelatively of the Universe and raises its own measure to an Absolute. He looks at the cosmos top-down, like at the periphery. He moves off *geocentrism* only in three-dimensional astronomy, otherwise he adheres to geocentrism. He would like to "revolve around himself", as a Master of the Universe, for he considers himself to be its centre. Such is *anthropocentrism*.[23]

---

23   Batishchev 1980b, § 4b.

It should be noted that during the period that Batishchev defined as 'anti-substantialist', he still stood for anthropocentrism.

According to Batishchev, philosophical use of the term 'anthropocentrism' is justified 'only if we mean the *absolute* (and not only local and relative) *ego-centrism*, embracing a claim on a human monopoly and exclusivity in the possession of values; that is, *axiological* anthropocentrism as well'.[24] Herewith Batishchev made a distinction between *two* types of anthropocentrism – *passive* and *active*.

> *Passive* anthropocentrism asserts itself in the form of *other-centrism* [*inakotsentrizm*]; in particular, this is theocentrism. It is self-measured recognition of the Higher Realms, included *inside* the same self-closed life, the same limited scope. Such is a *consumer* religiosity: it does not call man to overcome his imperfection and blindness and does not oblige him to transform his being in all aspects. It is included into a limited existence and placed next to his other sides as an annex, as an appendix, as their sanction, 'sacred' instrument and vestment. These sides are legalism, zealous formal ritualism, fanaticism and *fatalism*, self-abasement and servility for the sake of demise the responsibility, obedience to power for the sake of accommodation, intolerance and group exclusiveness.

> *Active* anthropocentrism excels in aggressive *self-measuring* [*svoemerie*], intrusion into the cosmos. Its pride stops at nothing; all is subject to *mastering* ... Hence the deceit: the living cosmic communication is mixed with consumer and social-functional religiosity.[25]

In his later work, Batishchev preferred to write *simply* about anthropocentrism without going into detail. In fact, he only ever meant the *active* version of it. Obviously, it was conditioned by his final plunge into Christianity, which, like any other theistic worldview, falls under the concept of *passive* anthropocentrism.

The 'Theses' also schedule the criticism of absolutisation of the objective-activity principle. In particular, Batishchev wrote,

> The main point is whether the objective activity is a certain ultimate, the *last* man's essence, the substance-subject, or whether it is merely a *way*

---

24   Batishchev 1986, p. 177, n. 4.
25   Batishchev 1974, 1980b, § 4b.

of disclosure via the creation of *inexhaustible potential depths* of the very subject, as well as of the Universe, in their mutual meeting.[26]

It seems that Ukhtomsky's concept of dominanta inclined Batishchev to make himself aware of the methodological and outlook limitedness of the activity-principle. Batishchev started to realise that objective activity does not cover the whole of human existence. In the mid-1970s, Batishchev reached the conclusion that 'activity is not the sole possible, universal *mode of being* of person, culture, sociality; it is not a unique and comprehensive way for man to interconnect with the world.'[27]

Ukhtomsky maintained that a 'person always approaches the reality via his dominants, his activities ... Man sees in the world and in other people that what is predetermined by his activity; that is, he sees himself anyway. And this may be his greatest condemnation!'[28] After the system of dominants has been formed, it blinds a man to the many significant realms of the world, unless the dominants are directed at them or if they head in another direction. Ukhtomsky called this a 'dominant abstraction'.

Batishchev tried to extend Ukhtomsky's concept across the sphere of interpersonal relations. The paradox was that if, at first, Soviet philosophers and psychologists for the most part resisted the principle of objective activity, fearing the alleged elements of subjectivism and idealism, then a later appeal to the principle of objective activity would become almost mainstream. A so-called 'activity approach' is also widely applied in psychology and theoretical pedagogy. As a result, the conceptual sense of the principle of activity appears to be diluted.

In Soviet humanitarian literature, Batishchev found, on the one hand, the almost total absolutisation of the category of objective activity, but on the other hand, the insufficient disclosure of its heuristic potential. The vulgar 'activity approach' spread, leading to the category of objective activity being, at heart, discredited.

Objective activity was interpreted commonly as a mere thingish activity, as objectification – as a process – directed from the 'inside' of the subject towards the outside (that is, simply as *exteriorisation*) and, correspondingly, deobjectification (that is, as *interiorisation*). 'In fact', Batishchev noted, 'such an embodiment of activity always occurs simultaneously with its objectification in

---

26   Batishchev 1980b, § 5b.
27   Batishchev 1990d, pp. 24–5.
28   Ukhtomsky 2008, pp. 546–7.

the structure of the subject's essential powers, when he transforms himself.'[29] In this context, Batishchev was referring to the need to protect 'extra-active [vnedeyatel'nostnye] layers of a subject's being ... from certain fashionable versions of the "activity approach" with their crude pretensions to universalism'.[30]

Yet another of Ukhtomsky's ideas had a strong influence on Batishchev. In human nature, Ukhtomsky found two opposite entities: the *Double*, or 'my solitary, *self-affirming, self-proofing* Ego', versus the *Interlocutor*, or alter ego. Ukhtomsky called for dominanta to be placed to the Interlocutor.

> It should be illusory to dream about a dominantless look at the world and another man, but it is quite real to educate and cultivate, by deliberate labour, the dominanta and the 'Copernican' behaviour, having placed the centre of gravity outside himself, *into the Other*. It means to organise and educate one's own behaviour and activity *to be ready at any moment to prefer the newly discovered laws of the world or the original features and interests of another Person to any of your own interests and theories about them*.[31]

After reading Ukhtomsky's writings, Batishchev introduced such negative concepts as 'self-measuring' and 'self-centrism' into his own work. Being an original philosopher, Batishchev developed and amended the ideas of others rather than simply borrowing them. Batishchev reached a conclusion about superiority of intersubjective relations over subject–object ones, and even over the artifiable (*proizvedencheskie*) relations of a subject with a work of art. It is not activity itself, but rather communication that links human beings with the Universe.

> The attitude to other members of society, or social relation, appears here as only an *intermediate* link and reliable *bearer* in man's relationship with the rest of the Universe. Hence, the creative *attitude* by itself, without any private or distorted forms, in essentially *non-geocentric* and *non-anthropocentric*.[32]

Reconsideration of the status of objective activity in human existence spills over into the 'axiologically oriented, hierarchical, *multi-layered* approach,

---

29   Batishchev 1985, p. 42.
30   Batishchev 1990d, p. 23.
31   Ukhtomsky 2008, p. 548.
32   Batishchev 1997, p. 69.

according to which the similar entities meet one with another. Higher levels cannot, in principle, be reduced to the lower ones, although they can penetrate them.'[33] According to Batishchev, such an approach makes it possible to find 'rootedness of human existence in the universally-general (substantial) characteristics'.[34]

Batishchev criticised the position that he himself had taken in *Deyatel'nost-naya sushchnost' cheloveka* (The Active Essence of Man, published in 1969), pointing out that in its light 'any extrahuman reality is to be more simple and crude, *lower* than human'.[35] It turned out, therefore, that *only* man in his object-ive activity inherits and develops the universal, substantial attributes of the Universe. This is the established *anthropocentrism*.

From a modern point of view (which coincides with the doctrine of Agni Yoga), the case looks much more complicated: there are subjects in the infinite Universe who are engaged in the same creative work. Considering himself the sole heir to the substance and the only builder of the world of culture, man is oriented towards the *lower* layers of the Universe.

> The more one succeeds in mastering only the lower levels of being – facts and objective laws – which are turned into means of his unilateral command, the stronger and more densely he bars himself from the higher levels, from all that resists this monopolistic dominance in cosmos.[36]

Early Batishchev interpreted the world of human culture as a unity of cognitive, ethical and aesthetic dimensions. At this later point in his career, he indicates, as their common profound root, 'the culture of *deep communication*, the onto-logical communion, the mutual determination of the essential aspirations of all through everyone and vice versa, the culture of shifting dominanta onto oth-ers'.[37] This is a *religious* culture, in the broad, non-confessional meaning, which is how it looks from the standpoint of Agni Yoga. From a Christian perspective, however, it is quite a concrete religious confession.

The late Batishchev discerned human beings into three levels: (1) pre-acti-vity, (2) activity and (3) over-activity. Objective activity takes the middle posi-tion in this hierarchy and, as such, it does not exhaust our being in the world. 'In fact', Batishchev noted, 'activity is a mode of being of the *only actualised*,

---

33   Batishchev 1989, p. 11.
34   Batishchev 1991a, p. 122.
35   Batishchev 1991a, p. 123.
36   Batishchev 1991a, p. 124.
37   Batishchev 1991c, p. 149. Compare Batishchev 1987, p. 33.

deobjectifiable *part* of the cultural-historical reality and of man himself.'[38] The level of the unconscious, for example, can hardly be interpreted as an *activity*-phenomenon. There are absolute and relative *limits* of objective activity, the 'thresholds of deobjectifiability', as Batishchev calls them. The relative thresholds may be separated by means of the *communication* of subjects, but some layers of the Universe are *principally* inaccessible to objective activity. Besides, within the activity itself, Batishchev prioritised deobjectification over objectification, saying, 'Only deobjectification breaks the vicious circle of activity.'[39]

However, Batishchev did not completely renounce his former conception of activity; he just tried to specify the scope of its relevance.

> The activity approach, as *one* possible approach, does not give rise to any objections. I have no doubts about its appropriateness. On the contrary, applying it in the maximal possible manner, every unbiased researcher should be persuaded that this approach also has its limits, beyond which it ceases to be fruitful.[40]

However, few people considered Batishchev's opinion.

Batishchev also made a distinction between *activity* and *communication*. Social relations are created by activity, whereas communication embraces pre-activity and over-activity levels. 'Communication', Batishchev wrote, 'is a meeting-process that unfolds simultaneously *at different levels*, which are, in principle, irreducible to one another and radically different in their degree of explicitness.'[41]

Redefining the status of objective activity led Batishchev significantly to rethink the essence of creativity: creativity was delimited from activity, including *creative* activity. Creativity

> *can* do exactly that what activity *cannot* do in principle, for it is progressive shifting the very thresholds of deobjectifiability, which restrict activity and lock it within its own sphere ... Of course, creativity is *also an act*, the creative act. But before it becomes an act and in order to become it, creativity is initially a special kind of the over-activity *relation* of subject to

---

38   Batishchev 1985, p. 42.
39   Batishchev 1991b, p. 145.
40   Batishchev 1990e, p. 169.
41   Batishchev 1990d, p. 30.

the world and to himself, the attitude to all things insofar as they are able to be *different*.[42]

Batishchev was treating creativity as an intersubjective relation, as 'co-creation', which has a *horizontal* (co-creation with other people) or *vertical* dimension (co-creation with higher levels of being in the infinite dialectics of the Universe). The higher creation is a deep communication with a Teacher – that is, a subject – having advanced in the way of self-improvement. The phenomenon of a Teacher is typical for the tradition of the esoteric East, particularly for Agni Yoga and Theosophy. The Christian position focuses on a different treatment of co-creation.

Creativity, as a harmonic-polyphonic relation, should have some immanent limits, as it is kept under the continuous control and trial of *conscience*. Batishchev questioned the *justification* of human creativity, or *creatodicy*, a problem that philosophers had largely ignored. Some of them, such as N.A. Berdyaev, correctly considered true creativity to be overcoming egoism and individualism, while at the same time declaring that creativity is an absolute, self-justifying power. 'The creative act justifies, but does not need to be justified. It vindicates itself, but does not need to be vindicated by something lying outside it.'[43]

Criticism of anthropocentrism forced Batishchev to reconsider the phenomenon of *humanism*. He suspected that the idol of 'spiritless faith' was hidden behind this notion. He shared Heidegger's and Dostoevsky's discontent with abstract humanism, agreeing that the notion of humanism 'is fraught with ambiguity, fateful antitheticity, perfidious and confusing duality'.[44] Absolute, unrestricted humanism is an apology of anthropocentrism. True humanism (*chelovechnost'*) is restricted by the human world, and, far from being humane, this world is crying out to be *humanised* more than ever before.

At that, Batishchev assigned to man the part of a 'gardener of cosmogenesis'. 'The Universum is a suspended world-building; there remains a lot to create in it, in the most fundamental sense.'[45] In an article written in his last years, 'To Find and Acquire Himself', Batishchev wrote about some 'all-embracing Person' (*vseob"emlyushchiy Lik*) who exists at the back of all individuals. It (or perhaps He?) forms an 'eternal bosom of the co-creative authorship' and a '*transcendental* absolutely creative Origin of any possible being and of *all* the

42   Batishchev 1990d, p. 29.
43   Berdyaev 1989, pp. 341–2.
44   Batishchev 1993, p. 90.
45   Batishchev 1989, p. 19.

Universe'.[46] To all appearances, this is a rare manifestation of outright Christian motifs in the works of Batishchev. This article was probably written in the last year of the philosopher's life.

It should be noted that, prior to this and throughout all his philosophical works, Batishchev had criticised any absolutes, however they were interpreted. He condemned 'all-wise wardship and assuring participation in a material or spiritual absolute'[47] and proclaimed false the common alternative: 'either squalor under the canopy of the Absolute, or self-deification'.[48] He stood up for those subjects who 'are able to start with themselves, precisely because they do not find themselves under the canopy of any kind of Absolute and do not have to measure themselves by any predetermined standard'.[49]

So the human being is treated now in a quite different vein:

> Man is by no means ready for the lofty prospect and destination, and he cannot make himself ready by his own power, from inside of himself ... Human beings have neither plenitude of perfection (this is easier to see and to make aware), nor even that integrity of essential core which could originate such a perfection. A human being does not originally possess the sufficiency of abilities and the authenticity of himself, of his inner *I*, of his internal prerequisites. Therefore, it is not enough to say that man is to find and acquire the approach to the Absolute, that he originally lacks it. We should add that man is to become a genuine person. He *must try to find and acquire himself yet, to a large extent.*[50]

Thus, having rethought his philosophical matters in the light of Christianity, Batishchev betrayed practically all his former beliefs and achievements. Nevertheless, they continue to live on in philosophy and resist religious annihilation.

---

46   Batishchev 1992, p. 21 (my emphasis).
47   Batishchev 1976, p. 112.
48   Batishchev 2003, p. 37.
49   Batishchev 2003, p. 35.
50   Batishchev 1992, p. 20.

CHAPTER 9

The Activity Approach in Soviet Philosophy and Contemporary Cognitive Studies

Vladislav Lektorsky

The activity approach was a popular part of Soviet philosophy and psychology between the 1960s and the 1980s, after which it was somewhat forgotten and criticised, even by some of its former followers. Nowadays, there is reason to attempt to understand some specific features of this approach in a contemporary context. At least three factors are connected with this re-examination of the activity approach.

Firstly, concepts such as 'embodied cognition' and 'enacted cognition', which stress the close relations between activity, cognition and cultural objectivations, are very popular in contemporary cognitive science and are subject to intense discussion. There are two variants of these concepts. The first, which is connected with the works of Francisco Varela, uses some ideas of the French phenomenologist Maurice Merleau-Ponty.[1] The second, represented primarily by the American philosopher Andy Clark, refers to the ecological theory of visual perception of James Gibson[2] and to the ideas of Lev Vygotsky, as well as of the Soviet school of cultural-historical and activity-psychology.[3] In connection with an analysis of the current situation in cognitive science, the famous Russian psychologist and specialist in cognitive science Boris Velichkovsky wrote about the need to return to the activity approach.[4]

Secondly, a number of Russian philosophers, psychologists and specialists in human sciences now share different constructivist conceptions (radical epistemological constructivism, social constructionism, and so on). From their point of view, constructivism is a more adequate interpretation of those phenomena that the activity approach dealt with previously. It is of interest to analyse the relations of the activity approach in Soviet philosophy in the 1960s–1980s and contemporary constructivism in epistemology and the human sciences.

---

1 Varela, Thompson and Rosch 1992.
2 Gibson 1979.
3 Clark 1997, especially p. 45.
4 Velichkovsky, vol. 2, p. 370.

Thirdly, there are nowadays several interesting examples of the fruitful application of a cultural-historical activity approach in psychology and other human sciences. Particularly relevant is the conception of the renowned Finnish psychologist Yrjö Engeström, who elaborated an original theory using ideas from the Soviet psychologist Aleksey Leontiev and the Soviet philosopher Evald Ilyenkov.[5] Every three years, the International Society for Cultural and Activity Research organises an international congress that includes psychologists, specialists in education and philosophers from different countries who share ideas about the current of cultural-historical psychology in the Vygotskian tradition and the activity approach.

This chapter attempts to analyse the main ideas of Soviet philosophers on the problems of activity and the activity approach between the 1960s and the 1980s in the context of their contemporary meaning and of the current discussions in epistemology and cognitive sciences.

An Early Variant of the Activity Approach in Soviet Philosophy and Psychology: S.L. Rubinshtein

In 1934, the well-known philosopher and psychologist S.L. Rubinshtein, referring to early works by Marx, formulated a conception of the unity of consciousness and activity. Rubinshtein stressed that, contrary to the ideas of introspective psychology about the immediacy of psychic life (claiming a direct access to subjectivity), consciousness is in reality mediated by activity: 'a new possibility is arising: to examine consciousness through human activity, in which consciousness is formed and developed'.[6] Rubinshtein drew special attention to one of the principal ideas in Marx's early works regarding the role of human-made things. Specifically, the human being does not simply double himself in things he makes and create a peculiar mirror in which he can see himself, but creates himself for the first time by this activity. This is the meaning of Marx's famous assertion, in the third thesis on Feuerbach, that practice must be understood as 'the coincidence of the changing of circumstances and of human activity or self-change [*Selbstveränderung*]'.[7] Proceeding from these philosophical principles, Rubinshtein elaborated a psychological conception according to which the psychological subject is formed in the process of his

---

5   Engeström 2005.
6   Rubinshtein 1934, p. 8.
7   Marx 1975, p. 422.

activity, and psychic processes are mediated by cultural objectivations. This conception became a basis for psychological (including experimental) investigations.

In 1969 appeared an article that Rubinshtein had written in Odessa in 1922, which had subsequently been forgotten; it was entitled 'Printsip tvorcheskoy samodeyatel'nosti' ('The Principle of Creative Activity'). There were no references to Marx or Marxism. The article criticised philosophical realism in general and materialism in particular (as well as subjective idealism). At the same time, the main idea of the future activity-conception of the author was already present in the article. In this version, Rubinshtein formulated some ideas that he did not develop at a later stage when he already had absorbed Marx's philosophy.

Rubinshtein criticised the viewpoint (which he ascribed to Kant's doctrine of the intelligible character) that viewed a subject as the subject of its actions (deyaniya) in which it expresses and manifests itself. Rubinshtein wrote, 'If a subject is only expressed in its actions, but is not also created by them, then it is presupposed that the subject is something ready-made, given before and outside of its actions, thus independent from them.'[8] According to Rubinshtein, if one accepts this position, it is not possible to understand a person as a coherent whole. 'It breaks down into two heterogenic constituting parts. The subject – that which in the personality constitutes its "selfhood", remains behind the actions which are its manifestations: the subject is transcendent to its actions.'[9] From this Kantian and transcendentalist point of view, 'actions are conceived of as belonging to a certain subject: they are its actions. But as actions are not included in the constitution of the subject, do not build up its structure, they do not determine the subject in question.'[10] Certainly, Rubinshtein wrote, there are such actions that do not determine the character of a subject or a personality. But there are also those which constitute a subject itself; otherwise, the latter could not exist.

Rubinshtein formulated his main position as follows: 'Thus, the subject not only becomes visible and manifests itself in the acts of its creative activity; it is also created and determined in them. Therefore, it is possible to determine what the subject is by that what it does.'[11] In creating a work of art, an artist

---

8   Rubinshtein 1989, p. 93.
9   Rubinshtein 1989, p. 94.
10   Ibid. In the original: 'Deyaniya myslyaetsya otnesennymi k opredelennomu subjektu: oni ego deyaniya. No, ne vkhodya svoim soderzhaniem v postroenie, v sostav ego, oni ne opredelyayut etogo subjekta.'
11   Ibid.

produces his individuality. Only in organising the world of thoughts is a thinker formed. 'The creator himself is produced in the creative process.'[12] 'There is only one way to create a grand personality: creating a grand work.'[13]

A striking similarity between the main idea of the 1922 article and the 1934 formulation is the principle of the unity of consciousness and activity. Criticism of Kant and subjective idealism in the 1922 article stimulated some authors to interpret that article as a break with Neo-Kantianism. Rubinshtein was known to be a pupil of Hermann Cohen, one of the leading figures of German Neo-Kantianism at the beginning of the twentieth century and the article was seen as an elaboration of ideas that were very close to those of Marx. In reality, however, Rubinshtein was in this article completely under the influence of the Marburg school of German Neo-Kantianism, which actually was not so much Kantianism as neo-Fichteanism, and even neo-Hegelianism. Marx was formed in the traditions of German idealism, which influenced not only many problems of Marx's philosophy, but even some of his solutions. I believe that this fact explains the easy transition of S.L. Rubinshtein from Neo-Kantianism to a reception of Marx's philosophical ideas and formulation of the principles of psychological activity theory.

The principle of the unity of consciousness and activity exerted considerable influence on Soviet psychology. In the 1960s, however, another well-known Soviet psychologist, A.N. Leontiev, formulated his own psychological theory of activity,[14] which in many respects was opposed to Rubinshtein's conception (there were, in addition, other conceptions of activity in the Soviet psychology of that time, such as those of P.Ya. Galperin and V.V. Davydov). Here I am not seeking to analyse the conceptions of activity in Soviet psychology, as I am currently interested in philosophical ideas about the activity approach and the principle of activity. I would simply note that Rubinshtein did not formulate the philosophical principle of the unity of consciousness and activity very clearly, and in his later years he started to criticise the activity approach, stressing that not only activity but also pure contemplation would provide contact with the 'Being'[15] (some Russian scholars even believe that Rubinshtein later rejected the activity approach).

---

12   Ibid. In the original: 'V tvorchestve sozidaetsya i sam tvorets.'
13   Rubinshtein 1989, p. 95.
14   Leontiev 1978.
15   Rubinshtein 1976, pp. 339–40.

General Features of the Activity Approach in Soviet Philosophy

I would like to formulate my own understanding of the role of the idea of activity, not only in Soviet philosophy and psychology, but also in other philosophical conceptions in the twentieth century. I believe that this role was connected with attempts to eliminate the sharp opposition between the subjective and the objective, between the 'inner' and the 'outer' worlds that philosophy and human science had presupposed since Descartes. This opposition determined the way of understanding the inner and the outer worlds and, in so doing, influenced research programmes in the human sciences. Different philosophical conceptions attempted to eliminate the opposition, including pragmatism, the phenomenology of Merleau-Ponty and Sartre, and the philosophy of later Wittgenstein. Despite their differences, all of these conceptions understood activity as a specific mediator between the 'inner world' of man and the world of outer objects, other persons and cultural artefacts. I believe it is possible to consider these as activity-conceptions, despite the fact that their interpretations of activity were very different.

In the Soviet Union, the understanding of the human being and activity was elaborated in the framework of tradition of Marx, but some ideas of German idealism from the early nineteenth century, primarily those of Hegel and Fichte, were also used. A specific feature of the activity approach in the Soviet philosophical literature consists of the important role given to the notion of object-oriented activity. This notion was understood not only as a means of eliminating the sharp opposition of the 'inner' and 'outer' worlds, but usually also as an openness towards the outer reality. In any case, it is important that a number of Western and Soviet philosophers who elaborated the activity approach dealt with the same problem, so that their conceptions are comparable. As noted earlier, the conceptions of activity in Soviet psychology have already been included in the development of world-psychology.

The activity approach was criticised by the official Soviet philosophy for several reasons. It was suspected of deviating from the theory of reflection and materialism. Moreover, the stress on creativity and freedom in the activity approach was understood as an attempt to doubt the leading role of the Communist Party and Marxist-Leninist ideology. The Soviet followers of the activity approach were suspected of closeness to the 'Praxis' group, which arose among Yugoslavian philosophers in the 1960s and claimed to express the authentic views of Marx and a humanistic interpretation of Marxism. Official Soviet ideologists considered this group to be revisionist. In fact, the two sides had several similarities. Both the Soviet adherents of the activity approach and the Yugoslav Praxis philosophers proceeded from the ideas of Marx (especially early Marx), and there were also some personal connections. For example, one of the leaders of the Praxis group, Mihailo Marković, visited the Soviet Union several times and had personal relations with some Soviet philosophers (Evald Ilyenkov, Genrikh Batishchev and myself). But there was also a difference. Philosophers from the Praxis group were mainly engaged in social criticism: their targets were bureaucratic socialism in the Soviet Union, authoritarian phenomena in Yugoslavia, the consumption-society in Western countries, and alienation all over the world. The Soviet followers of the activity approach had no such opportunities for social criticism, although they were, as a rule, very critical of the existing social reality in the Soviet Union. They too analysed the problem of alienation (in a famous article by Ilyenkov)[16] and of humanism (Batishchev wrote a lot about the theme).[17] But the interest of Soviet philosophers primarily focused on investigating the very structure of activity, and towards the methodological problems of science, particularly human sciences. Thus, the Soviet representatives of the activity approach were connected with psychology (Ilyenkov, G.P. Shchedrovitsky), with pedagogy (Batishchev) and with the history of natural sciences (V.S. Stepin, I.S. Alekseyev). An important final difference was that the philosophers of the Praxis group felt that interpreting praxis as the main feature of the human being eliminated the opposition between materialism and idealism. None of the Soviet followers of the activity approach rejected materialism, although official philosophers suspected them of doing so. (It is true that their interpretation of materialism differed from the primitive official understanding of it).

Main Variants of the Activity Approach in the Soviet Philosophy in the 1960s–1980s

From the 1960s, the activity approach became one of central subjects of a new movement in Soviet philosophy.

I believe that this is connected primarily with publications by E.V. Ilyenkov, particularly with his famous article on 'The Ideal' published in *Filosofskaya Entsiklopediya* in 1962 and the article 'Problema ideal'nogo' ('The Problem of the Ideal'), which was published in two subsequent issues of the journal *Voprosy filosofii* in 1979, after Ilyenkov's death. These articles were interpreted by the official Soviet philosophy as a major heresy. According to Ilyenkov, the ideal

---

16   Ilyenkov 1967.
17   Batishchev 1969.

exists in collective human activity and as a form of it; in other words, outside the individual head, as a form of a thing outside a thing. Objective reality, independent from a human being, is given to him through activity and in forms of activity. The subjective world, and such features of it as freedom, is determined by the inclusion of a human being in activity.

The ideal form is a form of a thing, but outside this thing, namely in man, as a form of his dynamic life-activity, as goals and needs. Or conversely, it is a form of man's dynamic life-activity, but outside man, namely in the form of the thing he creates, which represents, reflects another thing, including that which exists independently of man and humanity. 'Ideality' as such exists only in the constant transformation of these two forms of its 'external incarnation' and does not coincide with either of them taken separately. It exists only through the unceasing process of the transformation of the form of activity into the form of a thing and back – the form of a thing into the form of activity (of social man, of course).[18]

A human being, Ilyenkov continues:

> looks upon nature (matter) as the material in which his aims are 'embodied', as the 'means' of their realisation. This is why he sees in nature primarily what is 'adequate' for this role, what plays or may play the part of a means towards his ends, that is to say, what he has already drawn, in one way or another, into the process of his purposeful activity.

For example, he:

> first directs his attention upon the stars exclusively as a natural clock, calendar and compass, as means and instruments of his life-activity, and observes their 'natural' properties and regularities only insofar as they are natural properties and regularities of the material in which his activity is being performed, and with which he must, therefore, reckon as completely objective (in no way dependent on his will and consciousness) components of his activity.[19]

Ilyenkov's insights were accepted by many Soviet psychologists, primarily by those who continued to elaborate Vygotsky's ideas and were followers of the cultural-historical theory (including A.N. Leontiev and V.V. Davydov). More-

---

18   Ilyenkov 2012, translated by Alex Levant, in *Historical Materialism* 20:2, 193.
19   Ilyenkov 2012, p. 191.

over, I believe that Ilyenkov's interpretation of activity influenced the elaboration of the psychological theory of activity by A.N. Leontiev in the early 1970s. Mikhail Lifshits, a Soviet philosopher who was close to Ilyenkov in many respects but did not accept the activity approach, wrote that the Soviet psychologists had exerted a bad influence on Ilyenkov with regard to his ideas on activity. Lifshits was incorrect. In fact, the reverse was the case: it was Ilyenkov's philosophical ideas about activity that stimulated the further development of conceptions of activity in the Soviet psychology of that time.

In this connection, I would especially like to draw attention to the fact that Ilyenkov's philosophical ideas influenced not only the theoretical development of conceptions of activity in Soviet psychology, but also psychological experimental practices.

Consider the famous results of the Soviet psychologists connected with educating deaf-blind children, managing to awake them into a genuine psychic life. Ilyenkov was engaged in this practice: for him that meant an experimental testing of his philosophical ideas. Psychological experiments showed that apprehension of language-meanings by such a child is successful only if the child is involved in a collective activity. Attempts to teach language to such a child by simply referring language-signs to things were unsuccessful. It became successful when things were included in a collective activity (in this case, in a joint and distributed activity of a child and an adult). Activity is object-oriented, but it selects those features of objects that are important for activity. It is just the appropriation of the objective world in forms of activity, of which Ilyenkov wrote in his philosophical texts. It is evident in that case that communication is included in activity and is its essential component: without relation to another person(s), activity is impossible. In this process man-made things, such as spoons, cups, shoes and clothes, play a specific role. These are not simply things, but a means of inter-human communication. For Ilyenkov, the case of blind and deaf children was not something peculiar and specific (although there are a lot of specific features in it), but a distinctive 'hard experiment' of Nature itself, which made it possible to observe the role of human activity in forming psyche, consciousness and personality as if in 'a pure appearance'.[20]

The works of Genrikh Batishchev played an important role in elaborating a philosophical-anthropological interpretation of the activity approach. Many Soviet authors in the 1970s considered Batishchev to be the protagonist of the concept of activity. In the seminal article 'Deyatelnostnaya sushchnost'

20 Ilyenkov 1975, p. 82.

cheloveka' ('Activity-Nature of the Human Being', 1969), Batishchev investigated the structure of activity: interrelations between objectivation and de-
objectivation[21] (their unity is the essence of activity, as he wrote at that time),
objectivation and alienation, the mode of existence of cultural objectivations,
and the connections between the transformation of outer reality (subject–
object relations) and inter-human communication (subject–subject relations).
Batishchev especially analysed the creative nature of activity, its openness, the
overcoming of existing stereotypes in activity, and the connection of activity
with critical social attitudes and with human freedom:[22]

> Human reality, which is also the reality of the human being as the sub-
> ject, arises only as existing beyond the Nature – human reality is a spe-
> cific domain, where in principle new possibilities are created, which are
> impossible for the Nature as itself, in other words where creativity takes
> place. The human object-oriented activity is a process in which the sub-
> stantiality of the nature is 'completed' with the appearance of that which
> is impossible for the nature itself and the same time is appropriated as
> natural.[23]

Batishchev wrote a lot about the object-oriented nature of activity:

> Activity is an ability of a human being to act not according to the organ-
> isation of his body, not as a slave of specific features of his organism, but
> in accordance with a specific logic of every specific object; in other words
> it is an ability to be 'faithful' not to 'himself', but to the world of objects,
> as they exist by themselves. A human being becomes himself in this faith-
> fulness to the immanent logic of objects. He is not a body or thing besides
> other bodies, not a finite thing besides other finite things, but a 'being'
> with an object-oriented activity, an actor ... Object-oriented activity pro-
> ceeds and develops not from the peculiar specificity of an organism as a
> finite thing, but from the assimilation of objects as they are in themselves,
> in their measures and essences.[24]

---

21   In Russian, 'opredmechivanie' and 'raspredmechivanie', which correspond to the German
      terms 'Vergegenständlichung' and 'Entgegenständlichung', found in the young Marx's 'Paris
      manuscripts' of 1844.
22   Batishchev's analysis of 'revolutionary and critical activity' caused great displeasure
      among official ideologists, particularly M.A. Suslov.
23   Batishchev 1969, p. 89.
24   Batishchev 1969, p. 82.

I would like to draw special attention to a certain problem that was central to Batishchev's understanding of activity. It was the problem of relations between transformation of the outer reality (subject–object relations) and inter-human relations (subject–subject relations). At first, Batishchev considered these kinds of relations as two necessary components of activity ('The essence of the human being is activity as the identity of transformation and communication'[25]). Then he began to give priority to subject–subject relations (he interpreted subject–object relations at this stage of the evolution of his ideas as only a supplement to subject–subject relations). At the last stage (in the 1980s), he sharply distinguished these two kinds of relations and reached the idea that subject–subject relations and communication connected with them are a genuine mode of understanding the objective nature of the Universe. He began to write about the limitations of the activity approach and the existence of such levels in consciousness that in principle cannot be understood in the framework of activity: communication, intuition, and so on. He began to consider deep communication as the most adequate mode of conceiving the Universe: 'Activity is not only and not universal mode of being of a human, of culture and social life, is not only and universal mode of relations between a human being and the world.'[26] These ideas are connected with Batishchev's repudiation of Marxism at that time (he even wrote a text, as yet unpublished, criticising Marx's 'Theses on Feuerbach'[27]).

∴

Soviet philosophy specifically interpreted the activity approach at that time in some works in the sphere of philosophy of science. Philosophers who investigated these problems mainly analysed activity in respect of subject–object relations.

In the 1970s, V.S. Stepin developed a philosophical conception of scientific theory based on the results of analysing the structure and dynamics of a theory in physics. He specially investigated the relations of experimental actions and both formal and material operations in the process of constructing and developing of a scientific theory, relations between scientific ontologies and scientific 'world-pictures' and these operations. The originality of Stepin's conception was the idea that theories in natural sciences are built not by a hypothetic-

---

25   Batishchev 1969, p. 96.
26   Batishchev 1990d, pp. 24–5. See also Lektorsky 1990.
27   See Khamidov 2009, pp. 75–6.

deductive mode, as many specialists both in the USSR and the West believed, but by a genetic-constructive method that presupposes thought-experiments with ideal objects. Stepin suggested an idea of operational character and constructive substantiation of theoretical schemes.[28]

Stepin wrote about the possibility of understanding, in the framework of the activity approach, those objects that science deals with, but which a human being cannot influence. These include such objects of astronomy as the Sun, other stars, the planets of those solar systems, and so on. Stepin gave the following interpretation of this fact. First of all, he argued that there is a certain analogy between astronomical observations and a laboratory-situation when an interaction of a certain object with others is used as a kind of natural experiment.[29] The second part of his interpretation is connected with his general understanding of activity. He stressed that activity selects a limited class of features of objects from an indefinite set of actual and potential features. This applies to both practical and theoretical activity.[30]

Stepin discussed this problem with another Soviet specialist in the philosophy of science, I.S. Alekseyev, who said that any observable object does not exist outside the activity. Alekseyev defended an idea that the world does not consist of constant objects with actual properties, but is a set of possibilities, only some of which can be realised. Human activity is a way of realising what Nature by itself does not produce. Therefore, one could say that, in this sense, activity creates its objects; activity can even be understood as the primary substance.[31]

Alekseyev called his philosophical position 'subjective materialism'. Stepin opposed Alekseyev and defended the position of object-oriented activity. I think that Alekseyev's conception can now be interpreted as constructivist.

∴

A special role in the development of activity-ideas in Soviet philosophy and human sciences (psychology, pedagogy and others) was played by G.P. Shchedrovitsky. He wrote about the theme of activity throughout his career. At first (in the 1960s), he attempted to elaborate an original activity theory of thinking, which was understood as activity on several levels, with definite relations between different operations: generating the content and transformations of

---

28   Stepin 2005.
29   Stepin 1998, p. 662.
30   Stepin 1998, p. 663.
31   Ibid.

sign-forms. Operations of practical comparison of objects produce the content, after which the operating of the form begins. All thinking operations were decomposed into their constituent parts; the number of operations was presupposed to be finite.[32] Shchedrovitsky and his followers studied definite empirical cases of thinking and interacted with psychologists and specialists in pedagogy, giving concrete recommendations. In the 1970s, Shchedrovitsky developed a 'General Theory of Activity'. He argued that activity is a collective system that includes goals of activity, means of their realisation, norms, and division of positions of those who participate in it. The task of methodologists was understood as projecting different organised systems as systems of activity in several spheres of life, such as science, education and society. Shchedrovitsky and his followers established close relations with different spheres of practical life. This development of the activity approach led to the concept of the so-called organisation-activity-games (*organisatsionno-deyatel'nostnye igry*) that have developed successfully to the present day.

The problems of consciousness and personality is that they do not fall within the scope of interest for such forms of the activity approach. Shchedrovitsky was influenced by Marx, Hegel and the organisational theory ('tektology') of Aleksandr Bogdanov. Bogdanov created a specific technocratic variant of the activity approach that was in principle distinct from those of Ilyenkov and Batishchev. From Shchedrovitsky's point of view, activity can be understood as a certain substance that only uses human beings for its own goals and which has an autonomous logic of its development. Shchedrovitsky made some provocative statements about human beings. For example, 'Does creativity belong to an individual or to a functional place in a human organisation, to a structure? I will answer this question very strictly: certainly, not to an individual, but to a functional place.'[33] And, 'the main fraud is the idea of a human being with mind, and the second fraud is the idea of a subject'.[34]

Shchedrovitsky used the activity approach to oppose the 'natural attitude', which he criticised for supposing the existence of objects that are independent from activity. Therefore, I believe it could be said that some elements of constructivism can also be found in Shchedrovitsky's ideas.

In the Soviet philosophy of the 1960s–1980s, there were other influential conceptions of activity, produced by such philosophers as E.G. Yudin,[35]

---

32   Shchedrovitsky 1995, pp. 590–630, 34–49.

33   Shchedrovitsky 1997.

34   Shchedrovitsky 1997, p. 570.

35   Yudin 1978.

V.S. Shvyrev,[36] V.A. Lektorsky[37] and M.A. Rozov,[38] among others. There was something common between them, but they were very different and criticised each other and their positions as discussed in this article.

I think that these differences were not accidental, as they concerned real problems. My opinion is that these very problems are central to contemporary cognitive science and, in a broader sense, the human sciences.

The Activity Approach in Contemporary Epistemology and Cognitive Sciences

Firstly, let us consider the interpretation of the main thesis of the activity approach: that the world is given to a human being in the forms of his activity. Does this mean that objective reality is something like the Kantian *Ding-an-sich* and that a human being can deal only with those objects he has created (constructed) himself, as the philosophical-constructivism thesis claims?

I think that followers of I. Alekseyev and G. Shchedrovitsky answer this question in the affirmative. Another answer was offered by Evald Ilyenkov and early Genrikh Batishchev with reference to Marx. They argued that human activity is always object-oriented and is fulfilled not according to the specific features of a human body, but according to the specific logic of each object – it is connected with the 'universal nature' of a human being who is in principle distinct in this respect from all other living creatures.

The so-called 'embodiment' approach, which is now popular in cognitive science, opposes philosophical constructivism, as the former proceeds from the presupposition that each cognising and acting creature deals with the real world. According to the embodiment-approach, however, activity selects those features of the world that are essential for a certain kind of cognising creature, and this selection depends on the demands of the creature, its bodily size, affordances for its movements, and so on. Thus, it is important from this point of view to distinguish the physical world and the surrounding world and, further, within the latter different 'sub-worlds' or kinds and levels of reality (according to James Gibson, whose ideas essentially influenced the formation of the embodiment-approach).[39] For example, as Thomas Nagel famously

---

36   Shvyrev 2001.

37   Lektorsky 1984, 1990, 1999, 2009a, 2009b.

38   Rozov 2006.

39   Gibson 1979.

noted, the reality perceived by a human being is not the same as that perceived by a bat.[40] It seems that the embodiment-approach as a contemporary form of the activity approach and the thesis about the 'universal nature' of human activity contradict each other. However, this is only a seeming contradiction. The human relation to the world is not limited to the specific nature of a body and its demands: a human being as it leaves the confines of his body and creates a world of artificial things (beginning with simple tools and instruments and finishing with such 'tools' as language and theories). Man uses these artificial things in trying to understand the relations between these different worlds. This is the idea of the so-called 'extended' interpretation of cognition (A. Clark, R. Wilson and others), which is popular today.[41]

But there is yet another problem: what about the relations between contemplation and activity? I have stated in this article that such founders of the activity approach in Soviet philosophy as Rubinshtein and Batishchev in their later years contrasted contemplation and activity and stressed that the former cannot be reduced to the latter. It is true that there is a certain difficulty in understanding the relations between contemplation (particularly perception) and activity. Activity means a transforming of reality, while cognition is a conception of reality. Therefore, it is not possible to identify activity and cognition, as some theoreticians of cognitive science have tried to do, particularly Francisco Varela. However, it is important to consider that cognition is intertwined with activity from the beginning, as the latter connects a cognising subject and a cognised object and selects the essential features of the latter. If perception is understood as a simple result of the brain processing information received as an impact of the outer world, then ideas similar to the conception of 'methodological solipsism' by Jerry Fodor[42] (who suggested it as the methodology of cognitive science) are inevitable. In the framework of the activity approach, the new conception of perception has arisen. The activity approach refuses many ideas of classical interpretation of perception in philosophy and psychology. Perception is understood not as a result, not as a certain entity, but as a continuing process of extracting information from the world. In such interpretation, perception is not 'given' and not 'constructed', but is 'taken' by means of physical actions (James Gibson, Ulrich Neisser[43] and others).

---

40   Nagel 1982.
41   Wilson 2004.
42   Fodor 1980.
43   Neisser 1976.

A final problem is the relations between activity and communication. Such opponents of the activity approach as B. Lomov[44] in psychology and S. Rubinshtein and late Genrikh Batishchev in philosophy wrote that it is impossible to reduce subject–subject relations (communication) to subject–object relations (activity). It is true that the relation between a subject and another subject is not the same as its relation to an object. If I perceive another person as a real being, at that time I am aware that he perceives me in the same manner. This means that my perception of another includes my awareness of perception of me by another person. But why should activity be understood as the transformation of non-human reality only? Activity is transformation of different kinds of reality, including the reality of inter-human relations. Because the latter can be achieved by means of communication, it follows that communication is also activity, albeit of a very specific kind. In addition, it is important to stress that cognition and activity always presuppose communication, as a human being mediates his relations to the world by specific things made by other people. The use of such things necessarily includes communication with others (I have written about it in this text in connection with the problem of psychic development of deaf and blind children). Finally, every act of communication has a meaning in the broad system of activity. Conceptions of 'extended cognition' and 'extended mind' are connected with these problems.[45]

As noted at the start of this chapter, various constructivist conceptions are popular among philosophers, psychologists and other specialists in human sciences in present-day Russia. Especially popular are social constructionism (Kenneth Gergen[46] and others) and the narrative approach in philosophy and psychology[47] connected with it. I believe that this is a result of the fact that the followers of a constructionist approach claim to preserve some ideas of the activity approach, while at the same time going a step further and discovering new fields of research and suggesting new ideas. The followers of social constructionism stress the active, constructive nature of inter-human relations and the active role of an investigator of human beings. They write about the cultural and historical nature of psychic processes and personality and refer to works by Vygotsky and other Soviet psychologists. I think that, despite all that, social constructionism in reality is opposed to the activity approach and that the former cannot be a fruitful methodology of human sciences.

---

44   Lomov 1984.
45   Clark and Chalmers 1998, pp. 7–19.
46   Gergen 1994.
47   Sarbin 1986.

The point is that, in social constructionism, objects which an investigator of human beings deals with are not real, but constructions only. In this conception, communication has supplanted all other kinds of activity and become the main and independent force. From this point of view, research into human beings deals with two kinds of constructions. The first are results of different communications between humans having historical and cultural nature. The second are results of communicative interactions between a researcher and those whom he investigates. From this point of view, a researcher is not an investigator in the proper sense, but a participant in creating a certain ephemeral reality, about which one can speak only conventionally, as it exists only in the framework of these constructions. If we assume this viewpoint, experiment in human sciences becomes impossible, as an investigator and another person who is an object of research interact with each other through communication, which leads to an object of investigation being in principle transformed. According to social constructionism, it is impossible to speak about a theory in the strict sense of this word in human studies.

I think that the problems with which the activity approach deals in reality cannot be better understood within the framework of social constructionism. On the contrary, the facts to which the followers of social constructionism refer can be better explained in the framework of the activity approach.

There is something in social constructionism that is similar to the cultural-historical and activity approaches: the idea that mind, consciousness and personality are products of social interactions and communications and have a cultural-historical nature. Followers of social constructionism refer to the ideas of Lev Vygotsky and Mikhail Bakhtin, claiming that these ideas have been developed in constructionism. However, the assertion that a researcher cognises something that is not real, that he creates an object of investigation, differs in principle from the activity approach in Soviet philosophy and psychology. In fact, each construction presupposes a certain reality that forms the basis of the constructing and which the construction tries to transform. On the other hand, a subject selects some features of real objects through his constructive activity.

If something is a product of construction, this does not mean that it is something unreal or real only in an ephemeral sense. For example, if the 'ego' and the identity are social constructions, they are not unreal. The table I am sitting at is also a result of constructive activity, but it is real beyond any doubt. It is possible to say that all social institutions are results of human activity – in other words, constructions in some sense – but they are real. A human being creates such things (material and ideal), which escape his control and begin to live by themselves. As these are social institutions, it is possible and necessary to study their structures and make theories about them. It is also a subjective world – an object of both theoretical and experimental psychological research. It is a world of ideal products of human creativity, which develops according to their specific laws, although within human activity, as shown by Evald Ilyenkov. This ideal world becomes separated from its human creators to such a degree that some philosophers think it is meaningless to speak about an individual author of a certain ideal construction.[48]

In conclusion, the development of contemporary philosophy, psychology and cognitive science shows that further elaboration of the activity approach is urgently needed. The progress that was made in Soviet philosophy from the 1960s to the 1980s can be of interest in this respect. This does not mean that the Soviet philosophy of that time found answers to problems that are currently being discussed. It means only that the fruitfulness of some ideas formulated and elaborated in that philosophy can be understood in the present context.

---

48   Lektorsky 2009a.

CHAPTER 10

The Concept of the Scheme in the Activity Theories of Ilyenkov and Piaget

Pentti Määttänen

Evald Ilyenkov and Jean Piaget use the concept of the scheme in their theories of human mind. Scheme means for both of them general form or structure of action. Their conceptions have also at least partially common roots in the history of thought. There are also interesting connections between Ilyenkov's and Piaget's schematism and the pragmatism of Charles Peirce and John Dewey. The analysis of these views gives outlines for a theory of mind that is relevant also for contemporary debates in cognitive science. There is growing interest in theories of mind that do not consider mind a property of the brain or even of the body but of the concrete interaction between biological organisms and their environment.

Evald Ilyenkov on the Concept of the Scheme

The relation between thought and world is one of the perennial problems in philosophy. Benedict Spinoza's original contribution to this issue is, according to Ilyenkov, the appeal to the motion and activity of the human body as the crucial element of the solution. A human being, a thinking body, is able to accommodate its motion to the form of any other body. The form or scheme of the activity (motion) corresponds to the form of the object. For example, a hand moving along a round object is circular activity. The scheme of activity is also called the way or manner of action (*sposob deystviy*).[1] The active body reveals the true nature of the objects in the world, and the more active the body is, the more universal it is.[2] This entails that language is not the only manifestation of thought. The mode of existence of thinking is the activity of the body in the world.

---

1 Ilyenkov 1974, pp. 37–40. 'Habit of action' is also a possible translation here because habituality is involved in Ilyenkov's notion of scheme.
2 Ilyenkov 1974, p. 53.

Maybe the most important consequence of this is the consistent questioning of the dichotomy of internal and external that is typical for modern philosophy. Mind is not something internal as opposed to the 'external' world. The correct unit of analysis in investigating cognition is not the brain or even the body, but how the body acts in the system formed by the thinking body and nature as a whole.[3] As Felix Mikhailov puts it: 'My "mental" is above all the world of culture in which I live and act; it is the real existence of nature assimilated by man, every detail of which signifies for me that which it objectively represents. In other words, my mental world is, in fact, the being, the existence of which I am aware.'[4] Cognition is realised as concrete interaction between embodied beings and their natural and cultural environment.

Another consequence is that logic is not only about forms of (natural or artificial) languages. It is about forms of action. Ilyenkov refers here also to G.W.F. Hegel and Karl Marx. The topic of logic is not thinking as symbolic activity but thinking as activity that changes the object. Logic is about the history of science and technology. For Hegel logic is, according to Ilyenkov, manifested in deeds and acts. The products of work such as machines, devices and so on are a medium of the existence of thought.[5] In other words, thinking is activity that is expressed in invariant schemes of action. Logic is experiencing the world in actual practice that changes the world. This can be seen as a development of Spinoza's views, who describes in his essay 'On the Improvement of the Understanding' how we can get exact knowledge of our nature and nature in general. We have to collect the differences, the agreements and the oppositions of things, in order to learn how far they can or cannot be modified and to compare this result with the nature and power of man. This is the way to discern the highest degree of perfection that man is capable of attaining.[6]

Jean Piaget on Sensorimotor Schemes

Piaget's psychological theory emphasises the significance of motor action. A sensorimotor scheme is, according to Piaget, an organised series of motor-acts that is formed by reiterating action in the same or similar circumstances.[7] This

---

3 Ilyenkov 1974, p. 42.
4 Mikhailov 1980, pp. 141–2.
5 Ilyenkov 1974, pp. 117–21.
6 Spinoza 1955, p. 10.
7 Piaget and Inhelder 1969, p. 4.

is, by the way, very similar to the definition of a habit of action given by Charles Peirce. According to Peirce habits are acquired as consequences of the principle that 'multiple reiterated behaviour of the same kind, under similar combinations of percepts and fancies, produces a tendency – the *habit* – actually to behave in a similar way under similar circumstances in the future'.[8]

The sensorimotor schemes are genetically and cognitively independent and basic in regard to perceiving and thinking. They are formed during the child's early development in the course of sensorimotor interaction with the physical environment. Perceptions are regarded as subschemes integrated into the sensorimotor schemes. For example, the visual perceptions of Pavlov's dog are integrated into a reflex scheme.[9] Further, the structures of higher cognition are formed and organised on the basis of the sensorimotor structures. The child's concept of object-permanence is based on the ability to manipulate material objects. Visual coordination takes place on the ground of the sensorimotor scheme of grasping. Also logical operations have their ground in the properties of the sensorimotor schemes or 'practical intelligence'.[10] The extensive use of notions such as practical intelligence, practical concepts and logic of action entail that also for Piaget logic is not only about symbolic operations but action and practice.[11]

Piaget's overall strategy in developing his psychological theory was to avoid the extremities of rationalism and empiricism and build a reasonable synthesis on this basis. This strategy is the same that Immanuel Kant had in mind when writing his *Critique of Pure Reason*, and Piaget adopted it consciously from Kant. The same holds for the concept of the scheme. Several psychologists have after Piaget used the concept of the scheme, and the notion continued its way into cognitive science and studies of artificial intelligence. All this stems from Kant's chapter on schematism.

Immanuel Kant's Schematism

Schemes are methods for realising the constitutive synthesis of pure understanding. Synthesis constitutes nature as a possible object of experience. The origin of this idea is in the method of analysis and synthesis (resolution and composition) that stems from antiquity. In the Middle Ages it was the central

---

8   C.S. Peirce, Collected Papers, vol. 5, 487 (henceforward cited as *CP*).

9   Piaget 1971, p. 179.

10   Piaget 1980, pp. 164–5.

11   For further details see Määttänen 1993.

method of experimental science. On this account analysis is tracking the causes of phenomena and synthesis gives the explanation of the phenomena by deducing it from their causes.[12] Scientific knowledge of phenomena is demonstrative knowledge of their causes.[13] In this sense science is synthetic knowledge.

Thomas Hobbes defined philosophy as knowledge about phenomena that is based on knowledge about their causes or origin.[14] Also certain knowledge about geometric figures is possible because of the fact that we construct them. Hobbes uses the example of how we know whether a circle is a true circle or not. Sense perception alone is not enough for this. But if one knows that the curve is drawn with a solid body by pinning its one end and letting the other end draw the curve, then one knows for certain that it is a true circle.[15] Hobbes thus based the possibility of knowledge on the method of synthesis. Spinoza continued this tradition by maintaining that the only way to get true knowledge about a phenomenon is to acquire knowledge about its proximate cause.[16] Spinoza uses the same example of a circle. The adequate idea of the circle expresses the proximate cause of it, how it is constructed. The only difference is that Hobbes's solid body is changed to a line.[17]

Kant used the concept of the scheme in solving the problem of the connection between concepts and corresponding objects. How are objects subsumed under concepts? This is problematic because concepts are purely intellectual and objects purely sensible, and therefore they have nothing in common. There must be some kind of mediator, and the schemes of pure understanding take care of this. What are these schemes? The chapter about schematism is short and open to different interpretations. I have defended an interpretation that is based on how the Kantian schemes solve the problems of subsumption that remained unsolved in earlier philosophy. This interpretation is closely related to how Piaget and Ilyenkov use the notion. Shortly, schemes are methods of construction processes that proceed in space and time; they are ways of constructing sensible representatives of the concepts of pure understanding.[18]

John Locke considered the problem of how ideas in the mind are related to external objects. The significant background assumption of this way of posing the problem is Descartes's dualism: mind and matter are different sub-

---

12   Crombie 1953, pp. 317–19.

13   Crombie 1953, pp. 52–3.

14   Hobbes 1962, p. 3.

15   Hobbes 1962, p. 6.

16   Spinoza 1955, pp. 8, 11 and 34.

17   Hobbes 1962, pp. 35 and 395.

18   Määttänen 1983, 1988, 1973 and 2011.

stances. According to Locke the connection between ideas and objects is realised through sense-perception. Originally the mind is a *tabula rasa*, and ideas are formed on the ground of perceptions. The idea of the triangle is formed on the ground of various perceptions of different triangles. According to Locke, the connection between all simple ideas and their objects is based on conformity, and so it is with triangles.[19] It follows from the principle of conformity (coincidence of forms) that the idea of the triangle is triangular and that the idea of the circle is circular.[20]

The principle of conformity created a problem for Locke. In order to explain the connection between the idea of the triangle and different triangles in the world with this principle he had to postulate a general idea of the triangle that is 'neither oblique nor rectangle, neither equilateral, equicrural, nor scalenon; but all and none of these at once'.[21] Well, Locke could not imagine this kind of general triangle, and neither did George Berkeley who then concluded that abstract ideas simply do not exist.[22] This problem was called the one–many problem.

Kant solved the problem with his Copernican revolution and the concept of the scheme. The Copernican revolution states that the direction of sense-perception is not from the object of knowledge to the subject of knowledge but the other way round. Perceptions are active and constructive processes. The concept of the triangle gives the schematic method of constructing different triangles in different places at different times. This is simple: put three points on a plane and connect them with lines. Different realisations of this scheme are able to produce all kinds of triangles. Just place the dots differently. The relation between one concept and its different objects is in no way problematic. The one–many problem simply vanishes.

The main purpose of Kant's schemes is to explain the connection between concepts and their objects, between pure understanding and sensibility. The discussion of the one–many problem already shows that he had better success than classical empiricism. But there is more to it.[23]

---

19   Locke 1959, II, p. 230.

20   Locke 1959, I, p. 175.

21   Locke 1959, II, p. 274.

22   Berkeley 1994, pp. 246–7, 253.

23   See also Määttänen 1993, pp. 21–30.

Schemes and Generality

Ilyenkov regards general schemes as logical parameters and refers to Hegel's notion of concrete generality.[24] The form of the activity of a thinking body is general.[25] He has also written extensively about the Ideal as the form of activity.[26] But what is generality? What are the so-called universals?

There are various conceptions of generality. Nominalists deny the existence of universals; some realists have maintained the view that they are some kind of 'immaterial general particulars', whatever that may mean. Kant pointed out that generality is continuous activity (*stetige Handlung*).[27] For Kant mental entities are not immaterial units in a container called mind but mental functions are acts.[28] Charles Peirce says that Kant is a sort of pragmatist, although a 'confused one'.[29] One reason for this characterisation may be that Kant and Peirce had similar ideas about generality.

Peirce was a realist who affirmed that 'real generals' do exist. But how? As mentioned above Peirce's definition of the habit of action is the same as Piaget's definition of the sensorimotor scheme. According to Peirce habits are beliefs as well as meanings. For this the habits must involve generality. Activity proceeds in time; therefore it makes sense to ask how generality is related to time. Note that Kant defined schemes as transcendental time-determinations.[30] Time is (with space) for Kant a pure form of sensibility. Schemes are then a way to explain the connection between concepts and processes proceeding in space and time.

For Peirce habits consist of repeated individual acts. Similar action is repeated in similar circumstances, and this similarity between courses of action is generality. This repeated structure (form, scheme) is the mode of existence of generality. These acts are real processes in this real world in which we live. So there are real generals. The connection to time may be asked, as Peirce did, by asking when they exist. In the past there cannot be genuine generality because, for living creatures, in the past there can be only some definite number of instances of any habit. There can be only one instance of a habit in time, and

24   Ilyenkov 1974, pp. 120–3.
25   Ibid., p. 38.
26   Ibid., p. 168 ff.
27   Kant 1926, p. 615.
28   See Wolff 1963, p. 323.
29   *CP* 5.525.
30   Kant 1976 [1781/87], A pp. 138–139/B, pp. 177–8.

therefore generality cannot exist now. So there remains only the possibility that generality exists in the future. Peirce writes:

> For every habit has, or is, a general law. Whatever is truly general refers to the indefinite future; for the past contains only a certain collection of such cases that have occurred. The past is actual fact. But a general (fact) cannot be fully realized. It is a potentiality; and its mode of being is *esse in futuro*. The future is potential, not actual.[31]

It is important to note that Peirce speaks about an indefinite future instead of an infinite future. Peirce agrees with Kant that concepts can be applied to experience only. According to Kant the question of the beginning of time and that of the ultimate boundary of space are not meaningful because it would require the application of concepts over infinity. This is impossible for finite creatures such as human beings. In contemporary mathematical terms one can say that only potential, not actual infinity can be within the scope of concepts. Consider natural numbers. A number n can be indefinitely big. But it can always be exceeded by adding one to it. So there is no definite upper limit. This is potential infinity. However, the actually infinite set of all natural numbers is not accessible to concepts that are applied in experience.

Keeping this in mind one can say that Peirce's real generals are only potentially, not actually general entities. Human experience is only capable of potential generality. This is consistent with Peirce's terminology. Because generality is never actualised it can only be thought of. Generalities can only be objects of thought. So there is a genuine realm of thought. However, Cartesian dualism does not follow because all possible future acts take place in this material world. Generality, or the ideal, exists as forms (schemes, habits) of activity in this world, just as Ilyenkov put it. The ideal 'exists as human beings' ability to act'.[32] The ideal existence of things is not different from the real existence of things.[33] Descartes and Kant tried to solve the problem of the relation between ideas (concepts) and their objects by assuming that the ideal and the sensible have nothing in common. In Spinoza's and Ilyenkov's view this is not the case.

The object of thought is the ability to act. Or, in other words, thinking is anticipation of action.[34] 'What particularly distinguishes a general belief,

---

31   *CP* 2.148.
32   Ilyenkov 1974, p. 172.
33   Ilyenkov 1974, pp. 172–3.
34   Määttänen 2009, 2010 and 2015.

or opinion, such as is an inferential conclusion, from other habits, is that it is active in the imagination.'[35] For Peirce general beliefs are habits that are active in the imagination. According to Ilyenkov thinking is 'the ability to construct and reconstruct actively the schemes of overt action'.[36] All these phrases amount to the same thing: the world is experienced as possibilities of action (or affordances, to use J.J. Gibson's term). These future possibilities are thought of and evaluated on the ground of past practical experiences, and this thinking is manifested in the concrete interaction between human beings and their natural and cultural environment.

Questioning the Internal/External Dichotomy

Locke's epistemological problem was to explain the connection between objects in the world and ideas in the mind. He applied the principle of conformity and concluded that the idea of the circle is circular and the idea of the triangle is triangular. The problem was posed in the Cartesian framework where the dichotomy between internal and external is the starting point. Ideas are 'in' the mind and the objects 'out there'. One background idea behind this line of thought was knowledge about the eye functioning like a *camera obscura*. External objects create retinal images inside the eye, and this image is somehow changed into a mental image. On this view, ideas and objects resemble each other.

Spinoza is of a different opinion. He writes, '[B]y ideas I do not mean images such as are formed at the back of the eye, or in midst of the brain, but the conceptions of thought.'[37] He calls ideas images of things but 'they do not recall the figure of things'.[38] He explains that 'an idea (being a mode of thinking) does not consist in the image of anything, nor in words. The essence of words and images is put together by bodily motions, which in no wise involve the conception of thought.'[39] On this view, ideas and objects simply cannot resemble each other, which is quite understandable. Suppose, for the sake of argument, that some kind of servomechanism in the brain controls the hand's movements along a round object. Does it make sense to ask whether this servomechanism is round?

---

35   *CP* 2.148.
36   Ilyenkov 1974, p. 40.
37   Spinoza 1955, p. 120.
38   Spinoza 1955, p. 100.
39   Spinoza 1955 p. 122.

Ilyenkov changes the framework of the problem. Locke required conformity between ideas in the mind and objects in the external world, but Ilyenkov considers the relation between the form of the object and the form of activity, the form of the concrete interaction between a human being and objects in the world. This form of activity cannot, strictly speaking, 'reside' in the brain. It exists as forms of concrete activity. All talk about something being 'in the head' is purely metaphorical and colloquial. Mind is not a property of the brain or even of the body. Mind is a property of the interaction between living creatures and their environment.[40]

The form of activity may be a somewhat misleading notion. For example, when talking about a hand moving along a round object one might come to the conclusion that it is about the hand's circular movement. This is too simplistic. The form of activity is about the ability to act, about the whole body's organs, states and processes that make the activity possible. The example about circular movement is too simplistic also in the sense that most human activity is not just accommodation to the material world's spatial properties. Here we can refer to Spinoza once again. To have exact knowledge we must learn how far the objects can or cannot be modified and 'compare this result with the nature and power of man'.[41] The world is modified with the help of the body with its organs, but tools, instruments, machines and so on are also involved in the interaction. The notion of the form of activity refers to all this.

Ilyenkov is not the first one to question the dichotomy between internal and external. Charles Peirce was a consistent and sharp critic of Descartes's philosophy. According to Peirce habits of action are beliefs and meanings and, therefore, vehicles of cognition. Habits are best understood as structures (forms, schemes) of interaction.[42] Peirce distinguished between action and perception by saying that in perception the world's influence on us is greater than our influence on the world, and in action this is the other way round. Action and perception form a kind of mental loop.[43] John Dewey criticised as early as 1896 the concept of the reflex-arc and suggested that this concept should be replaced by that of sensorimotor circuit.[44] This can be expressed by saying that the external objects belong to 'the functional organization of

---

40   See Mikhailov 1980, pp. 141–2.
41   Spinoza 1955, p. 10.
42   Määttänen 2010.
43   Määttänen 2009.
44   Dewey 1975.

mind'.[45] Mind and consciousness emerge in the concrete interaction between living beings and their environment.

This pragmatic view of experience differs essentially from empiricism where the sense-organs form a kind of channel connecting the external world to the internal mind. In empiricism the object of experience and knowledge consists of perceived properties and the relations between perceived states of affairs. David Hume famously went so far as to say that causal relations and values are not facts in the world because one cannot literally perceive them. If action is involved in the very definition of experience then the definition of the object of experience changes.

The world is experienced as possibilities of future action. The object of experience is the relation between the present situation and the anticipated future situation that is the probable outcome of acting according to some habit (form or scheme) of action. The object of experience is thus the relation between two experienced situations, and this relation is mediated by some form of activity. This is the best way to get action into the definition of the object of experience (and knowledge). This change in the notion of experience has some important consequences.

As Ilyenkov points out, there can be no causal relation between thought and bodily behaviour.[46] Indeed, to take the brain to be the organ that thinks (in the head) by itself and causes external bodily behaviour is just a form of neo-Cartesianism.[47] The dichotomy of external and internal must be rejected, and the pragmatic definition of the object of experience takes care of it. This definition, with the view that mind is the property of interaction, leads to the following conception about the causes of bodily behaviour.

Needs and desires can be understood as internal bodily states, but they alone are not causes of behaviour. An organism may be hungry, but it is impossible to eat without the presence of some food. Perceiving the food is another cause, but even this is not enough to explain behaviour. The world is experienced as possibilities of activity. The anticipated outcome of eating, namely the satisfaction of hunger, is the desired future experience towards which the organism decides to act. The actual eating, the realisation of the scheme of eating, is itself a manifestation of thought. It makes no sense to say that this manifestation of thought is the cause of itself. The behaviour is caused by a complex system of causal relations between the organism and its environment. There is no one

---

45   Määttänen 1993, p. 105.

46   Ilyenkov 1974, p. 30.

47   See Bennett and Hacker 2003.

cause that could be singled out as *the* cause of activity.[48] The framework of the
very posing of the problem of mind as the cause of bodily activity is Cartesian,
and this framework is here rejected altogether.

Several contemporary authors maintain similar views. According to Merlin
Donald (2002) human mind is hybrid. The body with its brain is not enough.
The brain is not a device for manipulating symbols. Symbols are in the environment, and human mind emerges in the interaction with the various symbolic
systems. The hybrid mind consists of the brain in a living body and external
symbols. Alva Noë's (2009) title *Out of Our Heads* is informative in itself. According to Noë consciousness does not reside in the brain; it is something we
do. Timo Järvilehto (1998) investigates organism–environment systems. Andy
Clark (1997) wants to put the brain, the body and the world together again. This
list could be continued. The significance of the activity for cognition is receiving growing attention.

Dialectic, Logic and Epistemology

Ilyenkov puts forward the thesis that dialectic, logic and the theory of knowledge, epistemology, are the same. The meaning of this claim depends, of
course, on what one means by these terms. Each of them requires some discussion.

Traditional epistemology is the study of the prerequisites of knowledge. It
has been considered to be *a priori* conceptual analysis that is independent of
the world and our experience of it. Reason is categorically separated from the
world. Spinoza criticised this Cartesian dualism. This dualism is quite question-
able also from the viewpoint of the theory of evolution. How did one animal
species get this remarkable power to transcend nature? Various naturalistic
approaches have denied this possibility since the end of the nineteenth century.

In philosophical naturalism one can distinguish between two sorts of
approaches: soft naturalism and hard naturalism.[49] John Dewey maintained
simply that culture is a product of nature, a phenomenon developed by one
animal species. This is soft naturalism. Willard Van Orman Quine bases his
naturalism on a conception of natural science, hard science, so to say. In the
present context the most important difference between these approaches is

48   See Määttänen 2009.
49   Määttänen 2006.

that Quine supports reductionism (mind is reduced to the brain) while Dewey lays stress on the concrete interaction between living creatures and their environment (recall the notion of the sensorimotor circuit). What they have in common is the denial of any strictly aprioristic epistemology. According to Quine epistemology is a chapter of empirical psychology (considered as a branch of natural science). Dewey challenged the whole epistemological tradition by developing a view he called experimental empiricism or instrumentalism (stressing the role of scientific instruments and devices in acquiring knowledge). This is epistemology as a general theory of (practical) experience.

Also in Ilyenkov's materialism there is no room for *a priori* conceptual analysis that would be independent of the world and our experience of it. This follows immediately from the position that the ideal exists as forms (schemes) of activity. Consistent materialism cannot assume any kind of faculty of reason that would function entirely independently of our practical existence in this world, and this kind of faculty is necessary for *a priori* conceptual analysis. Language is sometimes considered to be a vehicle for such analysis, but for Ilyenkov language itself is not ideal (and neither are neural processes); it is only a way to express the ideal.[50] The conclusion is the same as in Dewey's naturalism. Epistemology is a general theory of experience, a theory of knowledge acquisition.

Logic is a general theory of thought. However, what logic turns out to be depends on what one takes thought to be. Thought as the use of language, the manipulation of symbols, leads to the view of logic as a formal theory of symbol manipulation. Ilyenkov, however, refers to Hegel and maintains that traditional logical theories do not describe thought that is realised as science investigating the world.[51] As noted above the topic of logic is the history of science and technology. Logical form is the form of action.[52] The general schemes are the parameters of logic.[53] Logic is, on this view, a general theory of the scientific investigation of the world. In other words, logic is about the right way of experiencing the world. The topic of logic and the topic of epistemology are thus the same, at least generally speaking.

Here, again, there is a connection with the pragmatism of Peirce and Dewey. Peirce is a prominent figure in formal logic, but this is not the whole story. A habit is for him a final *logical* interpretant.[54] Habit-formation is the way to acquire general conclusions by practical experience. Habit-formation in itself is

---

50   Ilyenkov 1974, p. 171.
51   Ilyenkov 1974, p. 114.
52   Ilyenkov 1974, p. 119.
53   Ilyenkov 1974, p. 120.
54   *CP* 5.591.

a form of inductive inference.[55] Induction as a formal procedure is 'the logical formula which expresses the physiological process of formation of a habit'.[56] Dewey published in 1938 the book *Logic: The Theory of Inquiry*. The title speaks for itself. In classical pragmatism logic is closely connected with habitual action and scientific inquiry.

Logic and epistemology turn out to be more or less the same doctrine, and dialectic as a real scheme of developing and growing knowledge[57] amounts to the same, at least generally speaking. Perhaps they concentrate on different aspects, but on the whole the object of inquiry is the same: the activity of human beings in this material world, activity that aims at the best possible knowledge of the world. However, the coincidence of dialectic, logic and epistemology does not entail the coincidence of the ideal and the material. The ideal is defined as the forms and schemes of activity that do not reach everything in the material world. Human beings are finite and historically limited creatures. There will always be parts and aspects of the material world that remain outside the scope of human experience in spite of the hard efforts to develop new kinds of scientific instruments and devices for observing and measuring unknown features and aspects of reality. The expanding limits of experience are determined by the limited powers and capacities associated with our practical interaction with the world.

---

55   *CP* 6.145.
56   *CP* 2.643.
57   Ilyenkov 1974, p. 109.

CHAPTER 11

The Ideal and the Dream-World: Evald Ilyenkov and Walter Benjamin on the Significance of Material Objects

Alex Levant

This article investigates the insights offered by Evald Ilyenkov's concept of the 'ideal' and Walter Benjamin's concept of the 'dream-world' on a recent formulation of an old problem: the relationship between thought and being. Marx and Engels's treatment of this problem has given rise to ambiguities that persist in current debates in continental philosophy. 'Life is not determined by consciousness, but consciousness by life',[1] they wrote in their critique of German idealist philosophy. The language of determination was subsequently cast in economic terms, in what is perhaps the most influential formulation of this problem: Marx's Preface to *A Contribution to the Critique of Political Economy* (1859). Here, 'life' appears as 'the economic structure of society':

> In the social production of their life, men enter into definite relations that are indispensable and independent of their will, relations of production which correspond to a definite stage of development of their material productive forces. The sum total of these relations of production constitutes the economic structure of society, the real foundation, on which rises a legal and political superstructure and to which correspond definite forms of social consciousness. The mode of production of material life conditions the social, political and intellectual life process in general. It is not the consciousness of men that determines their being, but, on the contrary, their social being that determines their consciousness.[2]

---

1 Marx and Engels 1991 [1846], p. 47.
2 Marx 1970 [1859], pp. 20–1.

This rich yet ambiguous passage has been the subject of much debate, and despite Engels's insistence to the contrary,[3] it has been largely understood in reductionist terms by the dominant currents in both the Second International and Soviet Marxism, which privileged 'the economic structure of society' over 'the social, political and intellectual life process' in their philosophy and politics.

In contrast, and partly due to the defeat of Bolshevik strategy in Western and Central European revolutions, Western Marxism – a tradition originating in the 1920s associated with names such as Lukács, Korsch, Gramsci and the Frankfurt School, as well as subsequent generations and currents of thinkers – sought to shift the focus of inquiry from political economy to cultural domination. Central to their approach was an effort to avoid economic reductionism. Long after the collapse of the Second International and the demise of Soviet Marxism, this effort continues in contemporary Marxist thought.[4]

This neat division of Marxist theory into Soviet Marxism and Western Marxism, however, is challenged by intellectual currents that existed on the margins of Soviet Marxism itself. One of the most interesting examples of these currents is 'activity theory' (*deyatel'nostnyj podkhod*). In the late 1960s, philosophers such as Evald Ilyenkov, Genrikh Batishchev and Yuri Davydov broke sharply with official Soviet Diamat and Histomat.[5] Although itself a current within Soviet Marxism, activity theory shares a common concern with Western Marxism to rescue Marxist thought from reductionism. In fact, similar to the key figures in Western Marxism, these thinkers likewise tried to refocus the

---

3   In his letter to J. Bloch of September 1890, Engels wrote, 'According to the materialist conception of history, the ultimately determining element in history is the production and reproduction of real life. More than this neither Marx nor I have ever asserted. Hence if somebody twists this into saying that the economic element is the only determining one, he transforms that proposition into a meaningless, abstract, senseless phrase' (quoted in Williams 1977, p. 79).

4   For instance, consider the recent debates surrounding John Holloway's work, as well as the journal *Open Marxism*, whose stated objective is to emancipate Marxism from positivism: 'to clear the massive deadweight of positivist and scientistic/economistic strata' (*Open Marxism* 1995, p. 1).

5   Soviet acronyms for dialectical materialism and historical materialism. Soviet Diamat and Histomat represented official Soviet Marxist philosophy, which was schematised in the fourth chapter of the *History of the Communist Party of the Soviet Union (Short Course)*, which is believed to have been written by Stalin. In this text, dialectical materialism is understood as 'the world outlook of the Marxist-Leninist party' (*History* 1938, p. 105), and historical materialism is presented as 'the principles of dialectical materialism applied to social life' (Bakhurst 1991, p. 96).

analysis from the economic structure to human activity in the development of consciousness. More fundamentally, and similar to their Western counterparts, they challenged the transformation of Marxism into Diamat and Histomat. Although vehemently resisted by proponents of official Soviet Marxism, these thinkers have left a body of work, as well as a living body of theorists who continue to develop their ideas.

The most influential of these philosophers was Evald Vasilievich Ilyenkov (1924–79), whose concept of the 'ideal' offers an original approach to an anti-reductionist understanding of the relationship between thought and being. His debates with the Soviet psychologist D.I. Dubrovsky are well known[6] – where Ilyenkov 'seeks to demonstrate that psychological characteristics are neither "written" in the brain, nor determined, not even in part, by its innate structures'.[7] However, the full force of his work has yet to be put into conversation with similar efforts to overcome reductionism in the tradition of Western Marxism.

If Ilyenkov were placed in the company of Western Marxists, it is unclear with whom his work would find the most affinity. An unlikely candidate is the early-twentieth-century literary critic from Germany, Walter Benjamin. However, there are interesting parallels in the relationship between these thinkers and their respective contexts. Most importantly, Ilyenkov's concept of the 'ideal' and Benjamin's concept of the 'dream-world' share a similarity in their original approaches to addressing the problem of reductionism in Marxist thought, as they both reframe the question of the relation between thought and being by approaching it in non-Cartesian terms.

Benjamin's anti-dualism has been famously misunderstood by Theodor Adorno as itself suffering from a pre-Marxist, reductionist materialism; however, when read through Ilyenkov, the influence of the materialist conception of history on Benjamin becomes more apparent. In his 1938 letter to Benjamin, Adorno explained the rejection of Benjamin's piece, 'The Paris of the Second Empire in Baudelaire', which he submitted for publication to *Zeitschrift für Sozialforschung*, the journal of the Frankfurt Institute for Social Research (which at that time had relocated to New York). He wrote, 'I regard it as methodologically unfortunate to give conspicuous individual features from the realm of

---

6 'In 1968, the journal *Voprosy Filosofii* [*Questions of Philosophy*] published an article by David Izrailevich Dubrovsky, 'Mozg I Psikhika' ['The Brain and the Psyche'], which attacked Ilyenkov's theory of the ideal and similar views shared by another philosopher, Feliks Trofimovich Mikhailov. Thus began a prolonged polemic about the nature of the ideal which has not ended to this day' (Maidansky 2005, p. 294).

7 Bakhurst 1991, p. 231.

the superstructure a "materialistic" turn by relating them immediately and perhaps even causally to corresponding features of the infrastructure.'[8] Ilyenkov's concept of the ideal, however, helps us to grasp Benjamin's approach as an anti-dualist, anti-reductionist Marxism, as opposed to vulgar materialism.

This article problematises the categories of Western Marxism and Soviet Marxism by focusing on a current within Soviet Marxism – activity theory – that shares a common concern with Western Marxism to avoid the reduction of 'life' to various structures. Specifically, it aims to demonstrate that Ilyenkov's work makes a significant contribution to anti-reductionist Marxist thought. His conception of the ideal provides a philosophical foundation to grasp the relationship between thought and being in non-Cartesian, non-reductionist terms. I illustrate this point by offering a reading of Benjamin's concept of the dream-world through Ilyenkov's concept of the 'ideal' on the question of the relation between base and superstructure. Although their concepts are very different, reading Benjamin through Ilyenkov helps us to see more clearly that Benjamin's concept of the dream-world seeks to grasp this relation in a manner that, similar to Ilyenkov, avoids the Cartesian dualism between body and thought, and recognises the central role of human activity.

1   Ilyenkov and Benjamin

Although Ilyenkov and Benjamin approached this problem in very different geo-political and disciplinary contexts, they nevertheless had much in common. Ilyenkov was a philosopher who made his most significant contributions in the late 1950s, 60s and 70s, primarily working in Moscow. Among his major influences were Hegel and Spinoza, as well as the 'cultural-historical school' of Soviet psychology.[9] Benjamin, on the other hand, was an eclectic literary critic of a previous generation, who wrote in the 1920s and 30s, predominantly in Berlin and Paris. His influences ranged from Freud to Surrealism to Jewish mysticism. However, both thinkers were, in some ways, on the margins in their respective contexts.

They were both widely published, but they also each had difficulties publishing their most innovative work. In an interesting parallel, both Ilyenkov's 'Dialectics of the Ideal' and Benjamin's 'The Paris of the Second Empire in

---

8   Adorno 2002, p. 129.

9   The cultural-historical school of Soviet psychology was founded in the 1920s by L.S. Vygotsky, and associated with names such as A.N. Leontiev and A.R. Luria.

Baudelaire' remained unpublished in their lifetimes. In Ilyenkov's case, in 1976, the Institute of Philosophy, headed by B.S. Ukraintsev, decided not to proceed with its planned publication of 'Dialectics of the Ideal'.[10] It remained unpublished in its complete form until 2009. Similarly, in 1938, Benjamin's essay was rejected for publication, chiefly by Adorno, in the Frankfurt School's journal, *Zeitschrift für Sozialforschung*.[11]

Both thinkers had difficult careers that tragically ended in suicide – in 1940 for Benjamin and in 1979 for Ilyenkov. They were also both critics of Soviet Diamat.[12] But most significantly, what brings these theorists together is a similarity in the innovations that they offer to the problem of the relationship between thought and being in Marxism.

Despite Benjamin's failure to secure a permanent academic position, his difficulties publishing his work and the tragic circumstances that cut his life short at the age of 48, he has posthumously become a well-known thinker who is studied across various disciplines, and often included in the canon of Western Marxism, usually in close proximity to the Frankfurt School.[13] In recent years, particularly since the publication of the first English translation of his major work, *The Arcades Project* (*Passagen-Werk*) in 1999, a substantial secondary literature has been produced, amounting to something like a Benjamin industry.[14]

Ilyenkov, on the other hand, despite having had a profound impact on Soviet philosophy in his own lifetime, has not been as influential in the West. For instance, in the introduction to the special issue of the journal *Studies in East European Thought*, dedicated to the work of Ilyenkov, Vesa Oittinen writes that Ilyenkov's philosophical insights have 'to this day remained a Soviet phenomenon without much international influence'.[15] Despite the fact that some of his work has been available in translation for many years, he has not had much impact on Western Marxist thought. However, there are many common features that should make Ilyenkov a substantial contributor to this tradition, most importantly their common concern to avoid vulgar materialism, a materialism that has led to various forms of reductionism.

---

10 Maidansky 2009a, p. 3.
11 Agamben 2007, p. 127; *Aesthetics and Politics* 1999, pp. 100–1; Benjamin 2003 [1940], p. 431.
12 Löwy 2005, p. 14.
13 'The largely posthumous publication of his later writings has made Walter Benjamin perhaps the most influential Marxist critic in the German-speaking world, after the Second World War' (*Aesthetics and Politics*, p. 100).
14 Benjamin began to be published in Russian in the 1990s (Buck-Morss 2000, p. xii).
15 Oittinen 2005a, p. 228.

There have been several attempts to place Ilyenkov in conversation with Western Marxist thought, and some work has been done in recent years that has facilitated this process. The earliest was a failed attempt in the early 1960s – the so-called 'Italian Affair'.[16] The only major English language book on Ilyenkov is David Bakhurst's *Consciousness and Revolution in Soviet Philosophy* (1991), written by a Canadian professor of analytic philosophy. In 1999, on the 20th anniversary of Ilyenkov's death, a symposium was held in Helsinki, the proceedings of which were published in 2000 in *Evald Ilyenkov's Philosophy Revisited* edited by Vesa Oittinen. This book was reviewed by Paul Dillon in 2005 in the London-based journal *Historical Materialism*. In that same year, the special issue of *Studies in East European Thought* on Ilyenkov advanced the discussion from the 1999 symposium. In 2009, the journal *Diogenes* published a special issue on Russian philosophy, which included an article by Abdusalam Guseinov and Vladislav Lektorsky that provides for English readers important insights into the historical context in which Ilyenkov wrote.

Some work has also been done in the Russian language that brings Ilyenkov into contact with Western Marxism. Of special mention is a recent publication by Sergey Mareev, *From the History of Soviet Philosophy: Lukács, Vygotsky, Ilyenkov* (2008), which places Ilyenkov in a line of development in Soviet philosophy that includes Georg Lukács, one of the principal figures of Western Marxism. This list is obviously not exhaustive; however, there is much more work to be done to bring the full scope of Ilyenkov's contributions on the problem of reductionism into conversation with the Western Marxist tradition.

2   Ilyenkov's Intellectual Context

A lot has been written about Benjamin's intellectual milieu – the Frankfurt Institute for Social Research (particularly Adorno, Horkheimer and Bloch), his close friend and accomplished playwright Bertolt Brecht and, of course, Georg

---

16   Oittinen 2005a, pp. 227–8. As Oittinen explains, the manuscript had been smuggled into Italy before it was published in Russia; however, it remained unpublished until its publication in Russia so as not to make 'life too difficult for Ilyenkov'. Oittinen writes, '[T]he foreword to the Italian edition was written by Lucio Colletti, a disciple of Galvano Della Volpe, who expressly wanted to develop a non-Hegelian version of Marxist philosophy. Such a position is extremely difficult to reconcile with Ilyenkov's Hegelian stance, which, far from abandoning dialectics, strives to make it the main tool of a reformed Marxism. So, both the Della Volpe school and Ilyenkov moved away from the Diamat, but, unfortunately, they went in different directions.'

Lukács, whose *History and Class Consciousness* (1923) was a towering point of reference for that generation of Marxist theorists. In comparison to Benjamin, relatively little is known about Ilyenkov's intellectual context in the West.

Ilyenkov's work is testimony to the fact that Soviet Marxism cannot be reduced to a rehearsal of state-sanctioned dogma in the form of Diamat and Histomat. There were significant counter-currents that made important contributions to Marxist theory, whose histories and lineages continue to be a subject of debate. However, much of this body of work continues to be largely unexamined in the West.

Ilyenkov was a pivotal figure in the opposition to the hegemony of the 'Diamatchiki',[17] who had dominated Soviet philosophy since 1931. Vadim Mezhuev writes, 'It is to him that my generation owes the conscious break with dogmatic and scholastic official philosophy.'[18] Similarly, Guseinov and Lektorsky identify a 'philosophical Renaissance in the Soviet Union' and Ilyenkov as one of its leading figures.[19] This history has also been well documented by David Bakhurst, Andrey Maidansky, Sergey Mareev and Vesa Oittinen, among others. After Stalin's death in 1953, during Khrushchev's 'thaw', a new group of theorists, who were part of the 'Shestidesiatniki' (of the Sixties generation), began to question some of the basic tenets of official Soviet Marxism. In a recently published edited volume entitled *Evald Vasil'evich Ilyenkov* (2008), V.I. Tolstykh writes, 'At the end of the 1950s begins the crisis of official Soviet ideology, and [Ilyenkov] is among other young philosophers [who] together with Aleksander Zinoviev, Georgy Shchedrovitsky, Merab Mamardashvili and others enter into polemics with philosophers of the type of Molodtsov and Mitin.'[20] In 1954, then junior lecturer Ilyenkov declared to the Chair of Dialectical Materialism at Moscow State University that in Marxism there is no such thing as dialectical materialism or historical materialism, but only a materialist conception of history.[21] Over the next 25 years, Ilyenkov worked as an engaged philosopher who challenged official Soviet philosophy. One of the most interesting and influential concepts to be developed in this context is his conception of the ideal.

---

17   Proponents of Soviet Diamat – the philosophy of dialectical materialism, as it had been developed by the 'Bolshevisers' following the support they received from the Central Committee in 1931 to work out the Leninist stage of dialectical materialism, and as it had been codified by Stalin in chapter four of the *History of the Communist Party of the Soviet Union* 1938 (Löwy 2005, p. 14).

18   Mezhuev 1997, p. 47.

19   Guseinov and Lektorsky 2009b, p. 13.

20   Tolstykh 2008, p. 6.

21   Mareev 2008, p. 8; Bakhurst 1991, p. 6.

3   Ilyenkov's Concept of the Ideal

The 1962 edition of the Soviet Encyclopaedia of Philosophy included several entries by Ilyenkov, one of which was a short article on 'The Ideal' (*Ideal'noe*). Developing this concept remained central to his work throughout the span of his career. In the mid-1970s, he completed his definitive work on this concept – 'Dialectics of the Ideal'. Its publication was blocked in 1976, although parts of it were subsequently published.[22] It remained unpublished in its complete form until 2009, 30 years after his death.[23]

In 'Dialectics of the Ideal' (2009), Ilyenkov recalls that in the postscript to the second Russian edition of *Capital*, Marx writes that 'the ideal is nothing other than the material when it has been transposed and translated inside the human head'.[24] Several obvious questions arise from this definition, including: What does this transposition and translation entail? What is the relationship between matter and the ideal inside the human head? In other words, how does the objective, material world assume significance? Ilyenkov's concept of the ideal offers an original approach to resolving these questions.

He grasps the relationship between the material and the ideal without reducing one to a consequence of the other. In contrast to vulgar materialists who posit the material as the determinant of the ideal, or the subjective idealists who privilege the ideal over the material, or even some Marxist theorists who are careful to note that the material and the ideal co-determine each other, as well as those who attempt a more nuanced analysis by including mediations in their interrelationship, Ilyenkov sidesteps the various problems associated with a dualist approach. He does this by demonstrating that the material and the ideal are both moments of a single process rather than two distinct substances.

Key to understanding this concept is another, perhaps less obvious question that arises from Marx's passage: that is, what did he mean by 'the human head'? In contrast to his intellectual opponents, who viewed the human head as the

---

22   It was prevented from publication in the USSR six additional times. However, in 1977 an 'abridged and amended' version was published in English as 'The Concept of the Ideal' by Robert Daglish (*Philosophy in the USSR: Problems of Dialectical Materialism*. Moscow: Progress, 1977, pp. 71–99). Another abridged version was published shortly following Ilyenkov's death in 1979 as 'The Problem of the Ideal' ['Probl'ema ideal'nogo'] in *Voprosy filosofii* (1979, 6: 128–40, and 7: 145–58). Two more abridged versions were published in the USSR, in *Art and the Communist Ideal* [*Iskusstvo i kommunisticheskiy ideal*] 1984 and in *Philosophy and Culture* [*Filosofia i kul'tura*] 1991 (Maidansky 2009a, p. 4).

23   Maidansky 2009a, pp. 3–5.

24   Marx, quoted in Ilyenkov 2009, p. 18.

physical brain, Ilyenkov grasped it as a cultural organ, not a natural one.[25] As Andrey Maidansky persuasively argues, 'Ilyenkov insisted that Marx had in mind not the bodily organ of an individual *Homo sapiens*, growing out of his neck at the mercy of Mother Nature, but precisely the *human* head – a tool of *culture*, not of nature.'[26] The human head referred to in Marx appears not to be simply the human *head* (the physical thing) but the *human* head (a collective or social phenomenon).

This assertion should not be controversial for readers of Marx, as he clearly posited human consciousness as a social phenomenon, something that does not develop automatically in each individual, but a capacity acquired through socialisation.[27] In his first major book, *The Dialectics of the Abstract and the Concrete in Marx's 'Capital'* (1960), Ilyenkov articulates this process as follows: 'Rising to conscious life within society, the individual finds a pre-existing "spiritual environment", objectively implemented spiritual culture.'[28] Prefiguring the development of his concept of the ideal, he writes that this spiritual environment ... 'structures from the very outset developing the consciousness and will of the individual, moulding him in its own image'. He continues: 'As a result, each separate sensual impression arising in individual consciousness is always a product of refraction of external stimuli through the extremely complex prism of the forms of social consciousness the individual has appropriated.'[29] From this perspective, the consciousness of the individual arises not from the physical head of a human, but from the process of the individual's appropriation of the ideal using the physical human head.

Some have remarked that this approach resembles Karl Popper's concept of 'World 3' – the world of human social constructions;[30] however, as Guseinov and Lektorsky convincingly argue, there is a significant difference between the two concepts. In a recent article in *Diogenes* (2009) they write, 'The substantive difference lay in the fact that, for Ilyenkov, ideal phenomena can exist only within the context of human activity.'[31] The role of human activity is one of the most distinctive features of Ilyenkov's concept of the ideal.

For Ilyenkov, the ideal does not exist in language or in other material phenomena, but in forms of human activity. His entry on the ideal in the 1962

---

25 Maidansky 2009b, p. 290.
26 Ibid.
27 Marx and Engels 1991 [1846], p. 51.
28 Ilyenkov 1960, pp. 40–1.
29 Ilyenkov 1960, p. 41.
30 Ilkka Niiniluoto, in Oittinen 2000, p. 8.
31 Guseinov and Lektorsky 2009b, p. 15.

edition of the Soviet Encyclopaedia of Philosophy defines it as 'the subjective image of objective reality, that is, a reflection of the external world in forms of human activity, in forms of its consciousness and will'.[32] One can think of the ideal as the significance that the material assumes in the process of its transformation by human activity. In other words, *it is only in and through human activity that matter takes on the character of an object with significance.*

To be clear, Ilyenkov is referring not only to parts of the material world that individuals directly transform, but to all matter that society comes 'in contact' with. *Idealisation* is for him a social phenomenon. In the same encyclopaedia-entry he writes:

> An ideal image, say of bread, may arise in the imagination of a hungry man or of a baker. In the head of a satiated man occupied with building a house, ideal bread does not arise. But if we take society as a whole, ideal bread and ideal houses are always in existence, as well as any ideal object with which humanity is concerned in the process of production and reproduction of its real, material life. This includes the ideal sky, as an object of astronomy, as a 'natural calendar', a clock and a compass. In consequence of that, all of nature is idealised in humanity and not just that part which it immediately produces or reproduces or consumes in a practical way.[33]

From this perspective, all matter appears in individual consciousness already transformed and idealised by the activity of previous generations, and this ideal informs the individual's activity in the present.

Perhaps the most striking feature of Ilyenkov's concept of the ideal is its articulation as part of a larger process, as a *phase* in the transformation of matter. This move allows him to avoid two forms of reductionism: the reduction of the ideal to the physical brain (characteristic of vulgar materialism) and the reduction of the ideal to some extra-human phenomenon such as 'nature' (characteristic of idealism). By understanding it as a phase of a process, Ilyenkov is able to grasp the ideal without severing it from human activity. In the 1962 article, he wrote, 'The ideal is the outward being of a thing in the phase of its becoming in the action of a subject in the form of his wants, needs and aims.'[34] Understanding it as a phase enables him to capture several moments of

---

32   Ilyenkov 1962, p. 222.
33   Ilyenkov 1962, p. 225.
34   Ilyenkov 1962, p. 223.

its existence – matter invested with meaning in the process of human activity, which comes to inform the subsequent transformation of the idealised material world. In 'Dialectics of the Ideal' (2009), he described it as follows:

> The process by which the *material* life-activity of social man [*sic*] begins to produce not only a material, but also an *ideal* product, begins to produce the act of *idealisation* of reality (the process of transforming 'the material' into 'the ideal'), and then, having arisen, 'the ideal' becomes a critical component of the material life-activity of social man [*sic*], and then begins the opposite process – the process of the *materialisation* (objectification, reification, 'embodiment') of the ideal.[35]

As individuals, we enter an already *idealised material world*, which we continue to transform, as we materialise the ideal we inhabit in our own activity.

Returning to the above question – What is the relationship between matter and the ideal inside the human head? – in light of Ilyenkov's concept of the ideal, we can say that the ideal inside the human head (that is, individual consciousness) is a product of the transformation of matter through social activity, which is acquired by the individual.

Far from conceptions that posit the material and the ideal as determining each other, in Ilyenkov's concept of the ideal, we have an approach that does not posit the ideal and the material as separate substances. The concept of the ideal offers a way of grasping the relationship between the material and the ideal in non-reductionist terms (which demonstrates affinity between Ilyenkov and Western Marxism), but it also understands this relationship in non-Cartesian terms.

Contemporary Ilyenkov scholars have noted the influence of Spinoza on Ilyenkov's thought. For instance, Vesa Oittinen writes, 'Ilyenkov stresses the methodological value of Spinoza's monism, which means a change for the better compared with the dualism of two substances in Descartes ... The Cartesians had posed the whole question of the psycho-physical problem in a wrong way: they desperately sought to establish some kind of a causal relation between thought and extension, although such a relation simply doesn't exist. Thought and extension are simply two sides of the one and same matter.'[36] He quotes Ilyenkov's essay 'Thought as an Attribute of Substance' from *Dialectical Logic* (1974): 'There are not two different and originally contrary objects of investig-

---

35   Ilyenkov 2009, p. 18.
36   Oittinen 2005b, p. 323.

ation – body and thought – but only *one single* object, which is the *thinking body* [which] does not consist of two Cartesian halves – "thought lacking a body" and a "body lacking thought" ... It is not a special "soul", installed by God in the human body as in a temporary residence, that thinks, but the *body of man* itself.'[37] This anti-dualist approach distinguishes Ilyenkov from similar critiques of reductionism in the Western Marxist tradition.

Ilyenkov's insights offer an original way of understanding the relationship between thought and being, which helps us to grasp the relationship between base and superstructure without slipping into reductionism. We can see from the above articulation of the concept of the ideal that for Ilyenkov thought does not simply reflect the material world. Rather than being separate substances that shape each other, they are both phases of a single process: the transformation of the material through human activity. In light of his conception of the ideal, the superstructure can be understood as an expression of the base in forms of human activity. Rather than a reflection, it appears as a special attribute of the base that is realised in human activity. The central role played by human activity reconfigures the question of the relationship between base and superstructure, where the superstructure appears less like a reflection of the base than a 'reflection' of the organisation of human activity.

Unlike Ilyenkov, Benjamin did not rigorously work out a historical-materialist conception of the ideal in the classical-philosophical tradition. However, when read through Ilyenkov, his insights reveal not only a common concern to avoid reductionism, but also a similar focus on human activity in the relationship between thought and being, as well as a similar approach to the problem.

4   Reading Benjamin's Concept of the Dream-world through
       Ilyenkov's Concept of the Ideal

Moving from Ilyenkov to Benjamin requires leaps across intellectual and political contexts. Although Benjamin did not formulate his ideas in the language of classical philosophy, he was certainly confronted by very similar problems to Ilyenkov, namely, how to grasp what appears more narrowly in Marxist thought as the relationship between base and superstructure. In Konvolut κ (entitled Dream City and Dream House, Dreams of the Future ...) of *The*

---

37   Ilyenkov 1974, pp. 31–2.

Arcades Project, Benjamin offered the following articulation of the relation between base and superstructure (what he calls infrastructure and superstructure):

> On the doctrine of the ideological superstructure. It seems, at first sight, that Marx wanted to establish here only a causal relation between superstructure and infrastructure ... The question, in effect, is the following: if the infrastructure in a certain way (in the materials of thought and experience) determines the superstructure, but if such determination is not reducible to simple reflection, how is it then – entirely apart from any question about the originating cause – to be characterized? As its expression. The superstructure is the expression of the infrastructure. The economic conditions under which society exists are expressed in the superstructure – precisely as, with the sleeper, an overfull stomach finds not its reflection but its expression in the contents of dreams, which, from a causal point of view, it may be said to 'condition.' The collective, from the first, expresses the conditions of its life. These find their expression in the dream and their interpretation in the awakening.[38]

This long passage requires some unpacking.

When read through Ilyenkov, one is struck by how similarly Benjamin approaches the relationship between base and superstructure to how Ilyenkov understands the relationship between the material and the ideal. Benjamin's understanding of the superstructure as an expression of the base in the dreams of an overfull sleeper is strikingly similar to Ilyenkov's conception of the ideal as an attribute of the material manifested in forms of human activity.[39] In light of Ilyenkov's concept of the ideal, we can understand Benjamin's superstructure as an *expression* of the base in collective human activity. Given the specific organisation of human activity in bourgeois society, the superstructure exhibits the characteristics of dreams.

Benjamin's concept of the dream-world is complex. In her influential book on the subject, *Dreamworld and Catastrophe* (2000), Susan Buck-Morss writes that Benjamin 'used [the concept of the dream-world] not merely as the poetic description of a collective mental state but as an analytical concept, one that was central to his theory of modernity as the reenchantment of the world'.[40] In

---

38   Benjamin 1999 [1927–40], p. 392.
39   As Naumenko 2005 and Oittinen 2005b have commented, Ilyenkov here is drawing on a particular reading of Spinoza.
40   Buck-Morss 2000, p. x.

order to fully appreciate Benjamin's concept of the dream-world, as we move from Ilyenkov to Benjamin, let us return briefly to their principal common influence, Karl Marx.

Consider Ilyenkov's concept of the ideal and Benjamin's concept of the dream-world in relation to the famous passage from Marx's *18th Brumaire*, 'People make their own history, but they do not make it just as they please; they do not make it under circumstances chosen by themselves, but under circumstances directly encountered, given and transmitted from the past.'[41] These 'circumstances' – which have often been understood in strictly economic terms, that is, as having a logic of their own that is separate from human activity[42] – appear, in light of Ilyenkov's work, as the idealised material world, which both empowers and directs us, and which is, at bottom, objectified human activity. Further on in the same passage, Marx makes one of his most often-quoted pronouncements: 'The tradition of all the dead generations weighs like a nightmare on the brain of the living.'[43] This 'tradition', these 'circumstances', this idealised material world weighs on us like a *nightmare*.

This notion of the idealised world as a nightmare has particular resonance when read alongside Benjamin's concept of the dream-world. In the 1935 version of his essay, 'Paris, Capital of the Nineteenth Century', he wrote, 'Balzac was the first to speak of the ruins of the bourgeoisie ... The development of the forces of production shattered the wish symbols of the previous century, even before the monuments representing them had collapsed ... They are the residues of a dream world.'[44] By inflecting his reading of Marx's conception of the 'nightmare' of history with Freud's conception of the unconscious, Benjamin produced an original understanding of how the idealised material world (to borrow Ilyenkov's language) in bourgeois society exhibited the characteristics of a dream-world.

To begin, Benjamin reworked Freud's proposition that consciousness acts not only as a receptor of stimuli, but also as a protector against stimuli. In his 1939 essay, 'On Some Motifs in Baudelaire' (a revised version of the 1938 piece that was rejected by Adorno), he investigated Freud's concept of consciousness, referencing the latter's 1921 work *Beyond the Pleasure Principle*.

---

41   Marx 1963 [1852], p. 15.

42   As the editors of *Open Marxism Volume 2* write, 'a common concern of our contributors is their rejection of an understanding of practice as merely attendant upon the unfolding of structural or deterministic "laws"' (Bonefeld et al. 1992, p. xi).

43   Marx 1963 [1852], p. 15.

44   Benjamin 1999 [1927–40], p. 13.

> In Freud's view, consciousness [has an] important function: protection against stimuli. 'For a living organism, protection against stimuli is an almost more important function than the reception of stimuli ... The threat ... is one of shocks. The more readily consciousness registers these shocks, the less likely are they to have a traumatic effect.'[45]

From this perspective, the role of consciousness is to apprehend stimuli in a manner that protects the individual from experiencing trauma. Benjamin, however, departed from Freud by grasping consciousness as a cultural-historical phenomenon, rather than an individual faculty.

He further de-reified Freud's concept by grasping it as an historical, rather than a natural, phenomenon. For instance, he tried to show how collective consciousness was shaped by human activity. He noted that bourgeois society involved an acceleration of shock-effects – 'the assembly line, photography, street lighting, film, the movement of crowds hurtling through great cities, bombardment by advertisements, the unfathomable mobilization of science and technology in war'[46] – resulting in consciousness becoming increasingly protective. He wrote, 'The greater the share of the shock factor in particular impressions, the more constantly consciousness has to be alert as a screen against stimuli; the more efficiently it does so, the less do these impressions enter experience.'[47] From this perspective, life under capitalism involves the experience of increasing shock-effects, which develop the shielding aspect of collective consciousness. Buck-Morss articulates this dynamic as follows: '[T]he aesthetic system undergoes a dialectical reversal. The human sensorium changes from a mode of being "in touch" with reality into a means of blocking out reality. Aesthetics – sensory perception – becomes *an*aesthetics, a numbing of the senses' cognitive capacity.'[48] Far from the natural and individual phenomenon we find in Freud, Benjamin posits consciousness as a social and a historical phenomenon.

One way to understand how this collective consciousness can be said to protect us from shock is by examining the narratives that organise experience. Following the innovative work of David McNally (2001), one could say that collective consciousness not only receives stimuli, but also protects against potentially harmful stimuli by producing 'a narrative which represses the memory of these sensory shocks and the fears they inspired. Consciousness, in other

---

45   Benjamin 1961 [1939], p. 161.
46   McNally 2001, p. 214.
47   Benjamin 1961 [1939], p. 163.
48   Buck-Morss 2000, p. 104.

words, spins a tale of security and stability in a dangerous and frightening world.'[49] The narratives with which collective consciousness grasps the world organise it in a manner that protects us from traumatic shocks. The more successfully such shocks are absorbed by these narratives, the less they are experienced consciously. 'Nevertheless', continues McNally, 'these shocks leave effects in the form of memory-traces stored in the unconscious.'[50]

Benjamin illustrated these memory-traces by drawing on Proust's concept of 'involuntary memory' from *In Search of Lost Time*. 'In the reflection which introduces the term', wrote Benjamin, 'Proust tells us how poorly, for many years, he remembered the town of Combray in which, after all, he spent part of his childhood. One afternoon the taste of a kind of pastry called *madeleine* (which he later mentions often) transported him back to the past, whereas before then he had been limited to the promptings of a memory which obeyed the call of attentiveness [*memoire volontaire*].'[51] These experiences of a sudden flash of memory are, according to Benjamin, unconscious memory-traces that have been triggered by something in the present. When consciousness acts as a shield that represses memories of sensory shocks, the unconscious acts as a storehouse of traces of these repressed memories.

In moving from the individual to the collective, Benjamin located the collective unconscious in certain products of human activity. The classic passage on 'involuntary memory' in Proust cited above concludes, 'The past is hidden somewhere outside the realm, beyond reach, of intellect, in some material object.'[52] One example of what Benjamin had in mind was the products that have been forgotten, things that have fallen out of fashion, the ruins of the bourgeoisie – what he called *the outmoded*: 'the first iron constructions, the first factory buildings, the earliest photos, the objects that have begun to be extinct, grand pianos, the dresses of five years ago, fashionable restaurants when the vogue has begun to ebb from them'.[53] Benjamin believed that the collective unconscious was practically written into the material world. Following the Surrealists, he wrote, '[C]onstruction fills the role of the unconscious.'[54]

Although belonging to the collective consciousness of a bygone era, these objects continue to haunt us in the present. McNally articulates this phenomenon as follows: 'Our old identifications and desires, the old selves we have

---

49   McNally 2001, p. 214.

50   Ibid.

51   Benjamin 1961 [1939], p. 158.

52   Proust, cited in Benjamin 1999 [1927–40], p. 403.

53   Benjamin 1986a [1929], pp. 181–2.

54   Benjamin 1986b [1935], p. 147.

left behind, leave traces in the physiognomy of the city and our dwelling places: in the outmoded buildings, clothes, art works, photos and so on. Thus, as consciousness absorbs new blows and lets go of old identities, it also regularly confronts monuments to its past dreams and the frustrations they endured.'[55] These traces of forgotten memories return in our collective dreams in the form of current fashions, styles, architecture, as well as wish-images of the future that seek to address past experiences of collective trauma.

Recall that for Freud, repressed memories often returned in dreams. Benjamin wrote, 'Freud's investigation was occasioned by a dream characteristic of accident neuroses, which reproduce the catastrophe in which the patient was involved. Dreams of this kind, according to Freud, "endeavour to master the stimulus retroactively, by developing the anxiety whose omission was the cause of the traumatic neurosis." '[56] Benjamin sought to use this approach to analyse collective dreams.

In the passage that introduces the image of the sleeper in Konvolut K of *The Arcades Project*, Benjamin moves from the individual dreamer to the dreaming collective. He analogises the sleeping body to that precursor of shopping malls – the arcades:

> But just as the sleeper ... sets out on the macrocosmic journey through his own body, and the noises and feelings of his insides, such as blood pressure ... and muscle sensation ... generate, in the extravagantly heightened inner awareness of the sleeper, illusion or dream imagery which translates and accounts for them, so likewise for the dreaming collective, which, through the arcades, communes with its own insides. We must follow in its wake so as to expound the nineteenth century – in fashion and advertising, in buildings and politics – as the outcome of its dream visions.[57]

In addition to the shift from the individual to the collective, this passage is also noteworthy for how it casts human activity. Fashion, advertising, buildings and politics – all products of human activity – constitute the body of the dreaming collective.

Our collective body, in the form of the ruins of the bourgeoisie, is a product of our activity. In the same section, Benjamin continues: 'Of course, much

---

55   McNally 2001, p. 214.
56   Benjamin 1986b [1935], p. 161.
57   Benjamin 1999 [1927–40], p. 389.

that is external to the former is internal to the latter: architecture, fashion – yes, even the weather – are, in the interior of the collective, what the sensorial of organs, the feeling of sickness or health, are inside the individual. And so long as they preserve this unconscious, amorphous dream configuration, they are as much natural processes as digestion, breathing, and the like. They stand in the cycle of the eternally selfsame, until the collective seizes upon them in politics and history emerges.'[58] In moving from the individual to the collective, Benjamin noted that phenomena such as architecture and fashion have an 'amorphous dream configuration' and that this state of affairs will continue until the collective does something about it and 'history emerges'.

One can see the influence of Marx, who saw all epochs including his own as prehistory.[59] History, of course, begins when collective human activity becomes consciously directed by the collective. This selection recalls Marx's well-known passage on the fetishism of commodities. In *Capital* Volume I, he writes, 'The veil is not removed from the countenance of the social-life process, i.e. the process of material production, until it becomes production by freely associated men [*sic*], and stands under their conscious and planned control.'[60] In other words, fetishism will persist as long as the collective is not in control of its activity.

Looking at the matter more closely – and this is the value of Ilyenkov's work – one can see why bourgeois society appeared to Benjamin as a dream-world. Of course, as individuals we are fully awake, but taken as a whole, and when read next to Marx above, the collective appears to be acting unconsciously. In light of Ilyenkov's work, one can understand the idealisation of the material as a dream-world because of the way activity is organised. This insight, which is implicit in Benjamin, is coherently articulated in the concept of the ideal (as a phase in the social transformation of the material). When read through Ilyenkov, the materialist conception of history becomes more apparent, as Benjamin's dream-world appears as the significance that matter has assumed in the course of its transformation by human activity. It appears as a dream-world because this activity is not being consciously directed.

58　Ibid.

59　'The prehistory of human society accordingly closes with this social formation' (Marx 1970 [1859], p. 22).

60　Marx 1977 [1867], p. 173. Similarly, he writes in the *Grundrisse*, 'The life-process of society, which is based on the process of material production, does not strip off its mystical veil until it is treated as production by freely associated men, and is consciously regulated in accordance with a settled plan' (Marx 1973 [1857], p. 92).

This reading of Benjamin through Ilyenkov appears in sharp relief against Adorno's critique of Benjamin's essay 'The Paris of the Second Empire in Baudelaire'. As we saw above, in his well-known rejection letter to Benjamin he accused the latter of 'vulgar materialism'.[61] However, reading Benjamin through Ilyenkov, one can appreciate a different type of anti-reductionism operating in Benjamin's work. Seeing the superstructure as an expression, as opposed to a reflection, of the base does not reduce it to the base itself, as with vulgar materialism; rather, it serves for Benjamin as a way to grasp the role of past human activity as the nightmare of history that forms the conditions under which people make history in the present. As an expression of bourgeois society, the 'ruins of the bourgeoisie' are not a superstructural reflection of the base, but a product of human activity. As Giorgio Agamben notes in his commentary on the exchange between Adorno and Benjamin about the 'Baudelaire' piece, '[w]hat looks upon us from the monuments and the rubble of the past ... is not then a relic of the ideological superstructure ... what we now have before us is praxis itself'.[62] Reading Benjamin through Ilyenkov helps to illuminate Benjamin's anti-dualist anti-reductionism.

When read through Ilyenkov, Benjamin's attempt to articulate a materialist conception of history emerges more clearly. His understanding of the superstructure as an expression of the base in products of human activity resembles Ilyenkov's approach to the ideal as an attribute of the material in forms of human activity. This attempt to avoid Cartesian dualism is an innovative way to approach the problem of base and superstructure.

Conclusion

Reading Benjamin's concept of the dream-world through Ilyenkov illuminates a common focus on human activity and a common concern to avoid vulgar materialism. These points of contact demonstrate that Ilyenkov's work is not only closely related to currents in Western Marxism, but makes a substantial contribution to anti-reductionist Marxist thought. Ilyenkov offers a rigorous working out of the relation of the ideal to the material in the language of classical philosophy. Deploying his insights to the problem of base and superstructure yields a coherent approach to the problem in non-reductionist terms, and helps us to identify an anti-dualist approach to the materialist conception of history that operates in Benjamin.

---

61   Agamben 1993, pp. 115–16.
62   Agamben 1993, p. 122.

Considering Benjamin's concept of the dream-world alongside Ilyenkov's concept of the ideal, one notes not only the substantial chasms that separate the two thinkers in terms of discipline, vocabulary, influences, intellectual and political contexts, and so on, but also a common 'anti-dualist anti-reductionism' operating in their thought. With Ilyenkov, we find that the 'human head' is not reducible to the material brain, nor is it posited as a substance separate from matter – a mind that reflects on its world. Instead of a Cartesian mind/body dualism, we find a Spinozist anti-reductionist materialism where thought is understood as an 'activity of the thinking body'.[63] Similarly, with Benjamin there is an articulation of the base/superstructure relationship as the body of the dreaming collective. His conception of the dream-world offers an original account of the relationship between base and superstructure. Although the two thinkers are working with very different points of reference, they share a similar anti-dualist approach to anti-reductionism.

This reading of Benjamin's concept of the dream-world through Ilyenkov's concept of the ideal not only demonstrates the originality of both thinkers, but also introduces a representative of a school of thought that challenged official Soviet philosophy which has largely remained absent from debates on these questions in Western Marxism. Soviet 'activity theory' offers a distinctive approach to the problem of reductionism that warrants further attention.

Ilyenkov's specific contribution to this problem can take further research in a number of directions. One of the distinguishing features of his concept of the ideal is the inflection of classical-Marxist thought with a Spinozist monism. Turning to Spinoza is not entirely original for Western Marxism. For instance, we can see attempts to turn to Spinoza as an alternative to Hegelian Marxism in the work of theorists such as Althusser, Deleuze and Negri.[64] As Eugene Holland notes, 'Antonio Negri has argued in favor of Spinoza's materialism, suggesting it is an important, early-modern precursor of Marx's fully modern materialism'.[65] Ilyenkov makes a similar assertion in *The Dialectics of the Abstract and the Concrete in Marx's 'Capital'* (1960): 'The rational kernels of Spinoza's dialectics ... were developed on a material basis only by Marx and Engels.'[66] What sets Ilyenkov apart from these theorists, however, is that he does not turn to Spinoza as an alternative to Hegel, but reads Marx through both Hegel and

---

63   Ilyenkov 1962, quoted in Oittinen 2005a, p. 321.
64   Holland 1998.
65   Ibid.
66   Ilyenkov 1960, p. 24.

Spinoza. Far from Hegelian Marxism, Ilyenkov's target is positivism. According to Oittinen, 'it seems that the role of Spinoza in his attempts to develop a "humanist," that is, an anti-positivistic and anti-scientistic form of dialectics, was greater than hitherto has been assumed'.[67] It may be fruitful to explore further the role of Spinoza in Ilyenkov in comparison to these thinkers.

A potential direction for further research in this regard would involve placing Ilyenkov in conversation with similar efforts to articulate an 'an anti-positivistic and anti-scientistic form of dialectics' in Western Marxism. For instance, the journals of Open Marxism sought to 'emancipate Marxism' from positivism and scientism, 'to clear the massive deadweight of positivist and scientistic/economistic strata'.[68] It also shares an affinity with a precursor of Open Marxism, Italian *operaismo*, a tradition within Western Marxism that is also critical of various forms of reductionism. Ilyenkov's Spinozist Marxism offers an interesting approach with which to think through the problem of reductionism alongside these traditions. This is but one of many directions for further research in this area.

---

67   Oittinen 2005b, p. 320.
68   Bonefeld et. al. 1995, p. 1.

Bibliography

Adorno, Theodor et al. 2002, *Aesthetics and Politics*, London: Verso.

Agamben, Giorgio 1993 [1978], *Infancy and History*, London: Verso.

Anscombe, G.E.M. (Elizabeth) 1957, *Intention*, Oxford: Blackwell.

Bakhurst, David 1990, 'Social Memory in Soviet Thought', in D. Edwards and D. Middleton (eds), *Collective Remembering*, 203–26, London: Sage.

———— 1991, *Consciousness and Revolution in Soviet Philosophy: From the Bolsheviks to Evald Ilyenkov*, Cambridge: Cambridge University Press.

———— 1992, 'Soviet Philosophy in Transition: An Interview with Vladislav Lektorsky', *Studies in Soviet Thought*, 44: 33–50.

———— 1995, 'Social Being and the Human Essence: An Unresolved Issue in Soviet Philosophy', symposium with V.S. Bibler, V.V. Davydov, V.A. Lektorsky and F.T. Mikhailov, *Studies in East European Thought*, 47: 3–60.

———— 1997, 'The Philosophy of Activity', in *Russian Studies in Philosophy*, 36, 1, 47–51.

———— 2005, 'Strong Culturalism', in *The Mind as a Scientific Object: Between Brain and Culture*, edited by David Martel Johnson and Christina Erneling, New York: Oxford University Press.

———— 2007, 'Meaning, Normativity and the Life of the Mind', *Language and Communication*, 17, 1: 33–51.

———— 2009, 'Reflections on Activity Theory', *Educational Research*, 61, 2: 197–210.

———— 2011a, *The Formation of Reason*, Oxford: Wiley-Blackwell.

———— 2011b, 'The Riddle of the Self Revisited', *Studies in East European Thought*, 63, 1: 63–73.

Batishchev, Genrikh S. 1963, *Protivorechie kak kategoriya dialekticheskoy logiki*, Moskva: Vysshaya shkola.

———— 1966, 'Deyatel'naya sushchnost' cheloveka kak filosofskiy printsip', in *Chelovek v sotsialisticheskom i burzhuaznom obshchestve. Simpozium. Doklady i soobshcheniya*, 245–86, Moskva: IF AN SSSR.

———— 1967, 'Tvorchestvo i ratsional'nost' (k opredeleniyu ponyatiya cheloveka)', in *Chelovek, tvorchestvo, nauka. Filosofskie problemy*, 83–98, Moskva: Nauka.

———— 1969, 'Deyatel'nostnaya sushchnost' cheloveka kak filosofskiy printcip', in *Problema cheloveka v sovremennoy filosofii*, 73–144, Moskva: Nauka.

———— 1976, 'Nravstvennyy smysl i soderzhanie vsestoronne-tselostnogo razvitiya cheloveka', in *Nravstvennyy progress i lichnost'. Metodologicheskie voprosy nravstvennogo progressa i sovershenstvovaniya lichnosti. Tematicheskiy sbornik*, 111–17, Vil'nyus: Mintis.

———— 1977, 'Ponyatie tselostno razvitogo cheloveka i perspektivy kommunisticheskogo vospitaniya', *Problema cheloveka v "Ekonomicheskikh rukopisyakh 1857–*

1859 godov" K. Marksa, 147–70, Rostov-na-Donu: Izdatel'stvo Rostovskogo universi-teta.

——— 1979, 'Dialektika kak logika mirovozzreniya tselostno razvitogo cheloveka', *Materialisticheskaya dialektika kak logika*, 113–22, Alma-Ata: Nauka KazSSR.

——— 1980a, 'Neischerpaemye vozmozhnosti i granitsy primenimosti kategorii deya-tel'nosti', in *Deyatel'nost: teorii, metodologiya, problemy*, Moskva: Politizdat, 21–35.

——— 1980b, *Tezisy ne k Feuerbakhu* (Lichnyy arkhiv A.A. Hamidova).

——— 1984, 'Samopoznanie cheloveka kak kul'turosozidatel'nogo sushchestva: tri urovnya slozhnosti zadach', in *Chelovek i kul'tura. Kriticheskiy analiz burzhuaznykh kontseptsiy*, 4–24, Moskva: IF AN SSSR.

——— 1985, 'Deyatel'nost i tsennosti. Kritika "deyatel'nostnogo" podkhoda i teorii interiorizatsii', *Voprosy filosofii*, 2: 41–4.

——— 1986, 'Dialektika pered litsom global'no-ekologicheskoy situatsii', in *Vzaimod-eystvie obshchestva i prirody. Filosofsko-metodolo-gicheskie aspekty ekologicheskoy problemy*, 175–97, Moskva: Nauka.

——— 1987, 'Osobennosti kul'tury glubinnogo obshcheniya', in *Dialektika obshchen-iya. Gnoseologicheskie i mirovozzrencheskie problemy*, 13–51, Moskva: IF AN SSSR.

——— 1989, *Dialekticheskiy kharakter tvorcheskogo otnosheniya cheloveka k miru*. Dis-sertatsiya v forme nauchnogo doklada na soiskanie uchënoy stepeni doktora filosof-skikh nauk, Moskva: IF AN SSSR.

——— 1990a, 'The Category of Activity: Inexhaustible Possibilities and Limits of Applicability', in Vladislav A. Lektorsky (ed.) 1990, *Activity: Theories, Methodology, and Problems*, Orlando, FL, Helsinki, Moscow: Paul Deutsch.

——— 1990b, 'The Activity Approach in the Captivity of Substantialism', in Vladislav A. Lektorsky (ed.) 1990, *Activity: Theories, Methodology, and Problems*, Orlando, FL, Helsinki, Moscow: Paul Deutsch.

——— 1990c, 'Not by Deed Alone', in Vladislav A. Lektorsky (ed.) 1990, *Activity: Theor-ies, Methodology, and Problems*, Orlando, FL, Helsinki, Moscow: Paul Deutsch.

——— 1990d, 'Neischerpannye vozmozhnosti i granitsy primenimosti kategorii deya-tel'nosti', in *Deyatel'nost: teorii, metodologiya, problemy*, 21–34, Moskva: Politizdat.

——— 1990e, 'Deyatel'nostnyy podkhod v plenu substantsializma', in *Deyatel'nost: teorii, metodologiya, problemy*, 169–76, Moskva: Politizdat.

——— 1990f, 'Ne deyaniem odnim zhiv chelovek', in *Deyatel'nost: teorii, metodologiya, problemy*, 317–29, Moskva: Politizdat.

——— 1991a, 'Poznanie, deyatel'nost, obshchenie', in *Teoriya poznaniya*, Volume 2, 119–35, Moskva: Mysl'.

——— 1991b, 'Poznanie i tvorchestvo', in *Teoriya poznaniya*, Volume 2, 136–69, Moskva: Mysl'.

——— 1991c, 'Filosofiya kak rabota cheloveka nad samim soboy', in *Filosofskoe sozn-anie: dramatizm obnovleniya*, 146–51, Moskva: Politizdat.

——— 1992, 'Nayti i obresti sebya', in *Stupeni samoobreteniya* (*Problemy obrazovaniya i kul'tury v malom gorode*), 18–27, Moskva: IF RAN.

——— 1993, 'Chelovechnost' ili antropotsentrizm? Antiteza mezhdu tsennostnoy posvyashchënnost'yu i gordym samodovleniem', in *Filosofskie nauki*, 1–3: 85–97.

——— 1997, *Vvedeniye v dialektiku tvorchestva*, Sankt-Peterburg: RHGI.

——— 2002, 'Vstupitel'noe slovo na zashchite doktorskoy dissertatsii', in *Mir cheloveka*, 2: 84–90, Almaty.

——— 2003, 'Dialektika bez al'ternativy: substantsializm ili anti-substantsializm. (Kritika panlogistskogo konstituirovaniya sub"ekta lish' kognitivnymi otnosheniyami, zakrytosti obrazovatel'nogo protsessa i logicheskogo preformizma voobshche)', in *Mir cheloveka* [Almaty] 2003, 2: 31–40.

Benjamin, Walter 1961 [1939], 'On Some Motifs in Baudelaire', in *Illuminations*, translated by Harry Zohn, New York: Schocken Books.

——— 1986a [1929], 'Surrealism', in *Reflections*, New York: Schocken Books.

——— 1986b [1935], 'Paris, Capital of the Nineteenth Century', in *Reflections*, New York: Schocken Books.

——— 1999 [1927–40], *The Arcades Project*, Cambridge, MA: Harvard University Press.

——— 2003 [1940], 'On the Concept of History', in *Selected Writings*, Volume 4: 1938–1940, Cambridge, MA: Harvard University Press.

Bennett, Max and Peter Hacker 2003, *Philosophical Foundations of Neuroscience*, Oxford: Blackwell.

Berdyaev, Nikolay A. 1989, *Filosofiya svobody. Smysl tvorchestva*, Moskva: Pravda,

——— 1991, *Samopoznanie* (*Opyt filosofskoy avtobiografii*), Moskva: Kniga.

Berkeley, George 1994 [1710], 'A Treatise Concerning the Principles of Human Knowledge', in *The Works of George Berkeley*, Volume I, edited by A.C. Fraser, Bristol: Thoemmes Press.

Bonefeld, Werner, Richard Gunn and Kosmas Psychopedis (eds) 1992, *Open Marxism*, Volume 2: Theory and Practice, London: Pluto Press.

Bonefeld, Werner, Richard Gunn, John Holloway and Kosmas Psychopedis (eds) 1995, *Open Marxism*, Volume 3: Emancipating Marx, London: Pluto Press.

Brandom, Robert 1994, *Making it Explicit*, Cambridge, MA: Harvard University Press.

Buck-Morss, Susan 2000, *Dreamworld and Catastrophe*, Cambridge, MA: MIT Press.

Bukharin, Nikolai 2005, *Philosophical Arabesques*, translated by Renfrey Clarke, New York: Monthly Review Press.

Bulatov, Mikhail A. 1984, *Dialektika i kul'tura*, Kiev: Naukova Dumka.

Chelovek i mir cheloveka (*Kategorii 'chelovek' i 'mir' v sisteme nauchnogo mirovozzreniya*) 1977, Kiev: Naukova Dumka.

Clark, Andy 1997, *Being There: Putting Brain, Body and World Together Again*, Cambridge, MA: The MIT Press.

Clark, Andy and David Chalmers 1998, 'The Extended Mind', *Analysis*, 58: 7–19.

Crombie, Alistair 1953, *Robert Grosseteste and the Origins of Experimental Science 1100–1700*, Oxford: Clarendon Press.

Daniel, Ute 2001, *Kompendium Kulturgeschichte: Theorien, Praxis, Schlüsselwörter*, Frankfurt/Main: Suhrkamp.

Davidson, Donald 2001 [1971], 'Agency', in Donald Davidson, *Essays on Actions and Events*, Oxford: Oxford University Press, pp. 43–63.

Davydov, Vasily V. 1990a, 'Yes, We Need a Monistic Theory of Human Existence', in Vladislav A. Lektorsky (ed.) 1990, *Activity: Theories, Methodology, and Problems*, Orlando, FL, Helsinki, Moscow: Paul Deutsch.

————— 1990b, 'Problemy deyatel'nosti kak sposoba chelovecheskogo bytiya i printsip monizma', in *Deyatel'nost: teorii, metodologiya, problemy*, Moskva: Politizdat, 239–50.

————— 1997, 'The theory of activity and social practice', *Russian Studies in Philosophy*, 36: 57–69.

Davydov, Yuri N. 1962, *Trud i svoboda*, Moskva: Vysshaya shkola.

Dewey, John 1975, 'The Reflex Arc Concept in Psychology', in John Dewey, *The Early Works*, Volume 5, Carbondale and Edwardsville: Southern Illinois University Press, 96–109.

Dialektika deyatel'nosti i kul'tura 1983, Kiev: Naukova Dumka.

Donald, Merlin 2002, *A Mind So Rare*, New York: Norton.

Dubrovsky, David I. 1971, *Psikhicheskie yavleniya i mozg*, Moskva: Nauka.

————— 1976, 'Informatsionnyy podkhod k probleme "soznanie i mozg"', *Voprosy filosofii*, 11: 41–54.

Elder, Crawford 2005, *Real Natures and Familiar Objects*, Cambridge, MA: MIT Press.

————— 2007, 'On the Place of Artifacts in Ontology', in *Creations of the Mind: Theories of Artifacts and their Representation*, edited by E. Margolis and S. Lawrence, Oxford: Oxford University Press.

Engels, Friedrich 1941 [1886], *Ludwig Feuerbach and the Outcome of Classical German Philosophy*, New York: International Publishers.

Engeström, Yrjö 2005, *Developmental Work Research: Expanding Activity Theory in Practice*, Berlin: Lehmanns Media.

Filosofs'ko-antropologichni studii 2003: Pizniy radyans'kiy marksizm ta s'ogodennya: do 70-richchya Vadima Ivanova 2003, Kiev: Stilos.

Fodor, Jerry 1980, 'Methodological Solipsism Considered as a Research Strategy in Cognitive Science', *Behavioral and Brain Sciences*, 3: 63–109.

Franks, Paul W. 2005, *All or Nothing: Systematicity, Transcendental Arguments, and Skepticism in German Idealism*, Cambridge, MA: Harvard University Press.

Frolov, I.T. (ed.) 1989, *Vvedenie v filosofiyu* (2 volumes), Moskva: Politizdat.

Fundamentals of Marxism-Leninism 1963, 2nd issue, Moscow.

Gergen, Kenneth J. 1994, *Realities and Relationships: Soundings in Social Construction*, Cambridge, MA: Harvard University Press.

Gibson, James J. 1979, *The Ecological Approach to Visual Perception*, Boston: Houghton Mifflin.

Gorsky, D.P. 1973, *Operezhayushchiy kharakter otritsaniya deistvitelnosti na urovne chelovecheskogo poznanijy*, in D.P. Gorsky et al. (ed.), *Praktika i poznanie*, Moscow, pp. 69–70.

Gould, Carol 1978, *Marx's Social Ontology: Individuality and Community in Marx's Theory of Social Reality*, Cambridge, MA: MIT Press.

Guseinov, Abdusalam and Vladislav Lektorsky 2009a, 'Filosofiya v Rossii: proshloe i nastojashchee', in Maja Soboleva (ed.), *Rossiyskaya postsovetskaya filosofiya. Opyt samoanaliza*. München-Berlin: Verlag Otto Sagner, pp. 13–39.

———— 2009b, 'Philosophy in Russia: History and Present State', *Diogenes*, 56, 3: 3–23.

Hegel, G.W.F. 1999, *Grundlinien der Philosophie des Rechts, Vorrede*, in *Hauptwerke in sechs Bänden*, vol. 5, Hamburg: Felix Meiner.

———— 2000, *Enzyklopädie der philosophischen Wissenschaften im Grundrisse*, Hamburg: Felix Meiner.

History of the Communist Party of the Soviet Union (Bolsheviks). Short Course 1943 [1938], edited by a Commission of the Central Committee of the CPSU(B), Moscow: Foreign Languages Publishing House.

Hobbes, Thomas 1962 [1655], *Elements of Philosophy. The First Section, Concerning Body. The English Works of Thomas Hobbes, I*, edited by Sir William Molesworth, Aalen: Scientia.

Holland, Eugene 1998, 'Spinoza and Marx', *Cultural Logic*, 2, 1.

Ilyenkov, Evald V. 1960, *Dialektika abstraktnogo i konkretnogo v "Kapitale" K. Marksa*, Moskva: Izdatel'stvo Akademii nauk SSSR.

———— 1962, 'Ideal'noe', in *Filosofskaya entsiklopediya*, Volume 2, Moskva: Sovetskaya entsiklopediya.

———— 1964, 'Vopros o tozhdestve myshleniya i bytiya v domarksistskoy filosofii', in *Dialektika – teoriya poznaniya. Istoriko-filosofskie ocherki*, Moskva: Nauka.

———— 1967, 'From the Marxist Point of View', in Nicholas Lobkowicz (ed.), *Marx and the Western World*, Notre Dame: University of Notre Dame Press.

———— 1968, *Ob idolakh i idealakh*, Moskva: Politizdat.

———— 1974, *Dialekticheskaya logika*, Moskva: Politizdat.

———— 1975, 'A.I. Meshcheryakov i ego pedagogika', *Molodoy kommunist*, 2: 80–4.

———— 1977 [1974], *Dialectical Logic*, Moscow: Progress.

———— 1979, 'Problema protivorechiya v logike', in *Dialekticheskoe protivorechie*, 122–43, Moskva: Politizdat.

———— 1982 [1960], *The Dialectics of the Abstract and the Concrete in Marx's 'Capital'*, translated by Sergei Kuzyakov, Moscow: Progress Publishers.

———— 1984a, *Iskusstvo I kommunisticheskiy ideal*, Moskva: Iskusstvo.

———— 1984b, 'Ob ehsteticheskoy prirode fantazii', in Evald Ilyenkov, *Iskusstvo i kommunisticheskiy ideal*, Moskva: Iskusstvo.

———— 1988, 'Marx i zapadnyy mir', *Voprosy filosofii*, 10: 99–112.

———— 1991a [1979], 'Dialektika ideal'nogo', in Evald V. Ilyenkov, *Filosofiya i kul'tura*, Moskva: Politizdat.

———— 1991b, 'Otkuda beretsya um?', in Evald V. Ilyenkov, *Filosofiya i kul'tura*, Moskva: Politizdat.

———— 1991c, 'O vseobshchem', in Evald Ilyenkov, *Filosofiya i kul'tura*, Moskva: Politizdat.

———— 1991d, 'O "sushchnosti cheloveka" i "gumanizme" v ponimanii Adama Shaffa', in Evald V. Ilyenkov, *Filosofiya i kul'tura*, Moskva: Politizdat.

———— 1997, 'The Question of the Identity of Thought and Being in Pre-Marxist Philosophy', *Russian Studies in Philosophy*, 36: 5–33.

———— 2002a, *Shkola dolzhna uchit' myslit'*, Moskva: MPSI.

———— 2002b, 'O prirode sposobnosti', in Evald V. Ilyenkov, *Shkola dolzhna uchit' myslit'*, Moskva: MPSI.

———— 2007, 'A Contribution on the Question of the Concept of "Activity" and its Significance for Pedagogy', *Journal of Russian and East European Psychology*, 45, 4: 69–74.

———— 2009, 'Dial'ektika ideal'nogo', *Logos*, 69, 1: 6–62.

———— 2012, *Dialectics of the Ideal*, translated by Alex Levant, in *Historical Materialism* 20, 2: 149–93.

Ivanov, Vadim P. 1977, *Chelovecheskaya deyatel'nost – poznanie – iskusstvo*, Kiev: Naukova Dumka.

Järvilehto, Timo 1998, 'The Theory of the Organism-Environment System', *Integrative Physiological and Behavioral Science*, 33, 317–38.

Jordan, Zbigniew 1967, *The Evolution of Dialectical Materialism: A Philosophical and Sociological Analysis*, New York: St Martin's Press.

Kagan, Moisey S. 1974, *Chelovecheskaya deyatel'nost (Opyt sistemnogo analiza)*, Moskva: Politizdat.

Kant, Immanuel 1926 [1762], *Reflexionen zur Metaphysik I. Kant's gesammelte Schriften 17*, Berlin and Leipzig: Preussische Akademie der Wissenschaften.

———— 1968 [1783], *Prolegomena*, in Immanuel Kant, *Werke*, Akademie-Ausgabe, Berlin: De Gruyter, Vol. III.

———— 1976 [1781/87], *Kritik der reinen Vernunft*, in *Werkaugabe*, Band III–IV, edited by Wilhelm Weischedel, Frankfurt am Main: Suhrkamp.

Kategorial'naya struktura poznaniya i praktiki 1986, Kiev: Naukova Dumka.

Kategorii dialektiki, ikh funktsii i razvitie 1980, Kiev: Naukova Dumka.

Kategorii filosofii i kategorii kul'tury 1983, Kiev: Naukova Dumka.

Khamidov, Aleksandr A. 2009, 'Put' otkrytiy kak otkrytie puti: filosofskie iskaniya G.S. Batishcheva', in *Genrikh Stepanovich Batishchev*, Moskva: Rosspen.

Kline, George 1988, 'The Myth of Marx's Materialism', in *Philosophical Sovietology: The Pursuit of a Science*, Sovietica 50, edited by H. Dahm, T.J. Blakeley and G.L. Kline, Dordrecht: Kluwer Publishing Co.

Kołakowski, Leszek 1968, *Toward a Marxist Humanism: Essays on the Left Today*, New York: Grove Press.

——— 1978, *L'esprit révolutionnaire, suivi de Marxisme: utopie et anti-utopie*, Bruxelles: Editions complexes.

Korovikov, Valentin I. 1990, 'Nachalo i pervyy pogrom', *Voprosy filosofii*, 2: 65–8.

Kucherov, P. 1930, 'Praktika i dialekticheskaya logika', *Pod znamenem marksizma*, 7–8: 75–90.

Kul'tura i razvitie cheloveka (Ocherk filosofsko-metodologicheskikh problem) 1989, Kiev: Naukova Dumka.

Kuznetsova, Nataliya I. and Yuliy A. Shreyder 1999, 'Rossiyskaya filosofiya vtoroy poloviny XX veka v litsakh', *Voprosy filosofii*, 2: 167–83.

Lazarev, Valeriy S. 2001, 'Krizis "deyatel'nostnogo podkhoda" v psikhologii i vozmozhnye puti ego preodoleniya', *Voprosy filosofii*, 3: 33–47.

Lektorsky, Vladislav A. 1984, *Subject, Object, Cognition*, Moscow: Progress Publishers (German translation: *Subjekt – Objekt – Erkenntnis. Grundlegung einer Theorie des Wissens*, Frankfurt am Main, 1985).

——— 1985, 'Status deyatel'nosti kak ob"yasnitel'nyy printsip', *Voprosy filosofii*, 2: 30–5.

——— (ed.) 1990, *Activity: Theories, Methodology, and Problems*, Orlando, FL, Helsinki, Moscow: Paul Deutsch.

——— 1999, 'Historical Changes of the Notion of Activity: Philosophical Presuppositions', in *Activity Theory and Social Practice: Cultural-Historical Approaches*, Aarhus: Aarhus University Press.

——— 2009a, 'Mediation as a Means of Collective Activity', in *Learning and Expanding with Activity Theory*, Cambridge: Cambridge University Press.

——— (ed.) 2009b, 'Realism, anti-realism, konstructivism, i konstructivny realism v epistemologii i nauke', in *Konstructivnyy podkhod v epistemologii I naukakh o cheloveke*, Moskva: Kanon+.

Lenin, Vladimir I. 1968, *Materializm i empiriokritritsizm*, in *Polnoe sobranie sochineniy*, Volume 18, Moskva: Politizdat.

Leontiev, Aleksey N. 1975, *Deyatel'nost, soznanie, lichnost'*, Moskva: Politizdat.

——— 1978, *Activity, Consciousness, and Personality*, New York: Prentice-Hall.

——— 2001, *Lektsii po obshchey psikhologii*, Moskva: Smysl.

Lifshits, Mikhail A. 1984, 'Ob ideal'nom i real'nom', *Voprosy filosofii*, 10: 120–45.

——— 1985, 'Bessistemnyy podkhod', in Mikhail A. Lifshits, *V mire ehstetiki*, Moskva: Izobrazitel'noe iskusstvo.

Locke, John 1959 [1689], *An Essay Concerning Human Understanding*, New York: Dover Publications.

Lomov, Boris F. 1979, 'Kategorii obshcheniya i deyatel'nosti v psikhologii', *Voprosy filosofii*, 8: 34–47.

———— 1984, *Metodologicheskie i teoreticheskie problemy psikhologii*, Moskva: Nauka.

Löwy, Michael 2005, *Fire Alarm: Reading Walter Benjamin's 'On the Concept of History'*, London: Verso.

Määttänen, Pentti 1983, 'Kant, Piaget ja skeeman käsite', *Tiede & Edistys* 8, 4: 47–52.

———— 1988, 'Mind, Reality and the Concept of Schema', in *Vom Werden des Wissens – Philosophie, Wissenschaft, Dialektik. Annalen der internationalen Gesellschaft für dialektische Philosophie*, Societas Hegeliana IV. Hrsg. Hans Heinz Holz and Juha Manninen, Köln: Pahl-Rugenstein, 29–32.

———— 1993, 'Action and Experience. A Naturalistic Approach to Cognition', in *Annales Academiae Scientiarum Fennicae B 64*, Helsinki: Suomalainen tiedeakatemia. https://tuhat.halvi.helsinki.fi/portal/en/publications/action-and-experien%280d5e485b-48b0-47af-a1cc-22797f10c313%29.html

———— 2006, 'Naturalism: Hard and Soft', in Heikki J. Koskinen, Sami Pihlström and Risto Vilkko (eds.), *Science – A Challenge to Philosophy?*, Frankfurt am Main: Peter Lang, 227–36.

———— 2009, *Toiminta ja kokemus, pragmatistista terveen järjen filosofiaa*, Helsinki: Gaudeamus.

———— 2010, 'Habits as Vehicles of Cognition', in Mats Bergman, Sami Paavola, Ahti-Veikko Pietarinen and Henrik Rydenfelt (eds.), *Ideas in Action, Proceedings of the Applying Peirce Conference. Nordic Studies in Pragmatism 1*, Helsinki: Nordic Pragmatism Network.

———— 2013, 'Luonto, ymmärrys ja skeemat Kantilla', in *Kant-antologia*, edited by Vesa Oittinen, Helsinki: Gaudeamus, 78–87.

———— 2015, *Mind in Action. Experience and Embodied Cognition in Pragmatism*, Cham: Springer.

Maidansky, Andrey 2005, 'Metamorphoses of the Ideal', *Studies in East European Thought*, 57: 289–304.

———— 2009a, 'Introduction', *Logos*, 69, 1: 3–5.

———— 2009b, 'Voskhozhd'enie k ideal'nomu', *Logos*, 69, 1: 63–73.

Mareev, Sergey 2008, *Iz istorii sovetskoy filosofii: Lukach – Vygotskii – Ilyenkov*, Moskva, Kul'turnaya revoliutsiya.

Margolis, Joseph 1986, 'Constraints on the metaphysics of culture', in *Review of Metaphysics*, 39: 653–73.

Markaryan, Eduard S. 1972, 'Sistemnoe issledovanie chelovecheskoy deyatel'nosti', *Voprosy filosofii*, 10: 77–86.

———— 1973, *O genezise chelovecheskoy deyatel'nosti i kul'tury*, Yerevan: Izdatel'stvo AN Armyanskoy SSR.

———— 1983, *Teoriya kul'tury i sovremennaya nauka*, Moskva: Mysl'.

Marx, Karl 1959 [1844], *Economic and Philosophic Manuscripts of 1844*, Moscow: Progress Publishers.

———— 1963 [1852], *The Eighteenth Brumaire of Louis Bonaparte*, New York: International Publishers.

———— 1966, 'Zametki po povodu knigi Jamesa Millya', *Voprosy filosofii*, 2: 113–27.

———— 1968 [1845], 'Theses on Feuerbach', in Karl Marx and Frederick Engels, *Selected Works in One Volume*, London: Lawrence and Wishart.

———— 1969a [1845], 'Theses on Feuerbach', in Karl Marx and Friedrich Engels, *Selected Works*, Volume I, Moscow: Progress Publishers, 13–15.

———— 1969b, *Das Kapital. Kritik der politischen Ökonomie*, Frankfurt-Berlin-Wien: Ullstein GmbH.

———— 1970 [1859], *A Contribution to the Critique of Political Economy*, translated by S.W. Rayazanskaya, New York: International Publishers.

———— 1973 [1857], *Grundrisse*, translated by Martin Nicolaus, New York: Vintage Books.

———— 1975, *Early Writings*, Harmondsworth: Penguin Books.

———— 1977 [1867], *Capital*, Volume I, translated by Ben Fowkes, New York: Vintage Books.

———— 1982, Ökonomisch-philosophische Manuskripte (Zweite Wiedergabe), in *Marx/Engels Gesamtausgabe* (MEGA). 1. Abt. Bd. 2, Text, 323–438, Berlin: Dietz Verlag.

———— 1986, *Karl Marx: A Reader*, edited by Jon Elster, Cambridge: Cambridge University Press.

Marx, Karl and Friedrich Engels 1961 [1859], 'Zur Kritik der politischen Ökonomie', in *Werke*, Band 13. Berlin: Dietz Verlag.

———— 1981, 'Exzerpte und Notizen, 1843 bis Yanuar 1845', in *Gesamtausgabe*, Band 2, Berlin: Akademie Verlag.

———— 1985, *Werke*, in 42 Bdn, Berlin: Dietz Verlag [cited as MEW, by volume and page number].

———— 1991 [1846], *The German Ideology*, New York, International Publishers.

McDowell, John 1994, *Mind and World*, 2nd edition 1996, Cambridge, MA: Harvard University Press.

———— 2005, 'Self-Determining Subjectivity and External Constraint', in John McDowell, *Having the World in View: Essays on Kant, Hegel, and Sellars*, Cambridge, MA: Harvard University Press.

McNally, David 2001, *Bodies of Meaning*, Albany, NY: State University of New York Press.

Megrelidze, Konstantin R. 1973, *Osnovnye problemy sotsiologii myshleniya*, Tbilisi: Metsniereba.

Melkov, Yuriy A. 2008, *Kievskaya shkola filosofii: osnovnye idei i kharakternye cherty*, http://www.nbuv.gov.ua/portal/soc_gum/Vnau_f/2008_2/melk.pdf

Mezhuev, Vadim M. 1977, *Kul'tura i istoriya (Problema kul'tury v filosofsko-istoricheskoy teorii marksizma)*, Moskva: Politizdat.

——— 1997, 'Evald Ilyenkov and the End of Classical Marxist Philosophy', in *Drama sovetskoi filosofii*, Moscow: The Russian Academy of Science Institute of Philosophy.

Mikhailov, Felix T. 1964, *Zagadka chelovecheskogo ya*, Moskva: Politizdat.

——— 1976, *Zagadka chelovecheskogo ya*, 2nd edition, Moskva: Politizdat.

——— 1980, *The Riddle of the Self*, Moscow: Progress Publishers.

——— 2001, 'Predmetnaya deyatel'nost ... ch'ya?', *Voprosy filosofii*, 3: 10–26.

Mikhailov, I.F. 1987, 'Subyekt, subyektivnost, kultura (k voprosu o sotsialno-kulturnoi determinatsii poznaniya)', in *Filosofskie nauki* (*FN*), 6: 30–40.

Mirovozzrencheskaya kul'tura lichnosti: filosofskie problemy formirovaniya 1986, Kiev: Naukova Dumka.

Mirovozzrencheskie orientiry myslitel'noy kul'tury 1993, Kiev: Naukova Dumka.

Mirovozzrencheskoe soderzhanie kategoriy i zakonov materialisticheskoy dialektiki 1981, Kiev: Naukova Dumka.

Nagel, Thomas 1974, 'What is it like to be a bat?', in Douglas Hofstadter and Daniel Dennett (eds.), *The Mind's I*, New York: Basic Books.

Naumenko, Lev K. 1968, *Monizm kak printsip dialekticheskoy logiki*, Alma-Ata: Nauka.

——— 2005, 'Evald Ilyenkov and World Philosophy', *Studies in East European Thought*, 57: 233–48.

——— 2008, 'V kontekste mirovoy filosofii', in *Evald Vasil'evich Ilyenkov*, 38–69, Moskva: Rosspen.

Neisser, Ulric 1976, *Cognition and Reality: Principles and Implications of Cognitive Psychology*, San Francisco: Freeman.

Noë, Alva 2009, *Out of Our Heads*, New York: Hill and Wang.

Ogurtsov, A.P. 1967, 'Praktika', in *Filosofskaya entsiklopediya*, vol. 4, Moscow: Sovetskaya enciklopediya, pp. 340–9.

——— 2010, 'Praktika', in *Novaya filosofskaya entsiklopediya*, vol. III, Moscow: Mysl', 321–5.

Oittinen, Vesa (ed.) 2000, *Evald Ilyenkov's Philosophy Revisited*, Helsinki: Kikimora Publications.

——— 2005a, 'Introduction', *Studies in East European Thought*, 57: 223–31.

——— 2005b, 'Evald Ilyenkov as Interpreter of Spinoza', *Studies in East European Thought*, 57: 319–38.

——— 2009, *Das Ding an sich – Stein des Anstosses der Bolschewiki? Zur philosophischen Polemik von Lenin und Bogdanow*, in Vesa Oittinen (ed.), *Aleksandr Bogdanov Revisited*, Aleksanteri Series 1/2009, Helsinki, 297–328.

Oizerman, T.I. 2003, *Marksizm i utopizm*, Moscow: Progress–Traditsiya.

Peirce, Charles S. 1931–58, *Collected Papers* [cited as CP followed by volume and paragraph number], edited by Charles Hartshorne and Paul Weiss, Cambridge, MA: Harvard University Press.

Piaget, Jean 1971, *Biology and Knowledge*, Edinburgh: Edinburgh University Press.

—— 1980, 'Schemes of Action and Language Learning', in *Language and Learning*, edited by Massimo Piattelli-Palmarini, Cambridge, MA: Harvard University Press, 164–7.

Piaget, Jean and Bärbel Inhelder 1969, *The Psychology of the Child*, New York: Basic Books.

Pinkard, Terry P. 2002, *German Philosophy 1760–1860: The Legacy of Idealism*, Cambridge: Cambridge University Press.

Plekhanov, Georgi 1976a [1908–10], *Materialismus Militans*, in Georgi Plekhanov, *Selected Philosophical Works*, vol. III, Moscow: Progress Publishers.

—— 1976b [1907], *Fundamental Problems of Marxism*, in Georgi Plekhanov, *Selected Philosophical Works*, vol. III, Moscow: Progress Publishers.

Porshnev, Boris F. 2006, *O nachale chelovecheskoy istorii*, Moskva: Feri-v.

Potëmkin, Aleksey V. 1973, *O specifike filosofskogo znaniya*, Rostov-na-Donu.

Praktika – poznanie – mirovozzrenie 1980, Kiev: Naukova Dumka.

Priddat Birger P. 2005, '"Reiche Individualität" – Karl Marx' Kommunismus als Konzeption der "freien Zeit für freie Entwicklung"', in *Karl Marx' kommunistischer Individualismus*, edited by Ingo Pies, Tübingen: Mohr Siebeck.

Rödl, Sebastian 2007, *Self-Consciousness*, Cambridge, MA: Harvard University Press.

Rozin, Vadim M. 2001, 'Tsennostnye osnovaniya kontseptsiy deyatel'nosti v psikhologii i sovremennoy metodologii', *Voprosy filosofii*, 2: 96–106.

Rozov, Mikhail A. 2006, *Teoriya socialnykh estafet i problemy epistemopogii*, Moskva: Novyy khronograf.

Rubinshtein, Sergey L. 1934, 'Problemy psikhologii v trudakh Karla Marksa', *Sovetskaya psikhotekhnika*, 1.

—— 1976, *Problemy obschey psikhologiy*, Moskva: Pedagogika.

—— 1989, 'Printsip tvorcheskoy samodeyatelnosti. K filosofskim osnovam sovremennoy pedagogiki', *Voprosi filosofii*, 4: 89–92.

—— 2005, *Osnovy obshchey psikhologii*, Sankt-Peterburg: Piter.

Sánchez Vázquez, Adolfo 1977, *The Philosophy of Praxis*, London/New Jersey: Merlin Press/Humanities Press.

Sarbin, Theodore R. 1986, *Narrative Psychology: The Storied Nature of Human Conduct*, New York: Praeger.

Schmidt, Alfred 1971, *The Concept of Nature in Marx*, London: NLB.

Searle, John 1995, *The Construction of Social Reality*, New York: The Free Press.

Shchedrovitsky, Georgy P. 1964, *Problemy metodologii sistemnogo issledovaniya*, Moskva: Znanie.

———— 1995, *Izbrannye trudy*, Moskva: Shkola Kul'turnoy Politiki.

———— 1997, *Filosofiya. Nauka. Metodologiya*, Moskva: Izdatel'stvo Shkoly Kul'turnoy Politiki.

Shvyrev, Vladimir S. 1976, 'Zadachi razrabotki kategorii deyatel'nosti kak teoreticheskogo ponyatiya', in *Metodologicheskie problemy issledovaniya deyatel'nosti*, Trudy VNII, Moskva: 66–74.

———— 1985, 'Deyatel'nost kak filosofskaya kategoriya', *Voprosy filosofii*, 2: 39–41.

———— 1990a, 'Deyatel'nost – otkrytaya sistema', in *Deyatel'nost: teorii, metodologiya, problemy*, Moskva: Politizdat, 159–68.

———— 1990b, 'The Concept of Activity as a Philosophical Category: Problems Involved', in Vladislav A. Lektorsky (ed.) 1990, *Activity: Theories, Methodology, and Problems*, Orlando, FL, Helsinki, Moscow: Paul Deutsch

———— 2001, 'O deyatel'nostnom podkhode k istolkovaniyu "fenomena cheloveka" (popytka sovremennoy otsenki)', *Voprosy filosofii*, 2: 107–15.

Sotsial'no-istoricheskie i mirovozzrencheskie aspekty filosofskikh kategoriy 1978, Kiev: Naukova Dumka.

Spinoza, Benedict 1955, *On the Improvement of the Understanding. The Ethics. Correspondence*, translated by R.H.M. Elwes, New York: Dover Publications.

Stepin, Vyacheslav S. 1998, 'V mire teoreticheskikh idei', in *Filosofiya ne konchaetsya. XX vek. 1960–80 gody*, edited by Vladislav Lektorsky, Moskva: Rosspen.

———— 2005, *Theoretical Knowledge*, Dordrecht: Springer.

Stout, Jeffrey 2007, 'On Our Interest in Getting Things Right', in Cheryl Misak (ed.), *New Pragmatists*, Oxford: Oxford University Press.

Surmava, Aleksandr V. 2009, 'Ilyenkov i revolyuciya v psikhologii', *Logos*, 1: 112–32.

Tabachkovsky, Valeriy G. 1976, *Kritika idealisticheskikh interpretatsiy praktiki*, Kiev: Naukova Dumka.

———— 1997 *Chelovecheskoe mirootnoshenie: dannost' ili problema*, Kiev: Naukova Dumka.

Thomasson, Amie 2007a, *Ordinary Objects*, Oxford: Oxford University Press.

———— 2007b, 'Artifacts and Human Concepts', in Stephen Laurence and Eric Margolis (eds.), *Creations of the Mind: Essays on Artifacts and their Representation*, Oxford: Oxford University Press, 52–73.

Thompson, Michael 2008, *Life and Action: Elementary Structures of Practice and Practical Thought*, Cambridge, MA: Harvard University Press.

Tiukhtin, V.S. 1984, *Dialektiko-materialisticheskiy printsip otrazheniya i tvorcheskiy kharakter poznaniya*, in D.P. Gorsky (ed.), *Tvorcheskaya priroda nauchnogo poznaniya*, Moscow: Nauka.

Tolstykh, Valentin I. (ed.) 2008, *Eval'd Vasil'evich Ilyenkov*, Moscow: Rosspen.

Trubnikov, Nikolay N. 1967, *O kategoriyakh 'tsel'', 'sredstvo', 'rezul'tat'*, Moskva: Vysshaya shkola.

Ukhtomsky, Aleksey A. 1973, Pis'ma, *Puti v neznaemoe. Pisateli rasskazyvayut o nauke*, Sb. КН, 371–434, Moskva: Sovetskiy pisatel'.

———— 2008, *Litso drugogo cheloveka*, Sankt-Peterburg: Izdatel'stvo Ivana Limbakha.

Van der Zweerde, Evert 1994, *Soviet Philosophy: The Ideology and the Handmaid*, diss., Nijmegen.

Varela, Francisco J., Evan Thompson and Eleanor Rosch 1992, *The Embodied Mind: Cognitive Science and Human Experience*, Cambridge, MA: MIT Press.

Velichkovsky, Boris M. 2006, *Kognitivnaya nauka. Osnovy psikhologii poznaniya*, Volume 2, Moskva: Smysl.

Vygotsky, Lev S. 1982–4, *Sobranie sochineniy*, 6 vols, Moskva: Pedagogika.

Williams, Raymond 1977, *Marxism and Literature*, Oxford: Oxford University Press.

Wilson, Rob 2004, *Boundaries of the Mind: The Individual in the Fragile Sciences: Cognition*, Cambridge: Cambridge University Press.

Wolff, Robert 1963, *Kant's Theory of Mental Activity: A Commentary on the Transcendental Analytic of the Critique of Pure Reason*, Cambridge, MA: Harvard University Press.

Yatsenko, Aleksandr 1977, *Tselepolaganie i idealy*, Kiev: Naukova Dumka.

Yudin, Erik G. 1978, *Sistemnyy podkhod i printsip deyatel'nosti: Metodologicheskie problemy sovremennoy nauki*, Moskva: Nauka.

Zakony i printsipy materialisticheskoy dialektiki 1989, Kiev: Naukova Dumka.

Zinchenko, Vladimir P. 2001, 'Psikhologicheskaya teoriya deyatel'nosti', *Voprosy filosofii*, 2: 66–88.

Index